HORSESTORY

VOLUME I:
THE EARLY YEARS

by

Vicki Watson

Where in this wide world can man find
nobility without pride,
friendship without envy,
or beauty without vanity?
Here where grace is laced with muscle
and strength by gentleness confined.
— Ronald Duncan

Table of Contents

Introduction

Imagine the history book horses could write if only they knew how to type! You see, they were there for it all, working for thousands of years alongside man as his strong and faithful partner. Man provided the brain power—and horses, the brawn. Together, they accomplished amazing things.

Through their bond with humans, horses shaped our past in ways no machine ever could. You'd think such a significant contribution would be highlighted in history books. However, in most, horses are strangely absent.

Their role in transportation, agriculture, communication, commerce, healthcare, and other vital areas has been largely unrecognized—or forgotten altogether.

From the days of the Spanish explorers to modern times, the three-volume Horsestory series brings the past to life from a unique perspective—the back of a horse—or perhaps a horse-drawn vehicle.

In the series, you'll learn the stories of a variety of horses—from Cortez's black stallion, El Morzillo, who was worshiped as a god by the ancient Mayans—to the modern-day Cinderella story of Harry de Leyer's Snowman[1], rescued from a slaughter truck to become a national jumping champion.

The journey begins with the arrival of horses in America in the 1500s.

Let's get started!

---

[1] *Snowman's story appears in Volume III.*

1

Arrival in America

Many consider the Mustangs out West to be wild horses, however there are no true wild horses in the United States. Horses aren't native to North America. How did they find their way here?

The name, Mustang, comes from the Spanish mesteño meaning wild, stray, or free. These animals are descendants of once-tame horses. Mustangs are feral horses—once tame, but having reverted to a "wild" state. Explorers brought the earliest horses from Spain to North America. These were generally known as Iberian horses, the ancestors of the Andalusian, Lusitano, Paso, and Criollo breeds. Many modern breeds have these horses somewhere in their ancestry.

- Columbus brought no horses on his first journey in 1492 when he landed in the West Indies (Caribbean). On his trip the following year, the ship carried fifteen stallions and ten mares. Columbus also brought several donkeys to the New World.

- Hernando Cortes brought the first horses to the mainland. Sixteen of those animals traveled to Mexico in 1519.

- In 1539, Hernando de Soto landed in Florida with 250 horses.

- Francisco Coronado brought as many as 1500 horses to Southwest America in 1540.

This influx of horses continued as other explorers arrived in following years. Initially, many Native Americans were afraid of horses. They had never seen such an animal and thought perhaps the

man on horseback was a new creature—a combination of horse and man. Recognizing the power and advantage horses gave them, the Spaniards didn't want Native Americans to own or ride horses.

Catholicism was the dominant religion of Spain. Catholic missionaries came with later explorers and established missions in the Southwest. In 1680, the Pueblo tribe rose up against the Spanish at Sante Fe, in the area of New Mexico, killing more than 400 Spanish soldiers and many of the Catholic priests.

After the Pueblo revolt, thousands of Spanish horses ran free or were taken by Native Americans. This spread of horses became known as the Great Horse Dispersal and is considered the official beginning of the Mustang herds. The horses spread northward from tribe to tribe. By 1690, horses had reached Idaho. The Comanches gained a reputation as the most skilled horsemen.

Recent blood typing of western Mustangs has shown that only a small percentage of the horses trace back to their Spanish ancestors. Over the years, the Spanish lines have been diluted by ranch stock and other horses that have mingled with the herds. The Kiger Mustangs in southeastern Oregon are one of the purest remaining Spanish strains.

In addition to the Mustangs out West, there are several breeds in the East that descended from the colonial Spanish horses. Carolina Marsh Tackies were used in the American Revolution by Francis Marion, known as the Swamp Fox. Marsh Tackies range in size from 13.2 to 15 hands and weigh 700 to 900 pounds. They have a unique gait known as the swamp fox trot. The British forces couldn't navigate the swampy land in that area, but the colonists' Marsh Tackies were accustomed to it. The Tackies were also used in the Civil War by Confederate forces. In World War II, Carolina Marsh Tackies patrolled the eastern coast of the U.S. on the lookout for attacks by sea.

Two breeds closely related to the Marsh Tacky are the Banker Horse found in the Outer Banks of North Carolina and the Florida Cracker Horse. In 1926, five to six thousand wild horses lived in the Outer Banks area of North Carolina. The Florida Cracker Horse was named after the crackers or cowboys known by the sound of the whip they cracked to drive cattle.

Several of these breeds have been chosen as official state horses.

- Florida - Florida Cracker Horse
- North Carolina - Colonial Spanish Mustang
- South Carolina - Carolina Marsh Tacky
- Oregon - The Kiger Mustang has been proposed but not yet officially adopted.

2

The Weather God

Hernando Cortez is remembered as a Spanish conquistador, but few know of his connection to the Mayan God of Thunder. Cortez, born in 1485 in Medellin, Spain, sailed for the New World in 1504 and landed at Santo Domingo in the Caribbean. The island was known then as Hispaniola.

In 1519, Cortez led an expedition to Mexico with hundreds of men and sixteen horses. The emperor, Montezuma, initially thought Cortez might be Quetzalcoatl, an Aztec god. Montezuma gave the Spaniard gold, hoping that would keep him from taking over the Aztec capital, Tenochtitlan, but Cortez and his men conquered the Aztecs the following year. Tenochtitlan was renamed Mexico City and became the capital of the Spanish territory.

In 1524, Cortez traveled south to Honduras in Central America. The expedition included ninety horses. His personal mount was a black stallion named El Morzillo (from the Spanish morcillo—black with reddish hairs). While traversing the rough terrain, Morzillo was injured and unable to continue. Cortez left the horse in the care of natives from a local tribe at Lake Peten-Itza. In a letter, the explorer wrote:

THE MEETING OF CORTEZ AND MONTEZUMA.

The natives didn't want to incur the wrath of Cortez who had promised to return for Morzillo. But, apparently they had no idea how to care for a horse. El Morzillo was housed in a temple and fed delicacies of fruit, nuts, chicken, and other meats, all topped with flowers. Whether due to this unusual diet or his foot injury, the stallion didn't live long.

Cortez returned to Spain in 1541 and never knew what happened to his favorite horse. He died six years later, never making it back to America.

When Spanish missionaries visited Peten-Itza in 1618, they found a strange sight. In the temple, was a statue of the stallion. The stone Morzillo was seated on his hindquarters with his forelegs stretched out in front of him. He was known by the Mayans as Tzimin Chac, the God of Thunder.

In the intervening years, El Morzillo had been worshiped as a weather god. The missionaries considered the stone horse a pagan idol and destroyed it.

3

Thoroughbred Family Tree

If horses cared about such things, every Thoroughbred could trace his genealogy back to one of three foundation stallions—the Byerley Turk, the Darley Arabian, or the Godolphin Arabian. The three sires arrived in England in the late 1600s to early 1700s.

The **Byerley Turk**, born around 1680, was the earliest of the foundation stallions. Little is known for certain of his early history. Some claim he was foaled and raised in England, while others insist on a more exotic background—that in 1686, the horse was taken by the British after winning the Battle of Buda against the Turks in Hungary.

The Byerley Turk was dark brown and unmarked. He may have been a purebred Arabian, however due to recent genetic testing, some believe he was an Akhal Teke. What's known for certain is his entry in the General Stud Book, the breed registry for horses in Great Britain and Ireland.

The record states that the Byerley Turk was the war horse of Captain Robert Byerley.

The captain and his horse fought in the Williamite War in which Catholics battled Protestants for control of Ireland, England, and Scotland. Military records indicate Byerley, served with distinction in Ireland, and having taken with him the Turk who bears his name, rode him as a charger in the campaign of 1689-90. At the Battle of the Boyne he was so far ahead reconnoitering the enemy that he narrowly escaped capture, owing his safety to the superior speed of his horse.

After his military career, Captain Byerley retired to Goldsborough Hall in Yorkshire, England. The Byerley Turk sired many foals, some of whom were successful racehorses. His most influential foal was a colt named Jigg, who sired Partner, a racing phenomenon. Partner sired Herod, one of the most influential stallions of the Thoroughbred breed. The Byerley Turk died in 1706 at approximately twenty-six.

The bloodline of the Byerley Turk is fading away in favor of the more successful racehorse descendants of the other two foundation stallions.

The second foundation sire, the **Darley Arabian**, was foaled around 1700 in the Syrian desert near Aleppo. The horse was part of the Mannicka strain of Arabians known for their speed. His original name was Ras el Fedowi, which means "The Headstrong One."

Thomas Darley, a merchant trader, purchased the stallion from Sheikh Mirza II in 1704. Some sources claim the Sheikh changed his mind and attempted to back out of the deal. If that was the case, Darley somehow managed to acquire the horse anyway and smuggled him out of Syria. The horse's life changed dramatically from that point. He left his home among the desert Bedouins and was shipped to the Darley stable at Aldby Hall near York, England.

Thomas included a note to his brother Richard regarding the horse.

> *Since my father expects I should send him a stallion, I esteem myself happy in a colt I bought about a year and a half ago with a design indeed to send him at the first good opportunity. He comes four at the latter end of March or the beginning of April next. His colour is bay and his near foot before and both his hind feet have white upon them. He has a blaze down his face something of the largest. He is about 15 hands high, of the most esteemed race among the Arabs both by sire and dam and the name of the said race is called Mannicka. I believe he will not be disliked for he is esteemed here where I could have sold him at a considerable price if I had not designed him for England.*

The horse arrived safely, however Thomas Darley died before he was able to return from Syria. The beautiful bay quickly became one of the leading sires in Great Britain and Ireland with many successful racing descendants.

The Darley Arabian is considered the most influential Thoroughbred sire. Some of his progeny include: Flying Childers, recognized as the first great Thoroughbred racehorse; Eclipse, who was undefeated in eighteen races; Sir Barton, the first Triple Crown winner (1919); and Secretariat.

In addition to his influence on Thoroughbreds, one of Darley's sons, Manica, became a foundation sire of the Cleveland Bay breed of horses in England.

In 1730, Bulle Rock, a son of the Darley Arabian, was the first Thoroughbred shipped to Virginia in America. That same year, the Darley Arabian died at the age of thirty.

The **Godolphin Arabian** or **Godolphin Barb** was foaled around 1724 in Yemen at the southern end of the Arabian Peninsula. The value of this third Thoroughbred foundation sire wasn't immediately recognized as he changed owners frequently in his early life, spending time in a stable in Tunisia, North Africa.

From there he and three other stallions were given to Louis XV of France in 1728. The horses arrived in France sickly and half-starved. Needless to say, they didn't make a good impression on the king.

A year later, the stallion was purchased by Edward Coke and moved to his stable in Derbyshire, England. When Coke died unexpectedly at thirty-two, the stallion was purchased by the 2nd Earl of Godolphin in Cambridgeshire. The horse derived his lasting name from this owner.

The Godolphin Arabian was 14.2 to 15 hands tall, a bay with one small white marking on his right, back leg near the heel. He had an unusually high, arched neck. A veterinarian who examined him had this to say.

> *It is not to be wondered at that the excellence of this horse's shape was not in early times manifest to some men, considering the plainness of his head and ears, the position of his fore-legs, and his stunted growth, occasioned by want of food in the country where he was bred.*

His first foal, out of Lady Roxana in 1731, proved the Godolphin's desirability as a sire. The colt, Lath, won the Queen's Plate nine times in nine tries and was considered the best racehorse of his day.

A daughter of the Godolphin, Selima, was brought to America in 1750. A fine racehorse herself, she became one of the Thoroughbred foundation mares, raising ten foals.

The great racehorse, Eclipse, undefeated in eighteen races, traces back to the Godolphin and Darley Arabians. Other famous descendants include Seabiscuit, War Admiral, and Man o' War.

Many of the great horses whose sires go back to the Darley Arabian had dams descended from the Godolphin Arabian.

In his later years, the Godolphin Arabian's constant companion was a cat named Grimalkin. The stallion died in 1753 at the age of twenty-nine.

4

Old Billy

According to Guinness World Records, the oldest verifiable age for a horse is sixty-two—an English horse called Old Billy. Well, the "Old" part was probably tacked onto his name after a considerable number of years. Billy was brown with a white star and resembled a big cob or Shire horse. Multiply Billy's age by three for a rough equivalent of his age in human years!

Billy was born in 1760 in Woolston, Lancashire, UK and died on November 27, 1822.

Could a horse really live that long? Is Billy's age reliable?

It seems so. Billy was raised by Edward Robinson, a farmer in Woolston. At two, Billy was trained by seventeen-year-old Henry Harrison to be a plow horse.

William Bradley, a portrait artist, painted Old Billy in his retirement in 1821, the year before the horse's death. Henry Harrison is also pictured in that portrait. They included the following description with copies of the painting.

Harrison was given the job of caring for Old Billy in his retirement, which didn't last long. Amazingly, the horse worked until he was almost sixty years old.

Although as a young horse, Billy was trained for farm work, at some point he was purchased by the Mersey and Irwell Navigation Company. Some accounts claim he was a barge horse, pulling boats along the canals. That may have been a seasonal job, but he also worked as a "gin" horse—gin being the short form of engine. In the days before electricity and steam engines, horses provided the power for many tasks through gins. The horse walked around and around, rotating a central drum connected to a system of cables and pulleys. Billy likely worked a gin used to raise goods from the decks of ships.

Until he reached the age of fifty, Old Billy had a bad temper, particularly shown when, at the dinner hour or other periods, a cessation of labor took place; he was impatient to get into the stable on such occasions and would use, very savagely, either his heels or his teeth (particularly the latter) to remove any living impediment… that happened, by chance, to be placed in his way…

Another artist, Charles Towne, painted Billy in June, 1822. At that time, Billy had

the use of all his limbs in tolerable perfection, lies down and rises with ease; and when in the meadows will frequently play, and even gallop, with some young colts, which graze along with him. This extraordinary animal is healthy, and manifests no symptoms whatever of approaching dissolution.

But five months later, the old horse passed away. Oddly enough, Old Billy's skull is on display at England's Manchester Museum while his stuffed head is exhibited at the Bedford Museum.

5

Eclipsing the Competition

A solar eclipse on April 1, 1764 was the inspiration for the name of one of the greatest racehorses of all time. Eclipse was foaled that night in Berkshire County, England. The colt's owner was Prince William Augustus, Duke of Cumberland. His sire was Marske and dam Spilletta. Eclipse's great-great-grandsire was the Darley Arabian. His mother's line traced back to the Godolphin Arabian.

When the Duke died the following year, all his Thoroughbreds were sold. Eclipse was purchased by William Wildman. Eclipse, a chestnut, was unusually tall for the time at 16 hands. He had a narrow blaze and a white stocking on his right hind leg nearly up to his hock.

He was not considered beautiful with his long legs, overly long neck, and large head. When younger, he was difficult to handle, but through training and challenging work, he became manageable enough to begin racing. He didn't race until fully mature at the age of five.

At that time, races were grueling events, testing a horse's endurance as well as his speed. Eclipse entered the racing world at Epsom in May of 1769 ridden by jockey, John Oakley. The race consisted of three heats; each of which was four miles. Between heats, the horse rested for half an hour, then ran again.

In his first outing, Eclipse easily won all three heats. His performance impressed Dennis O'Kelly who stated, "Eclipse first, the rest nowhere." After his second race, O'Kelly purchased half of Eclipse. The following year, he purchased the horse outright.

Eclipse raced from May, 1769 to October, 1770. In that time, he was undefeated, winning eighteen races, including eleven King's Plates. His brief career of seventeen months might have lasted longer, but he won such commanding victories that other owners refused to race their horses against him.

Some races were called "plates," such as the Queen's Plate, for the prize awarded to the winner—a gold plate or cup. It's unknown how fast

Eclipse could have run, since he was never seriously tested by any of his competitors. One person who watched him race wrote.

He never in his life felt whip or spur, or even the control of the bit; and although no jockey could hold him against his will, neither of the two, who only had the honour of riding him, ever experienced the least difficulty in pulling him up at an ending post. Nor was there any difficulty in training, at least after he had raced, although the most resolute and headstrong of horses.

Among his foals, Eclipse produced 343 recorded winners. One of Eclipse's sons had a clever name—Potooooooooo. Do you know how it was pronounced?[1]

It's estimated that ninety percent of all Thoroughbred racehorses are descended from Eclipse. Eclipse died of colic in 1789 at the age of twenty-four. His hooves were made into ink stands. There have been claims of as many as nine such ink stands floating around. The horse's skeleton is on display at the Royal Veterinary College in Hertfordshire, England.

After Eclipse's death, his heart was found to be nearly twice as large as that of a normal horse. Eclipse passed this tendency for a large heart on to his descendants, Secretariat and Phar Lap.

An average horse's heart weighs approximately eight to nine pounds. The heart of Eclipse and Phar Lap weighed fourteen. Secretariat had the largest known horse heart. Although never actually weighed, it was estimated to be twenty-two pounds.

This tendency for a large heart in horses has been called the X-Factor. Some Thoroughbred mares are thought to have a recessive gene that, when matched with a stallion who also carries the trait, results in a foal with a larger-than-average heart.

SAINT BEL'S ANATOMICAL STUDY OF ECLIPSE

---

[1] *Potatoes, Po-t-8 o's*

6

Delivering the Good News

Of all the things horses carried and delivered in the days before motorized vehicles, one that is often overlooked is the Christian faith. More precisely, horses carried the men that preached God's word. These men were known as circuit riders. They were usually Methodists, although a few Baptist pastors also rode preaching circuits.

Methodists are a Protestant denomination, based upon the practices of John and Charles Wesley. In 1729, the Wesley brothers formed the Holy Club at the University of Oxford in England. Other students scoffed at the young men's determination to study the Bible, pray, fast, and live a disciplined life. The scoffers considered them religious fanatics and labeled them "methodists."

In 1735, John and Charles traveled to the colony of Georgia in America. After that rather unsuccessful two-year missionary trip, both Wesleys returned to England, questioning the genuineness of their own faith. On May 24, 1738, John Wesley had a spiritual experience while meeting with a group of Moravian Christians. He felt his "heart strangely warmed" and considered this the moment when he truly became a Christian.

In the evening I went very unwillingly to a society in Aldersgate Street, where one was reading Luther's Preface to the Epistle to the Romans. About a quarter before nine, while he was describing the change which God works in the heart through faith in Christ, I felt my heart strangely warmed. I felt I did trust in Christ, Christ alone for salvation, and an assurance was given me that he had taken away my sins, even mine, and saved me from the law of sin and death.

—John Wesley

Charles Wesley had experienced something similar three days prior to John's conversion. Although the Wesleys never left the Church of England, they were banned from preaching in Anglican churches. Along with George Whitefield, they began holding open-air services, preaching in fields, barns, homes, or anywhere they could attract an audience. The Methodists broke away from the Anglican Church after John Wesley's death.

Francis Asbury

Although the Wesleys hadn't been effective missionaries to America, other Methodists would soon follow. Among them was Francis Asbury.

Francis was born to Joseph and Elizabeth Asbury in Staffordshire, England in 1745. Three years later, Asbury's older sister, Sarah, died. After her daughter's death, a preacher helped Mrs. Asbury overcome her grief and depression. She acquired a deep faith that was passed on to her son, however her husband was apparently not a Christian. Francis learned to read the Bible by age seven, but left formal schooling at twelve to be apprenticed to a metalworker.

Asbury began traveling a preaching circuit in England in 1765 at the age of nineteen and may have preached occasionally for several years before that. In 1771, Asbury traveled to America. During his first years in America, he preached along the east coast.

When the Revolutionary War broke out, the loyalty of all British citizens in the colonies was questioned. Nearly all the British Methodist preachers returned to England. Asbury and James Dempster were the only two who remained in the colonies throughout the war. Asbury attempted to remain neutral, not wanting to take the side of either the British or the colonists.

Once the war was over, John Wesley named Francis Asbury and Thomas Coke the first American Methodist bishops (1784).

The Methodist preachers were not usually college-educated. They shared a natural affinity with the people they preached to. A circuit rider often traveled days before reaching a farm or village. Asbury, who never married, averaged 6,000 miles a year on horseback, preaching at different stops nearly every day. Most Methodist circuits consisted of 200 to 500-mile routes. It took four to six weeks to complete the entire circuit.

At a time when a minister in the East earned $400 a year, a Methodist circuit rider was paid $80. They relied on the hospitality of the families on their circuit for food and lodging. The traveling preachers usually served two years on a circuit, then switched to a new one. This allowed them to use the same sermons repeatedly. Sometimes, two riders worked the same circuit, roughly two weeks apart. In that case, during a four-week circuit, the people would hear a sermon every two weeks, but it could be on any day of the week.

Asbury despised slavery and ordained Richard Allen, the first black minister in the United States. At the 1784 Methodist conference, slave holders were declared ineligible for membership. This decision split the denomination into northern and southern factions. Asbury personally asked George Washington to free the slaves he owned.

> *I preached to any audience I could find, even when seriously ill or threatened by angry mobs. I preached hundreds of sermons with my throat so sore I could barely speak and fever burning so hot I could barely think. I was once so sick I had to be tied to my horse so I wouldn't fall off.*
>
> *My closest companions were my horses. First Jane, then Fox after I wore Jane out, followed by Spark when Fox gave way. Yet it was a privilege to suffer what little I did for God's sake. I wanted Him to find me faithful.*
>
> —*Francis Asbury*

A circuit rider carried a variety of books with him. In addition to the Bible, these might include: a hymnal, prayer book, journal, the *Constitution and Discipline of the Methodist Church*, and *Primitive Physic* by John Wesley which contained home remedies for illnesses. It was quite common for the men to read and study as they rode. Hopefully, Asbury wasn't studying when he experienced the following incident, recorded in his journal.

A new horse, Fox, was given to him by friends. Those friends neglected to inform Asbury that Fox had previously been used as a racehorse. On one of their journeys, Fox recognized an area where he'd raced in the past. The horse took off, and Asbury clung to the saddle for dear life.

On my way to Andrew Purdin's, (Delaware), I came on a race ground, where the sons of Belial had been practicing my horse; he ran away with me when he came to the end of the paths, but stopped, and I received no harm. I lifted my heart to God; and by the mercy of the Lord he stopped near a point of woods, which, had he entered, I might probably have lost my life: my heart was deeply humbled before the Lord, who preserved me from such imminent danger.

Apparently, Asbury had no further problems with the horse. Fox remained one of his regular mounts. Additional excerpts from Asbury's journal give a glimpse of the arduous life of the circuit rider for both man and horse.

After preaching on John vii. 17. we set out on our return: I was much fatigued, and it rained hard; my poor horse too, was so weak from the want of proper food, that he fell down with me twice; this hurt my feelings exceedingly—more than any circumstance I met with in all my journey beside.

Since Thursday we have rode sixty miles along incredibly bad roads, and our fare was not excellent. O what pay would induce a man to go through wet and dry, and fatigue and suffering, as we do?—souls are our hire.

We have had rain for eighteen days successively, and I have rode about two hundred miles in eight or nine days; a most trying time indeed. My horse lost a shoe on a bad road, and next day on the mountains dropped two more; so I rode my old baggage horse along a most dreary, grown-up path to brother C___'s

We went on through devious roads and arrived at Guess's—here I set on a scheme to prevent my horse from falling lame, that had yesterday lost a shoe; it was to bind round his foot a piece of the neck of a bull's hide—my contrivance answered the purpose well.

We hasted to O___'s in the Cove, where we met with a most kind and affectionate reception. But O the flies for the horses, and the gnats for the men! And no food, nor even good water to be had.

Asbury has been called the "George Washington of American Christianity." During his years of leadership, the Methodist church grew from 1,200 to 214,000 members with 700 ordained preachers. Later in his life, when Asbury could no longer ride due to rheumatism, he continued preaching but traveled by carriage. The faithful circuit rider preached his last sermon in Richmond, Virginia on

March 24, 1816 and died a week later. President Calvin Coolidge honored Francis Asbury in 1924, with an equestrian statue in Washington, D.C.

Peter Cartwright

Peter Cartwright came from a different background than Francis Asbury, but he eventually acquired that same fire to saddle a horse and preach the Gospel. Born in Virginia in 1785, Cartwright's father, Peter, Sr. later moved his family to Kentucky. In his autobiography, Peter Cartwright describes himself as a wild youth.

> *I was naturally a wild, wicked boy, and delighted in horse-racing, card-playing, and dancing. My father restrained me but little, though my mother often talked to me, wept over me, and prayed for me, and often drew tears from my eyes; and though I often wept under preaching, and resolved to do better and seek religion, yet I broke my vows, went into young company, rode races, played cards, and danced. At length my father gave me a young race-horse, which well-nigh proved my everlasting ruin.*

Cartwright's mother, Christiana, continued to pray for her son. At the age of sixteen, during a camp meeting, Peter felt convicted about his sin.

> *An awful impression rested on my mind that death had come and I was unprepared to die. I fell on my knees and began to ask God to have mercy on me. I gave up my race-horse to my father, and requested him to sell him, I went and brought my pack of cards, and gave them to mother, who threw them into the fire, and they were consumed. I fasted, watched, and prayed, and engaged in regular reading of the Testament.*

GOING TO CONFERENCE.

Cartwright wrestled with God for several weeks after that meeting, but was finally converted. He began preaching two years later at the age of eighteen. In 1806, he was ordained by Francis Asbury and given his own circuit. Here he describes the difficulty of those early years.

> *I will here state something like the circumstances I found myself in, at the close of my labors on this hard circuit. I had been from my father's house about three years; was five hundred miles from home; my horse had gone blind; my saddle was worn out; my bridle reins had been eaten up and replaced, (after a sort) at least a dozen times; and my clothes had been patched till it was difficult to detect the original.*

> *I had concluded to try to make my way home, and get another outfit. I was in Marietta, and had just seventy-five cents in my pocket. How I would get home and pay my way I could not tell.*

16

Cartwright did make it home, with a little more than six cents to spare.

Next day I reached home with the six and a quarter cents unexpended. Thus I have given you a very imperfect little sketch of the early travel of a Methodist preacher in the Western Conference. My parents received me joyfully. I tarried with them several weeks. My father gave me a fresh horse, a bridle and saddle, some new clothes, and forty dollars in cash. Thus equipped, I was ready for another three years' absence.

Cartwright describes an unexpected dunking during one of his journeys.

Brother Summers and myself concluded to cross at the upper ford on Rock River. About midway in the river was a very slippery rock, which could be avoided by keeping up stream considerably, but somehow I missed the safe track, and my horse got on this slippery rock, and all of a sudden he slipped and fell. My saddle turned, off I went, and the first thing I knew I saw my saddle-bags floating down with great rapidity, for the water ran very swift. I left my horse to get up as best he could, and took after my saddle-bags. I had a tight race, but overtook them before they sunk so as to disappear. They were pretty well filled with water.

My books and clothes had all turned Campbellites[1], for there was much water; and I escaped, not by the skin of my teeth, but by the activity of my heels. My horse rose, and, with all the calmness of old Diogenes, waded out, and left me to do the same. Brother Summers could not maintain his usual gravity, but I assure you all his fun was at my expense. I had scarcely a dry thread about me, but on we went, and reached Pope River settlement that night.

The circuit riders carried with them a simple message of repentance and faith in Jesus Christ. A Methodist preacher in those days, when he felt that God had called him to preach, instead of hunting up a college or Biblical institute, hunted up a hardy pony or a horse, and some traveling apparatus, and with his library always at hand, namely, Bible, Hymn Book, and Discipline, he started, and with a text that never wore out nor grew stale, he cried, "Behold the Lamb of God, that taketh away the sin of the world,"

In this way he went through storms of wind, hail, snow, and rain; climbed hills and mountains, traversed valleys, plunged through swamps, swam swollen streams, lay out all night, wet, weary, and hungry, held his horse by the bridle all night, or tied him to a limb, slept with his saddle blanket for a bed, his saddle or saddle-bags for his pillow, and his old big coat or blanket, if he had any, for a covering.

Often he slept in dirty cabins, on earthen floors, before the fire; ate roasting ears for bread, drank butter-milk for coffee, or sage tea for imperial; took, with a hearty zest, deer or bear meat, or wild turkey, for breakfast, dinner, and supper, if he could get it.

His text was always ready, "Behold the Lamb of God."

—Peter Cartwright

Unlike most circuit riders, Peter Cartwright married. He and his wife, Frances, had two sons and seven daughters. Like Asbury, Cartwright was opposed to slavery. In 1823, he and Frances sold their Kentucky farm and moved to Sangamon County, Illinois, because they didn't want any of their

---

[1] *Campbellites were members of a conservative faction known as the Churches of Christ. They did not believe musical instruments should be used in worship.*

daughters to marry a slave owner. Unfortunately, as they traveled to their new home, the Cartwright's youngest daughter was killed by a falling tree.

Peter Cartwright briefly turned to politics, hoping to ensure slavery would never find its way to Illinois. Cartwright was elected to the state legislature in 1828. When he ran for a second term, he defeated Abraham Lincoln. Then, in 1846, Lincoln defeated Cartwright for a U.S. House seat.

Despite being political opponents, in Abraham Lincoln's last case as an attorney, in 1859, he defended Peter Cartwright's grandson, Quinn "Peachy" Harrison in a murder trial. Cartwright testified in his grandson's defense, and Harrison was found not guilty.

Peter Cartwright passed away on September 25th, 1872 at eighty-seven.

7

Arriving With Bells On

S ome associate the word "Conestoga" with the covered wagons traveling west along the Oregon Trail. But Conestogas were larger, heavier wagons used from the 1700s to about 1840 to haul freight in the eastern colonies.

Conestoga originally referred to a Native American tribe living in the area of southern New York and extending into surrounding states. These people were also known as the Susquehanna. Their numbers were reduced greatly due to exposure to European diseases.

In one of the more appalling incidents of American history, the sixteen remaining Conestoga people in Lancaster, Pennsylvania, were killed by a group of Scotch-Irish men known as the Paxton Boys in December, 1763. Many colonists were outraged by the senseless murders.

The Conestoga name lived on as a river in Lancaster. The wagons built in Lancaster County in the early 1800s by skilled German craftsmen also carried the Conestoga name.

The average Conestoga wagon was sixteen to eighteen feet long, four feet wide, the bed four feet deep, with a height of eleven feet to the top of the cover. When hooked to a six-horse team, the entire outfit stretched sixty feet in length.

The heavy-duty wagons were designed to carry up to six tons of freight over rough roads. A variety of woods were used in their construction: oak for the frame and wheel spokes, gum for the wheel hubs, hickory or oak for the axles, and poplar for the floor boards.

The floor angled up at the front and back to gravitate cargo toward the center when the wagon was in motion. Gates at each end were opened for loading and unloading. The wagon's seams were caulked with tar to prevent them from leaking when crossing creeks or shallow rivers. The bodies were typically painted peacock blue with the wheels a scarlet red.

A heated iron ring was fitted around the outer edge of each wheel. When the iron cooled, it shrank and was held tightly in place. These iron-rimmed wheels were more durable than wheels made only from wood. The two front wheels were smaller than the rear ones. The fronts were forty to forty-five inches in diameter, the rear ones ten to twenty inches larger. The smaller front wheels allowed for sharper turns. The larger rear wheels made the wagon easier for horses to pull. The wagon wheels were removed periodically to grease the axles.

A canvas cover stretched across six or more wooden hoops that arched from side to side over the wagon bed. The hoops at both ends were taller than those in the center. The cover, often coated with linseed oil for waterproofing, protected the contents of the wagon from bad weather.

A toolbox, normally attached to the center, left side, held the tools for wagon repair. A slanted lid kept rainwater out of the box. Often, decorative ironwork latches were used on the tool box. A lever to activate the rear brake was also located on the left side, along with something called the lazy board. This board slid in and out under the wagon bed and was located below the toolbox. The lazy board was often the only seat the driver had. From the name, you can probably guess it wasn't used all the time.

One or more water buckets were hung from the back or side of the wagon. A farmer carrying produce might also haul feed for his team. Professional drivers bought horse feed when they stopped. A feed box for the horses was carried, suspended by chains from the back of the wagon. It was removed and attached to the wagon tongue to create a feed trough. The horses were tied two or three on each side of the tongue with their heads facing the center to enjoy a well-deserved meal after a hard day's work.

16. The Conestoga horse. This is the only extant drawing of the first native American breed of draft horse. The drawing was published in the 1863 *Annual Report* of the U.S. Department of Agriculture. *Courtesy of the U.S. Department of Agriculture.*

Conestoga Horses

Although never formally recognized, the Conestogas are considered the first unofficial breed developed in America, beginning around 1700.

The bloodlines of the Conestoga horses received a boost when in 1730, a wealthy businessman, Samuel Gist, purchased Bulle Rock from England. Bulle Rock was the first Thoroughbred stallion brought to America. The bay, former racehorse was aged, already twenty-one, when he arrived in America. Descended from the Darley Arabian, Bulle Rock and his descendants, were instrumental in developing a line of large horses that would become known as the Conestogas. Draft-like in stature, the horses averaged 16 hands and weighed up to 1800 pounds.

Conestoga horses were particularly suited to pulling the heavy wagons. A team of four to six horses pulled each wagon, although sometimes the team contained an odd number with a single horse up front. The Conestoga horses were in high demand and might cost more than $250 each. The teams averaged ten to fifteen miles a day, sometimes part of a train of thirty or more wagons.

> *It was indeed an animating sight to see five or six well-fed horses, half covered with heavy bear skins, or decorated with gaudily fringed housings, surmounted with a set of finely-toned bells, their bridles adorned with loops of red trimming, as they moved over the ground. With a brisk, elastic step they snorted disdainfully at surrounding objects, as if half-conscious of their superior appearance.*
>
> —John Omwake, Conestoga Six-Horse Teams of Pennsylvania

Driving a Conestoga Wagon

Since Conestoga wagons weren't designed for passengers, they typically had no seats. Drivers, also known as waggoners, had three options. They could:

- Walk along the left side of the horse team or beside the wagon
- Ride the left wheel horse
- Stand or sit on the lazy board

When walking, the driver controlled the horses by voice commands. He might carry a whip, but rarely used it.

The horse the driver rode was the near (left) wheel horse. The right side is called the off side. Wheel horses were those at the back, closest to the wagon. When riding the wheel horse, drivers used a saddle, described by John Omwake as,

> *low, but ample, after the English type, having a rounded pommel and brass-bound cantle with rings to fasten packages. The skirt was quite long and square cornered, while the stirrups were of brass or iron, although later they sometimes had wooden ones with leather guards.*

When mounted, the driver was technically known as a postilion. He rode the left horse of the pair because horses are traditionally mounted from the left. When hitched, there was no easy access to the right-hand horse from its left side.

Many of the wagon drivers smoked cigars. The cigars became known as Conestogas—or stogies for short. The driver controlled the horses using a jerk line. This single line or rein fastened only to the bit of the lead horse, but ran through rings in the harnesses of the other animals in a variety of configurations.

A piece of wood known as a jockey stick, connected from the harness of the near lead horse to the bit of the off lead horse. When the near horse turned, the stiff jockey stick signaled the other lead horse to turn in the same direction, and the horses behind them followed suit.

The lazy board, made from strong oak, was located between the front and rear wheels on the left side. Riding on the lazy board gave the driver a chance to rest. Its location also provided easy access to the brake handle.

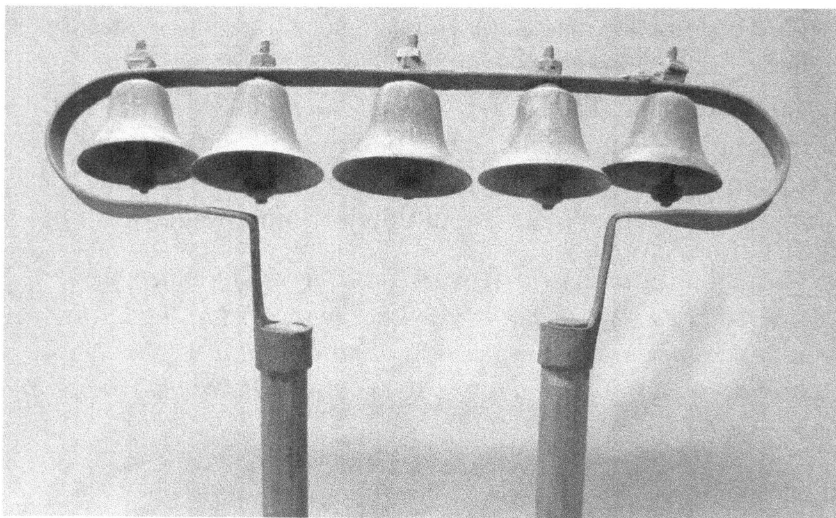

Colonial roads were quite narrow, therefore it was important to know when another wagon was approaching. Warning bells on the horses' harnesses announced their arrival, allowing one of the teams to move aside. Oncoming traffic moved to their right to make room for another wagon. This started the American tradition of driving on the right side of the road. The bells also gave people and animals time to clear out of the way.

Bells served not only as a warning; they became a personal statement and source of pride for the waggoners. The open-ended bells were made from a variety of metals and came in different sizes and shapes. They were suspended from an arched wire attached to the collar near the horses' withers. With a six-horse team, the front pair typically wore five bells, and the middle horses, four. The off wheel horse had three bells. If the near wheeler was ridden, he might have no bells, so they wouldn't interfere with the rider. Each set of bells had a different tone, growing lower in pitch toward the horses closest to the wagon.

If a wagon broke down, became stuck, or was otherwise disabled, it was usually another driver who came to the rescue. As an expression of appreciation, waggoner etiquette dictated that the one who received assistance would give his bells to the man who had rescued him.

To arrive at one's destination with a team's bells on, indicated that all had gone well on the trip. But, to show up without bells was a source of shame for the driver. Thus, the origin of the expression, "I'll be there with bells on."

The Conestogas faced formidable competition with the opening of canals and the development of railroads. Beginning around 1830, the wagons were relegated to local use, bringing produce from farms into the small towns.

The Conestoga wagon was too heavy to be used for traveling west on the Oregon or California Trails. Those journeys would be taken in lighter wagons with flat bodies and lower sides, known as prairie schooners.

Today, Conestoga wagons are rare, found mainly in museums or private collections.

Conestoga (top) compared to the smaller, lighter prairie schooners

8

A Midnight Ride

Although Henry Wadsworth Longfellow's poem, "Paul Revere's Ride," popularized the historic ride of the silversmith from Boston, it contains several inaccuracies.

Listen, my children, and you shall hear
Of the midnight ride of Paul Revere,
On the eighteenth of April, in Seventy-Five:
Hardly a man is now alive
Who remembers that famous day and year.

…

A hurry of hoofs in a village-street,
A shape in the moonlight, a bulk in the dark,
And beneath from the pebbles, in passing, a spark
Struck out by a steed that flies fearless and fleet:
That was all! And yet, through the gloom and the light,
The fate of a nation was riding that night;
And the spark struck out by that steed, in his flight,
Kindled the land into flame with its heat.

Revere didn't ride by himself that night. He most likely didn't even own a horse. But, first let's examine the events that led up to this historic ride.

The French and Indian War was fought from 1754 to 1763. The war pitted England and the colonies against the French and several Native American tribes in a battle for control of territory in the Ohio Valley. England was victorious. At the conclusion of the war, the British rulers decided to enact a series of taxes on the American colonists to help England pay the debts they'd incurred during the war.

Taxation began with the Sugar Act in 1764, followed by several more taxes as well as additional restrictions placed on the colonies. The colonists despised this "taxation without representation."

They wanted a say in the government which was passing laws that affected them. But England wasn't interested in sharing the governing role. Tension between the colonists and their mother country continued to increase.

In an event known as the Boston Massacre in 1770, five colonists were killed by British soldiers. In 1773, colonists dumped 340 chests of tea weighing approximately forty-six tons into Boston Harbor in what would come to be known as the Boston Tea Party.

By March of 1775, war seemed inevitable. The fiery patriot, Patrick Henry, pushed for revolt with his famous words, "I know not what course others may take, but as for me, give me liberty or give me death!"

Fearing arrest by the British authorities, leaders such as Samuel Adams and John Hancock moved out of Boston. Dr. Joseph Warren, a local surgeon, was one of the patriots who remained in the city, watching and listening for suspicious British activity.

In April 1775, the doctor learned that British regulars were preparing to march to Concord, Massachusetts to capture ammunition and militia supplies. He suspected the British planned to stop in Lexington to arrest Adams and Hancock.

At ten o'clock on the night of April 18, Dr. Warren asked Revere to warn the two men. William Dawes had started a half hour earlier toward Lexington. Dr. Warren advised Revere to take a different route in case Dawes was captured.

At the start of his journey, friends rowed Revere across the Charles River. The Sons of Liberty in Charleston had seen Revere's prearranged signal in the church tower—one lantern if the British were leaving Boston by land or two lanterns if by sea. Another error in Longfellow's poem—the lanterns were a signal *from* Revere *to* the patriots, not the other way around. Two lanterns were hung in the Old North Church two days before Revere's ride.

In Charleston, Revere borrowed a horse from Samuel Larkin. In his writings, Revere never mentioned the horse's name, only referring to her as "a very good horse." But, according to the Larkin family records, she was named Brown Beauty.

Revere rode northwest toward Lexington, a distance of twelve miles, alerting homes along the way. It's unlikely he shouted, "The British are coming! The British are coming!"

British troops were referred to as "regulars" and Revere wouldn't have wanted to call attention to himself in case there were troops patrolling the area.

When Revere arrived in Lexington just after midnight, a sentry, Sergeant Monroe, stood guard outside the house where Adams and Hancock were lodging. Monroe warned Revere not to make so much noise, since everyone in the house was asleep.

Revere replied, "Noise! You'll have noise enough before long! The regulars are coming out!"

John Hancock, who was not asleep, heard the commotion and convinced the sentry to allow Revere inside. A half hour later, William Dawes arrived. Revere and Dawes then left together to continue their journey to Concord. They were met along the way by a local patriot, Dr. Samuel Prescott, who offered to help spread the warning.

Around one in the morning on April 19, the three men were stopped by a British patrol. Prescott and Dawes escaped immediately, but Dawes was later thrown from his horse. Dr. Prescott was the only one of the three to reach Concord.

Revere was held and questioned at gunpoint by the British soldiers. He returned to Lexington with them but was eventually released. The British soldiers kept Brown Beauty. There is no record of what happened to the mare after that.

While retrieving a trunk containing papers that belonged to John Hancock from a local tavern, Revere heard gunshots fired on Lexington Green.

The Revolutionary War had begun.

Brown Beauty's role in carrying Paul Revere on that legendary ride is memorialized by a statue in Boston, Massachusetts.

9

Independence

On July fourth, 1776, the Second Continental Congress issued the Declaration of Independence, declaring the thirteen American colonies to be free and independent states, no longer under the rule of Great Britain. That declaration, in itself, didn't make the colonies free. It would take eight years of war to win that freedom.

The Revolutionary War had begun a year earlier at Lexington and Concord in Massachusetts. After those first skirmishes, the colonial government created the Continental Army and selected George Washington as its commander.

Washington was chosen for his military experience and leadership skills. Twenty years earlier, Washington had fought in the French and Indian War. At the age of twenty-three, he narrowly escaped death in the Battle of the Monongahela (near Pittsburgh). Washington wrote about that battle.

> *But by the All-Powerful Dispensations of Providence, I have been protected beyond all human probability or expectation; for I had four bullets through my coat, and two horses shot under me, yet escaped unhurt, although death was leveling my companions on every side of me!*

Horses played an important role in early wars. Not only could soldiers travel faster on horseback, horses were also used to transport weapons and supplies. And the sight of a commander sitting tall upon his horse gave the soldiers courage.

Thomas Jefferson considered Washington "the best horseman of his age, and the most graceful figure that could be seen on horseback."

Washington had many years to hone his riding skills. As a teen, he surveyed land, traveling great distances on horseback. Washington also enjoyed fox hunting. A fast horse with endurance and the ability to jump was required for the hunts which might last seven or eight hours.

Although Washington preferred light-colored horses, his favorite mount in the Revolutionary War was a flashy chestnut stallion given to him by Thomas Nelson, a friend from Virginia.

Washington named the horse after his friend. Nelson was 16 hands tall with a wide blaze and white legs. The horse was approximately fourteen years old when Washington received him. Nelson was described as a "splendid charger."

Washington's second favorite horse was Blueskin. He was described as iron-gray, almost blue in color. Blueskin was also a gift and was believed to be half Arabian. Many paintings of Washington in battle depict him riding a light gray or white horse, but Blueskin proved to be skittish and difficult to control under fire. The gray was often used for ceremonial events, but Nelson was Washington's preferred mount during the war. Nelson's bravery in battle matched that of his master.

A soldier wrote of General Washington astride Nelson on a bridge during the Battle of Trenton in 1777.

As I crossed the bridge crowded with fellow soldiers, I brushed up against the boot of the man and flank of the horse. Both seemed to exude courage.

During the Battle of Princeton in 1777, Washington rode Nelson within thirty yards of the British lines. Colonel Richard Fitzgerald later said.

I covered my face with my hat for fear of seeing my general hit. But upon replacing my hat, I saw many men dead or dying but miraculously the General was still astride his horse and unharmed.

Nelson also carried George Washington on October 17, 1781 at Yorktown, Virginia when the British army under the command of General Charles Cornwallis surrendered, ending the Revolutionary War.

Nelson and Blueskin were only two of the many horses that served faithfully in the Continental Army during the Revolution. Both of Washington's horses survived the war unharmed and were retired to his farm, Mt. Vernon. Blueskin was returned to his previous owner in 1785.

Nelson, especially, seemed to return Washington's affection. According to Washington's adopted son, George Washington Parke Custis, when Washington stopped at Nelson's paddock, "the old warhorse would run, neighing, to the fence, proud to be caressed by the great master's hands."

Nelson lived at Mt. Vernon until his death in 1790.

10

First in the Heart of His Mules?

Firrst in war, First in peace, First in the hearts of his countrymen." That is how "Light Horse Harry" Lee described George Washington. Washington is also credited with another first—our country's first American mule breeder.

The mule is the product of a cross between a male donkey (jack) and a female horse (mare). A similar animal, although less common is the hinny, the result of crossing a female donkey (jenny) with a male horse (stallion).

During the 1700s, donkeys and mules often worked the hilly farm lands of France and Spain. At the time, those countries weren't interested in exporting their animals to the colonies for fear of providing an advantage to their mutual enemy, England. Therefore, there were few mules in the American colonies, and the existing ones were too small to accomplish much work.

After gaining independence from Britain, America's relationships with France and Spain improved. One result was that in 1785, King Charles of Spain sent George Washington an unusual gift—two jennies and an Andalusian jack named Royal Gift.

The following year, the Marquis de Lafayette of France sent Washington a black Maltese jack, Knight of Malta, and several jennies.

Washington's goal was to establish a herd of larger donkeys which could be crossed with draft horses to produce large, working mules. The crossing of the Andalusian and Maltese lines succeeded in developing some of the best donkeys and mules in the country, the American Mammoths.

Washington's enthusiasm for the project is evident in this excerpt from a letter to Arthur Young in 1788.

> *The Spanish Jack seems calculated to breed for heavy, slow draught; and the others for the Saddle or lighter carriages. From these, all together, I hope to secure a race of extraordinary goodness, which will stock the Country. Their longevity & cheap keeping will be circumstances much in their favor. I am convinced from the little experiments I have made with the ordinary Mules, (which perform as much labour, with vastly less feeding than horses) that those of a superior quality will be the best cattle we can employ for the harness. And, indeed, in a few years, I intend to drive no other in my carriage: having appropriated for the sole purpose of breeding them, upwards of 20 of my best Mares.*

In 1785, there were 132 horses at Washington's Mt. Vernon estate—and no mules or donkeys. At the time of his death in 1799, the equine distribution had shifted. There were twenty-seven horses, twenty donkeys, and sixty-three mules.

By the early 1800s, there were over 800,000 mules in the United States. Mules were not popular with farmers in the North, but were the preferred farm animal in the South. By 1897, the mule population had grown to 2.2 million and reached a high of 6 million in the 1920s.

Mules served the developing country in a variety of ways including farm work, towing canal boats, pulling covered wagons and stagecoaches, and assisting soldiers during war.

"MAGNUM BONUM." Copied from an old Painting.

11

Figure

A sturdy, bay colt was born in West Springfield, Massachusetts in 1789, not long after the Revolutionary War. Three years later, Justin Morgan, a Vermont farmer, acquired the horse as payment for a debt. Morgan named him Figure. Justin Morgan was also a school teacher and music composer. He created musical renditions of poetry and psalms known as fuguing tunes or psalmody.

The parentage of Figure is uncertain, but the best guess is that his mother was a daughter of Diamond of the Wildair bloodline—a mix of Thoroughbred and Dutch Cob. His sire—True Briton, a bay Thoroughbred stallion, was once owned by British colonel, James DeLancey. The horse was stolen from Delancey by colonial patriots during the war and renamed Beautiful Bay.

At 14 hands, Figure was not a tall horse, but he was stocky and extremely strong for his size. He was a dark bay with an arched neck. Figure carried his refined head high with a proud look. He was strong, athletic, intelligent, and kind. Mr. Solomon Yurann of Randolph, Vermont, described Figure.

If Justin Morgan had realized what he had in this beautiful and versatile horse, he might have held on to him. No one, back then, fully appreciated the greatness of this stallion. Over the years, Figure changed hands many times.

- In 1795, Morgan leased Figure to Robert Evans for $15 a year to work clearing rocks and stumps from land in Randolph, Vermont.

- The stallion was traded to Samuel Allen.

- Allen sold him to William Rice of Woodstock, Vermont. In 1796, Figure raced in Brookfield, Vermont, beating all other horses to win $50.

- Figure was traded in 1797 to James Hawkins.

- From 1801 to 1804, he was owned by Robert Evans.

- Colonel John Goss received Figure as part of the payment of a debt owed to him by Evans. Figure was used by the colonel to review troops. Goss also entered the horse in a pulling bee, which Figure won.

- In 1805, Goss traded Figure to his brother David.

- David Goss owned Figure from 1805 to 1811 and used him for farm work.

- In 1811, he was sold to Philip Goss, then to Jacob Sanderson, then Jacob Langmeade.

- Langmeade used the aging Figure to haul freight. It's believed Langmeade abused Figure.

- At the end of 1811, Langmeade sold Figure to Joel Goss and Joseph Rogers.

- Samuel Stone purchased Figure in 1817 and exhibited him at the Randolph fair. That same year, President James Monroe rode Figure in a parade. Figure was twenty-eight years old.

- Levi Bean of Chelsea, Vermont was Figure's last owner, acquiring the horse in 1819. He may have still used Figure to haul freight as part of a six-horse team. While turned out in a pasture for the winter of 1821, Figure was kicked by another horse and died at the age of thirty-two.

As time passed, Figure came to be known by the name of the man who had owned him early on. He was called the Morgan horse or simply Justin Morgan.

Each of Figure's owners used him as a breeding stallion. Figure strongly stamped his offspring with the same looks and qualities he possessed. Figure's best-known sons were Bulrush, Sherman, and Woodbury. Their descendants created a highly desirable type of horse that would later become the Morgan breed. Not only could the sturdy Morgans clear and work farmland, they also excelled as harness horses.

Although details of Figure's life are sketchy, more is known about some of his famous descendants.

Ethan Allen, foaled in 1849, was a great grandson of Figure. He was a bay with a star, narrow stripe, and three white socks. A trotter, his harness racing career lasted an incredible twenty years—in the days when each race consisted of physically taxing, multiple heats.

Ethan Allen was poisoned at least three times to keep him from winning. The thought of anyone poisoning a horse is sad. Even worse, it's believed two of the incidents occurred at the hands of his owner, Joel Holcomb, so he could win more money by betting against his own horse.

Allen set several sub 2:30 mile records, but he's best remembered for a three-horse race conducted in 1867. At the advanced age of eighteen, Ethan Allen was to be double-hitched with a running mate, a Thoroughbred mare named Charlotte. The pair would race Allen's rival, Dexter.

Charlotte was not a trotter. She would gallop, pulling most of the weight of their sulky. While that might seem to be an advantage—two horses against one, it's difficult for paired horses to match their pace, especially at different gaits. Ethan Allen would be tempted to break from his trot to run at a gallop like Charlotte.

Dexter, a Hambletonian descendant, was half Ethan Allen's age. He was considered the favorite and would be hitched alone. The race was set up as the best of five heats.

The day before the race, Charlotte injured herself and could not run. Many debated whether to call the race off or have Ethan Allen run with a substitute. It was decided to pair Allen with another horse. This new partner was one Allen had never run with before.

Nearly 40,000 spectators watched the race. Driven by Dan Mace, Allen and his partner won the first mile heat in 2:15, the second in 2:16, and the third in 2:19. A rematch was held two weeks later, and the same two horses beat Dexter again in three straight heats.

Ethan Allen was featured in five Currier and Ives prints. He was also the model for a popular copper weather vane. It's believed Ethan Allen had the X-Factor which causes a larger than normal heart.

Ethan Allen died on September 10, 1876, at the age of twenty-seven. Although he lived a relatively long life, it's believed his death was due to the loss of a lower tooth. Horses' teeth grow continually. With nothing to oppose its growth, Allen's upper tooth cut nearly an inch into his lower jaw bone. If that had been discovered earlier and treated, Ethan Allen might have lived several more years.

12

All Men Are Created Equal

We hold these truths to be self-evident, that all men are created equal, that they are endowed by their Creator with certain unalienable Rights, that among these are Life, Liberty and the Pursuit of Happiness."

Ironically, the man that drafted those words held 600 people in slavery during his lifetime. In addition to writing the first draft of the Declaration of Independence, Thomas Jefferson served two terms as America's third president from 1801 to 1809. As president, Jefferson was instrumental in getting an act passed by Congress in 1807 that banned the importing of additional slaves.

Jefferson's expressed views on slavery are difficult to reconcile with his continued ownership of slaves at the Monticello plantation.

I tremble for my country when I reflect that God is just and his justice cannot sleep forever.

— *Thomas Jefferson*

Thomas Jefferson was a lifelong horse lover. In his younger days, he was known as a bold and fearless rider. He once stated that he couldn't tolerate any form of exercise except riding. Unlike many leaders who liked white horses, Jefferson was partial to bays.

A grandson of the Godolphin Arabian, the stallion, Fearnaught was a bright bay, 16 hands tall. The Thoroughbred stallion was born in England where he had a successful racing career, winning the King's Plate. At the age of nine, Fearnaught, was brought to America, settling at a farm in Caroline County, Virginia. Many of the stallion's American offspring were successful at racing or served as military horses in the Revolutionary War.

Jefferson's favorite horse was Caractacus, the foal of his mare, Allycroker, and sired by Fearnaught. In 1781, Jefferson broke his arm when he was thrown by the six-year-old Caractacus.

During the Revolutionary War, British general Cornwallis and his troops captured Jefferson's horse farm. Cornwallis took some of the mares and killed their foals. Jefferson was furious about this for the rest of his life.

Jefferson was a detailed record keeper and his horses were no exception. He maintained a list of the horses he owned over the years. His saddle horses included:

- Allycroker
- Gustavus
- Cacullin
- The General
- Crab
- Everallyn
- Alfred
- Caractacus (sire Fearnaught, May 1775)
- Ethelinda (sire Fearnaught, 1776)
- Silvertail
- Orra Moor (sire Fearnaught, 1778)
- Peggy Washington (sire Fearnaught)
- Zanga (sire Fearnaught, 1778)
- Odin (sire Fearnaught, 1778)
- Polly Peachum
- Silveret (sire Caractus, 1780)
- Assaragoa
- Raleigh
- Tarquin
- Brimmer
- Remus & Romulus (carriage horses)
- Matchless
- Fitzpartner
- Wildair
- Castor
- Diomed
- Bremo
- Wellington
- Tecumseh
- Peacemaker
- Eagle

The second president, John Adams, was the first to live in the White House. Adams had a matched pair of black harness horses—Cleopatra and Caesar. The team pulled the carriage taking President Adams and his wife to the inauguration. When Jefferson was elected in 1800, John Adams wrote him a letter offering his horses and carriage.

> *In order to save you the trouble and Expence of purchasing Horses and Carriages, which will not be necessary, I have to inform you that I shall leave in the stables of the United States seven Horses and two Carriages with Harness the Property of the United States.*
>
> *These may not be suitable for you: but they will certainly save you a considerable Expence as they belong to the studd of the Presidents Household.*

Jefferson declined Adam's offer. He believed the president should provide his own carriage, horses, and horse feed, rather than that being a government expense.

On May 20, 1800, a notice was posted requesting proposals for the construction of the White House stable.

> *Proposals will be received at the Commissioner's office until Second Day of June next (1800) for building a brick Stable (to contain Stalls for 12 Horses, Carriage House to contain three Carriages, and a small Room for Grain.*

Half the price was paid on signing the contract and the remainder on completion of the building. They received seven proposals and the project was given to William Lovell. The project was completed on August 11, 1800 at a cost of $1600.

The White House Stable housed the president's horses and a few others for government use. The president's horses were kept in large box stalls, while the additional horses were given smaller tie stalls.

During his presidency, Jefferson rode nearly every day and enjoyed attending horse races at the National Race Course, located two miles north of the White House. After serving two terms, Jefferson retired to Monticello.

Wormley Hughes was a slave who worked for Jefferson as a gardener. He was also a carriage driver and caretaker of the horses. According to Henry Randall, Jefferson's biographer, Hughes had a knack with horses. He could distinctly remember, and describe the points, height, color, pace, and temper of every horse.

Eagle was Jefferson's last horse. Jefferson continued to ride until he required assistance to mount the horse.

He retained to the last his fondness for riding on horseback; he rode within three weeks of his death at age eighty-three, when from disease, debility and age, he mounted with difficulty. He was fond of solitary rides and musing.

—Henry Randall, 1851

Jefferson died fifty years after the signing of the Declaration of Independence, on July 4, 1826. Wormley Hughes dug the grave. Hughes was freed at this time, but his wife and children were some of the 126 men, women, and children who were sold from Jefferson's estate in 1827.

13

Lewis & Clark

Sacagawea is one of the few Native American women to make it into American history textbooks. While some may recognize her name, further details about this woman are murky. With the Louisiana Purchase in 1803, President Thomas Jefferson acquired a vast area of land for the United States from France for fifteen million dollars. This territory extended west from the Mississippi River to the Rocky Mountains and doubled the country's size.

The Louisiana Purchase contained 828,000 square miles of land—what would later become fifteen states. Because the exact boundary at its western edge was in question, President Jefferson was eager to have the area explored and mapped.

He also hoped to locate a usable water route to the Pacific, establish trade with the Native American tribes, and document new forms of plant and animal life. An expedition was organized to explore the new territory.

Meriwether Lewis, Jefferson's personal secretary, and Lewis' friend, William Clark, were chosen to head the Corps of Discovery Expedition, now referred to as the Lewis and Clark Expedition.

Lewis, Clark, and a team of over forty military men aged nineteen to thirty-five set out from Camp Wood in Illinois on May 14, 1804. A Newfoundland dog, Seaman, was also part of the expedition.

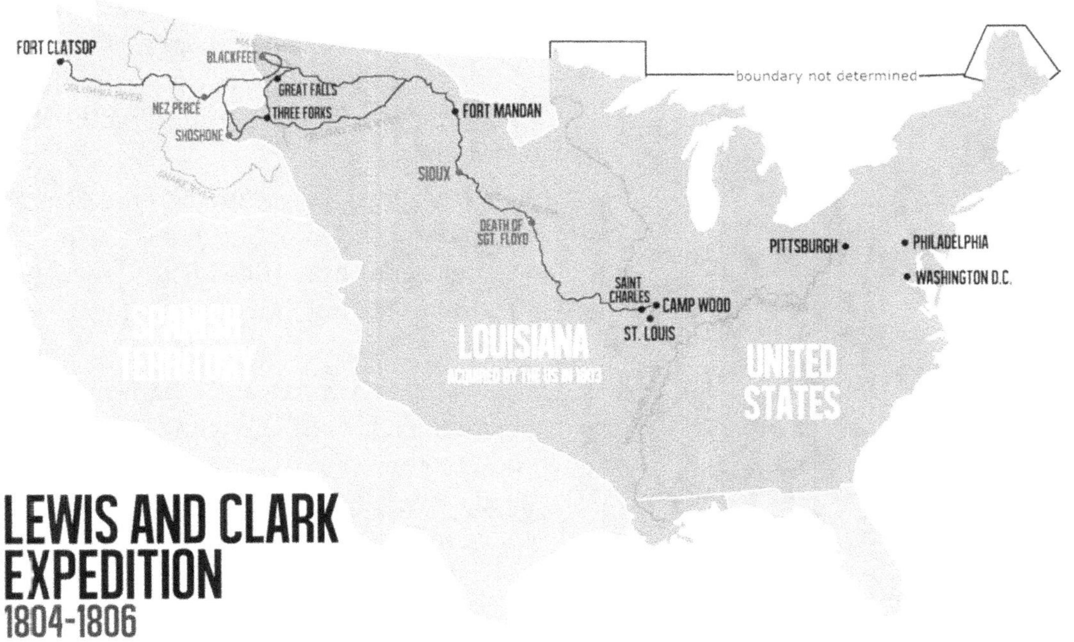

Much of their journey involved traveling by keel boat and other small boats or on foot carrying the boats to the next navigable river section. This process was known as portaging. The journey began by traveling up the Missouri River from St. Charles, Missouri. Further west, they would also travel on the Yellowstone and Columbia Rivers.

By the winter of 1804, the men had reached central North Dakota. Unable to travel in the frigid, forty-below-zero weather, they spent the winter there in a Mandan Indian village. Lewis and Clark hired an interpreter, Toussaint Charbonneau, a French-Canadian fur trader who lived with the Mandans.

Charbonneau's wife, Sacagawea (Bird Woman or Boat Launcher), was a Shoshone. She had been captured from her home in the Rocky Mountains by the neighboring Hidatsa tribe. A son was born to Sacagawea and Charbonneau at Fort Mandan in February 1805. The boy was named Jean Baptiste but was called Pomp.

Two months later, the expedition started west again, this time with Charbonneau and Sacagawea as their guides. Sacagawea carried Pomp in a cradle board on her back. In May, when one of the boats nearly overturned, Sacagawea helped save important items from the water. Expedition members were so grateful, they named a river after her.

The presence of Sacagawea and her child identified them as peaceful travelers and protected the expedition from attack. Charbonneau was not viewed favorably by the other men. Lewis described him in his journal as "a man of no peculiar merit."

With the vast majority of the expedition's miles traveled by boat, there was little need for horses. However, horses were essential for one section of the journey—crossing the Rocky Mountains.

In August, Lewis and half the expedition's members arrived in Shoshone territory, Sacagawea's homeland (Idaho). They encountered a band of Native Americans led by Chief Cameahwait.

Since Sacagawea and Charbonneau were further back, traveling with Clark, Lewis did his best to convey to the chief that he and his men had come in peace. He gave the Natives gifts and tried to communicate with sign language and the few Shoshone words he knew.

When Sacagawea arrived, she learned that her parents had died, and her brother Cameahwait was the new Shoshone chief. Lewis recorded the reunion in his journal.

> *Shortly after Capt. Clark arrived with the Interpreter Charbono, and the Indian woman, who proved to be a sister of the Chief Cameahwait. The meeting of those people was really affecting, particularly between Sah cah-gar-weah and an Indian woman, who had been taken prisoner at the same time with her, and who had afterwards escaped from the Minnetares and rejoined her nation.*

Lewis and Clark acquired horses from Cameahwait, and native guides led them over the Rocky Mountains. The expedition reached the Pacific Ocean on November 15, 1805.

Each member, including Sacagawea, and Clark's slave, York, voted on the location for their winter stay. They built Fort Clatsop and remained there until beginning the return trip on March 23, 1806.

Several entries from Lewis' journal indicate recurring lameness of the horses on the return trip — and his interesting remedy for it. Native Americans were known to use hoof boots, an alternative to metal shoes. Lewis calls them "mockersons." Equine boots are regaining popularity in modern times.

Tuesday July 15, 1806

the horses feet are very sore many of them can scercely proceed on over the stone and gravel in every other respect they are sound and in good sperits.

Wednesday July 16, 1806

…we did not set out untill 9 a m. we had not proceeded on far before i saw a buffalow & sent Sharnon to kill it this buffalow provd. to be a very fat bull i had most of the flesh brought on an a part of the skin to make mockersons for some of our lame horses.

saw a large gangue of about 200 elk and nearly as many antilope also two white or grey bear in the plains, one of them i chased on horse back about 2 miles to the rugid part of the plain where i was compelled to give up the chase two of the horses was so lame owing to their feet being worn quit smooth and to the quick, the hind feet was much the worst. i had mockersons made of green buffalow skin and put on their feet which seams to releve them very much in passing over the stoney plains.

This excerpt from the journal includes observations of feral horses in the area.

They appear to be of an excellent race, lofty, elegantly formed, active and durable: many of them appear like fine English coursers; some of them are pied with large spots of white irregularly scattered, and intermixed with a dark brown bay: the greater part, however, are of an uniform color, marked with stars and white feet, and resemble in fleetness and bottom, as well as in form and color, the best blooded horses of Virginia.

Horses are said to be found wild in many parts of this extensive country. The several tribes of Shoshones who reside towards Mexico, on the waters of the Mutlomah river, and particularly one of them, called Shaboboah, have also a great number of mules, which the Indians prize more highly than horses.

An elegant horse may be purchased of the natives for a few beads or other paltry trinkets, which in the United States, would not cost more than one or two dollars. The abundance and cheapness of horses, will be extremely advantageous to those who may hereafter attempt the fur trade to the East Indies, by the way of Columbia river, and the Pacific ocean.

The round-trip Lewis and Clark Expedition covered approximately 8,000 miles. Only one man was lost. Sergeant Charles Floyd died from a ruptured appendix.

The details of Sacagawea's life after the expedition are uncertain. She may have had a daughter, Lisette. Some records indicate Sacagawea died in 1812. Others claim she lived with a Comanche tribe or returned to the Shoshone. Either way, William Clark became the legal guardian of both Lisette and Sacagawea's son, Jean Baptiste (Pomp).

In May 1805, Seaman, the Newfoundland dog was bitten by a beaver. The two men operated on his leg, and the dog recovered. The last mention of Seaman in the journal is from July 1806. It's said that in 1809, Seaman refused to leave the graveside of his master, Meriwether Lewis, and that the dog died of grief on Lewis' grave.

14

Marengo & Napoleon

Although he loved horses, Napoleon Bonaparte was not known as a good rider. He hadn't grown up with horses and only began riding when he started his military career. One observer noted that he rode, "like a butcher… his body rolling backwards and forwards and sideways, according to the speed of his horse."

Napoleon is considered one of the greatest military leaders of all time. He rose to power during the years of the French Revolution. In Paris, in 1789, the common people rebelled against the royal government of France. The French king Louis XVI and his wife, Queen Marie Antoinette, were executed along with other noblemen and former rulers.

Napoleon joined a revolutionary group in France known as the Jacobins. They gained control of the government, and at the age of twenty-four, Napoleon was made a general.

In 1799, Napoleon and several allies restructured the French government. Theoretically, there were to be three consuls in charge, but as First Consul, Napoleon assumed the power of a dictator. As if that wasn't enough, in 1804, he made himself Emperor of France.

In order to expand his empire, Napoleon entered various wars with Britain and several European countries. These were known as the Napoleonic Wars. Over the years of his reign, it's estimated that Napoleon used 130 horses, twenty of which died in battle.

Napoleon preferred Arabians and particularly white ones. He had up to fifty light-colored Arabians in his stable. One of his favorite horses was a light-gray, 14.1 hand Arabian stallion, acquired as a six-year-old in 1799 from Egypt. He was named Marengo after Napoleon rode the horse to victory in a battle in Marengo, Italy. He would go on to ride Marengo in many battles.

In 1812, Napoleon rode Marengo over 3,500 miles from Paris to Moscow and back in a failed attempt to conquer Russia. Many soldiers died from exposure or starved along the way.

After the disastrous Russian campaign, Napoleon was forced into exile on the island of Elba in 1814. He returned briefly to take control of Paris for what is called the Hundred Days. His return to power was short-lived, as a European army, led by the British Duke of Wellington, defeated Napoleon at the Battle of Waterloo in June of 1815. The Duke rode a famous horse, Copenhagen, in that battle.

Napoleon fled the battlefield at Waterloo in a horse cart, leaving Marengo behind. A British lieutenant, Henry Petre, found the wounded Marengo lying in the road. He recognized the horse as belonging to Napoleon by the imperial brand on his flank—an 'N' with a crown above it. Considered a "spoil of war" by the British, Petre brought the horse to England and nursed him back to health.

Marengo had fought in many battles and was wounded several times. A bullet was found lodged in his tail bone, and five long scars crisscrossed his body. The

brave war horse died on the estate of William Angerstein at the age of thirty-eight in 1831, ten years after the death of Napoleon.

Angerstein had Marengo's front hooves shod in silver and turned into silver and gold snuff boxes. He gave the remainder of the horse's skeleton to the National Army Museum in London, England where it is still on display. Later, the hooves were reunited with Marengo's skeleton at the museum.

Some doubt that Marengo was actually one horse. They believe Napoleon rode a series of different white stallions over the years.

Another Arabian stallion, Le Vizir, was also a favorite of Napoleon's. Le Vizir traveled with Napoleon to exile in Elba in 1814, but by the time of Napoleon's return during the Hundred Days, Le Vizir was too old for battle and was retired at the imperial stables.

When Le Vizir died in 1826 at the age of thirty-three, he was stuffed by a taxidermist. With continuing unrest in France, it was feared the remains of the horse might be destroyed. The stuffed LeVizir was sold to William Clark, an Englishman living in France.

In 1839, Clark decided to bring Le Vizir to England. To avoid being detected by customs officials, he removed the horse's stuffing and placed the hide in a trunk. In England, Le Vizir was later re-stuffed and displayed at the Manchester Natural History Society in 1843.

Le Vizir returned to France in 1868, when a nephew of Napoleon, Napoleon III, came to power. The horse was displayed at the Army Museum of Paris. Two years later, Napoleon III was overthrown by the Prussians. Le Vizir was put into a storage room for thirty years before being moved to the Army Museum where he is now on display.

The names of some of Napoleon's other horses include:

- Arabella
- Babylonian
- Brother
- Cleopatra
- Distinguished
- Endurant
- Graceful
- Hector
- Judith
- Lyre
- Major
- Navigator
- Nickel
- Ramier
- Russian
- Sahara
- Shy
- Sportsman
- Sultan
- Triumphant

15

Copenhagen at Waterloo

I don't know what I shall do with my awkward son Arthur. He is food for powder and nothing more." It's not clear what Anne Wellesley meant by describing her son as "food for powder," but she apparently didn't have high expectations for him. One can only hope she later admitted how wrong she had been.

Arthur Wellesley became one of Britain's most successful military leaders. After his death, Queen Victoria called him, "the greatest man this country ever produced."

In 1814, Arthur Wellesley was named the Duke of Wellington. He served as the British prime minister in 1828 and 1834.

The Duke of Wellington's favorite war horse was Copenhagen. Born in 1808, the dark chestnut was a mixture of Arabian and Thoroughbred racing lines. Copenhagen's sire was the Thoroughbred racehorse, Meteor, a son of Eclipse. His dam, Lady Catherine, had been ridden by Thomas Grosvenor in the Battle of Copenhagen in 1807.

In addition to carrying Grosvenor in that battle, Lady Catherine carried her foal. When the colt was born, he was given the name Copenhagen, since indirectly he had also participated in the battle.

During his brief racing career, in 1811 and 1812, Copenhagen won two races. At 15.1 hands, he was strong and sturdy, but not exceptionally fast. The stallion had a peculiar habit that, at first, alarmed the grooms, who assumed he was sick. The horse liked to eat while lying down. Copenhagen was also temperamental and prone to kicking. But, the Duke of Wellington was able to handle him and said of Copenhagen.

There may have been many faster horses, no doubt many handsomer, but for bottom and endurance I never saw his fellow.

Copenhagen joined the Duke in many battles. In fact, Wellington won every battle he rode the horse in. But Copenhagen is most famous for the Battle of Waterloo.

During the Hundred Days of Napoleon's return to power in France in 1815, Wellington was given command of the allied force. The British, German, Dutch, and Belgian troops faced the French, led by Napoleon, at Waterloo. After seventeen hours, Napoleon was defeated, and France's attempts to conquer Europe were brought to an end.

The victory came at a high cost. On the French side, 26,000 soldiers were killed or wounded while the Allies suffered 22,000 casualties. Wellington was deeply disturbed by the losses.

My heart is broken by the terrible loss I have sustained in my old friends and companions and my poor soldiers. Believe me, nothing except a battle lost can be half so melancholy as a battle won.

The Duke and Copenhagen returned to an inn that night around 11:00 pm. Copenhagen, perhaps exhausted and nervous from the long battle, was caught off guard by his master's touch. The Duke recalled.

Well, on reaching headquarters, and thinking how bravely my old horse had carried me all day, I could not help going up to his head to tell him so by a few caresses. But, hang me if, when I was giving him a slap of approbation on his hind-quarters, he did not fling out one of his hind legs with as much vigor as if he had been in the stable for a couple of days!

It would have been horribly ironic if the Duke had survived the bloody battle only to have been killed by a kick from his own horse.

Having fought their last battle, the Duke and Copenhagen returned to England in 1818. Copenhagen was considered nearly as much of a hero as the Duke. Women picked strands of the horse's hair to turn into jewelry. Copenhagen was retired to the Duke's 7,000-acre estate, Stratfield Saye in Hampshire County, England. There, he was visited daily by the Duchess who always brought him a treat.

The stallion mellowed with age, enough that women were able to ride him around the estate. Children were sometimes permitted to ride Copenhagen—with adult supervision, but the Duchess forbade her own sons to ride him. As an adult, the Duke's oldest son, Arthur, admitted he had sometimes snuck out to the stable to ride the old war horse.

In 1828, when the Duke became Prime Minister, Copenhagen was pulled from retirement for one last job. He carried his master through the streets of London, taking Arthur to his new position in the government.

Toward the end of his life, Copenhagen became blind and deaf. He died in 1836 at twenty-eight.

When news of the horse's death reached Arthur, he went to the stable to say a final goodbye to his faithful friend. He was furious when he saw Copenhagen's right forefoot was missing. A servant had cut off the hoof to keep as a souvenir.

Copenhagen was buried with full military honors in his paddock at the Hampshire estate. The grave was unmarked in order to protect Copenhagen from other souvenir hunters. It wasn't until 1852, that a headstone was added.

Here lies
COPENHAGEN
The charger ridden by the Duke of Wellington
The entire day at the Battle of Waterloo.
Born 1808, Died 1836.
God's humbler instrument, though meaner clay,
Should share the glory of that glorious day.

The horse's missing hoof was returned after the Duke's death.

16

The Dream Horse

Simón Bolívar, known as The Liberator, traveled nearly 100,000 miles on horseback, many of those miles on a horse that came to him as the result of a woman's dream.

Bolívar was born to a wealthy Criollo[1] family in Caracas, Venezuela on July 24, 1783. Both of his parents died when Simón was young—his father when he was two, and his mother when he was eight. Simón was raised by the family's slave, Hipólita, whom he called "the only mother I have known." As a teen, Simón was educated in Spain and France, where he picked up ideas of liberation and independence.

In his twenties, Bolívar returned to his home country and joined Venezuela's fight for independence from Spain. He fought in hundreds of battles in Latin American countries including Bolivia, Colombia, Ecuador, Peru, and Venezuela.

His favorite horse was a stallion named Palomo. The horse was described as being as white as a snowflake.

The surprising story of Bolívar's acquisition of Palomo begins in 1814 when he approached the village of Santa Rosa, riding a horse who was so exhausted he refused to go any farther.

The man who appeared to help him informed Bolívar that his wife, Casilda, had recently dreamed she would give a colt to serve a famous general. When the man learned Bolívar's identity, he was astonished. Bolívar requested that Casilda keep the colt and raise it for him.

Five years later, shortly before the Battle of Vargas Swamp, near Bogota, Columbia, Bolívar returned for Casilda's

____

[1] Criollo: Latin American of Spanish descent

colt. He named him Palomo, and the horse was Bolívar's mount for ten years.

In 1829, Bolívar loaned Palomo to one of his officers who rode the horse on a grueling march, causing the stallion's death.

Simón Bolívar died of tuberculosis the following year at the age of forty-seven.

The famous war horse's shoes are on display at the Museum of Mulaló in Colombia.

17

Cabriolet

In today's motorized world, we've lost sight of all the services that were once provided by horses. Horses pulled carriages, coaches, carts, sleighs, and wagons of all sorts to perform work and to get both people and goods where they needed to go.

In the days before trains and automobiles, the options for travel were limited to walking, riding horseback, or as a passenger in a horse-drawn carriage. Not everyone could afford a horse and carriage or had a place to keep one. And many, particularly women, didn't have the skills or confidence to ride a horse.

Horse-drawn cabs were popular in large cities. The use of cab horses in London, England is detailed in Anna Sewell's novel, *Black Beauty*, in which she describes the life of the often overworked horses and drivers.

> *It is always difficult to drive fast in the city in the middle of the day, when the streets are full of traffic, but we did what could be done; and when a good driver and a good horse, who understand each other, are of one mind, it is wonderful what they can do. I had a very good mouth— that is I could be guided by the slightest touch of the rein; and that is a great thing in London, among carriages, omnibuses, carts, vans, trucks, cabs, and great wagons creeping along at a walking pace; some going one way, some another, some going slowly, others wanting to pass them; omnibuses stopping short every few minutes to take up a passenger, obliging the horse that is coming behind to pull up too, or to pass, and get before them; perhaps you try to pass, but just then something else comes dashing in through the narrow opening, and you have to keep in behind the omnibus again; presently you think you see a chance, and manage to get to the front, going so near the wheels on each side that half an inch nearer and they would scrape.*
>
> *Well, you get along for a bit, but soon find yourself in a long train of carts and carriages all obliged to go at a walk; perhaps you come to a regular block-up, and have to stand still for minutes together, till something clears out into a side street, or the policeman interferes; you have to be ready for any chance—to dash forward if there be an opening, and be quick as a rat-dog to see if there be room and if there be time, lest you get your own wheels locked or smashed, or the shaft of some other vehicle run into your chest or shoulder. All this is what you have to be ready for. If you want to get through London fast in the middle of the day it wants a deal of practice.*
>
> —Black Beauty, chapter 35

Cab is short for cabriolet, a light vehicle with two wheels and a folding hood. The cabriolet, dating back to the late 1700s, carried two people—a passenger and the driver.

In the 1800s, there were two main types of
cabs in England. Two-wheeled Hansom cabs
were designed in 1834 by Joseph Hansom. The
driver sat up high at the back of the cab behind
his passengers. These speedy, nimble cabs, pulled
by a single horse, were considered the sports cars
of the cab world. Passengers paid the driver
through a hatch at the rear of the cab. The driver
opened and closed the cab's passenger door with
a lever near his seat. That way, he could keep the
cab door closed until the fare was paid. Fictional
detective Sherlock Holmes and his assistant
Watson often traveled in a hansom cab.

> *Hosmer came for us in a hansom, but as
> there were two of us he put us both into it
> and stepped himself into a four-wheeler,
> which happened to be the only other cab in
> the street.*
>
> —*The Red-Headed League*

Clarence cabs, introduced in the
1840s, were named for Prince
William, the Duke of Clarence. These
four-wheeled vehicles were larger
than the hansoms. They carried up to
four passengers on two seats which
faced each other. The driver of a
Clarence cab sat up front, outside the
enclosed carriage, directly behind the
horses, typically a team of two. These
cabs came to be known as growlers
because of the noise their wheels
made on the cobblestone streets.

Cabs were not as popular in the
United States because of the sparse
population. To cover longer
distances, stagecoaches were used in
the US until rail travel became more
widespread. But cabs were used to
some extent in more populated areas
such as New York City. Central Park
included roads designed specifically
for the use of horse-drawn carriages.

18

School Buses

In the 1800s, schools were designed to support families within a four or five-mile radius. Initially, no public transportation was provided. Students walked to school, rode a horse or pony, or perhaps a parent transported them in a horse-drawn wagon.

In 1890, a girl who lived two and a half miles from the Riverhead School rode her pony to school each morning.

> *Upon arriving, she turned the pony back down the road and gave it a whack. As she went into the school, her pony found his way back home by himself. When school let out in the afternoon, the girl rode home in a wagon with the other students.*

—Times Union Brooklyn, New York, Oct 28, 1890

Not only was getting to and from school different in the 1800s, the schools themselves were different. One-room schoolhouses were common in rural areas. The buildings, heated by a single wood stove, were as small as twenty by thirty feet. Student desks or benches took up most of the space. The teacher's desk was often on a raised platform at one end of the room with a blackboard on the wall behind her.

Most teachers were female, between the ages of sixteen and twenty. The teachers taught all subjects to all grades with as many as forty students in attendance. The school year was shorter, about five months long, since children helped with planting in the spring and harvesting in the fall on their families' farms.

In 1869, Massachusetts passed the first law in the United States allocating public funds to transport children to and from school. In 1892, Wayne Works made an early version of a school bus, a horse-drawn carriage known as a "school hack" or "school car." Students entered through a door at the rear of the wagon in order to avoid the equine team

providing the horsepower. As many as twenty-five students sat facing each other on benches along the sides of the bus. These vehicles tended to be cold in the winter, with only curtains or a tarp covering the windows. In cold months, bricks were heated, wrapped in cloth, and placed on the floor to keep children's feet warm.

The interesting version of a school bus below, from northern Pennsylvania, looks more like a small house on wheels. It came equipped with a wood stove to keep the students warm in the winter.

By 1914, as automobiles became more common, Wayne Works revised its design. The motorized version looked like the horse-drawn school car, but it was mounted on a truck frame. In 1930, the company went even further, introducing an all-steel bus with safety glass windows. Yellow was adopted as the standard bus color at a 1939 safety conference.

Not many children ride horses or ponies to school today, except in Amish communities. Children attending an Amish school may walk, ride a pony, drive a pony cart, or ride a bike or scooter to school.

Although not Amish, senior Austin McGill rode his mother's twenty-seven-year-old Arabian, Sonny, two miles to his high school in Gloucester, Virginia in November 2021. He didn't stop with riding the horse "to" school, but proceeded to ride Sonny "into" the school.

"In the rule book, there's nothing that doesn't allow you to ride a horse into the building," Austin claimed.

No harm was done, but Austin received a ten-day suspension for his prank.

School Bus 1930

19

Funeral Horses

Even the transportation of a deceased person for a funeral or to a cemetery for burial was done in the past by horses pulling a hearse. Black horses were most often used as hearse horses. White ones might be used for a child's death.

In London, England, the funeral horses were known as the Black Brigade. At their peak, there were seven hundred of them in London. They were imported as three-year-old Flemish stallions and were most likely the breed we recognize today as Friesian. The most desirable animals were about 16 hands tall, coal-black with no white markings, and had a long, flowing tail. A horse with small patches of white might be accepted if the white could be dyed or painted over. If the tail was not as impressive as desired, a fuller, false tail was attached when the horse was at work. To ensure their coats remained glossy, the horses were fed special diets.

Black Brigade horses were kept by stablemen known as black masters and were rented by funeral undertakers as needed. During cholera or influenza epidemics, the horses might be used four times a day, six days a week.

The Dottridge Brothers, the most famous of the black masters, kept about eighty horses at their stable. The Dottridges named all their horses after famous people. Some of their horses were Charles Dickens, Henry Ward Beecher, John Wesley, Louis Pasteur, Aldous Huxley, and General Booth, as well as a mixture of poets, politicians, artists, actors, and musicians.

Each horse's personality was well known by the men who worked with them. It was noted that General Booth (named for William Booth, the founder of the Salvation Army) was "most amiable, and will work with any horse."

Other horse personalities did not get along so well.

Huxley will not work with Tyndall, but gets on capitally with Dr. Barnardo. Tyndall, on the other hand, goes well with Dickens, but has a decided aversion to Henry Ward Beecher.

—*The Horse World of London (1893) by W.J. Gordon; Chapter XI, The Black Brigade; p. 138-147*

In 1911, E.F. Parks, an undertaker in Bryan, Texas, purchased a Canadian team of perfectly matched white horses, full brothers five and six years old. Parks ran a contest in the local paper, the Bryan Eagle, offering a prize of a handsome piece of furniture to the girl who could come up with the best names for the pair.

The winning entry was from Bernadine McKnight.

Dear Sir: I think Prince and Pilot would be appropriate names for your beautiful team of hearse horses. These names are short, easily pronounced and will soon be recognized by their owners. The horses are very closely related as well as very similar in appearance. … It is in death these horses are to serve their chief function. And it is in death that we hope of a Pilot and a Prince for us all. … The very color of these horses as well as the purpose they are to serve suggest the appropriateness of these names. For do we not find in sacred literature many references to the white robed Prince and the Pilot that is to be?"

—*The Bryan Eagle Bryan, Texas Mar 02 and 16, 1911*

Although funeral horses received extensive training, accidents sometimes happened, serving to compound the sorrow family and friends were already experiencing. Newspapers of the time include many stories of accidents involving funeral horses including this one caused by a sudden hailstorm.

The funeral of Joseph Berger had just started up the Charles Street Hill when the great chunks of ice began to pelt down. Six carriages in addition to the hearse were lined up. As soon as the horses felt the hailstones, they became unmanageable and a wild stampede up the hill ensued.

A brand new carriage from the undertaking establishment of Kress Brothers led the charge and all of the horses ran at the top of their speed.

The length and steepness of the hill was the only thing that prevented a frightful accident as all of the horses were thoroughly terrified and wholly beyond the control of their drivers. But by the time the frightened animals, beaten and urged forward by the merciless pelting of the great pellets of ice, reached the top of the hill, they were so much exhausted that the drivers managed to get them under control again.

The hearse was considerably damaged, but the casket had remained in its place.

—*The Pittsburgh Press, Pittsburgh, Pennsylvania May 21, 1893*

In 1889, five men were killed in an explosion in Rockland, New York. When the procession of five hearses headed to the burial grounds, the team attached to the rear hearse became frightened and bolted. According to the Springville Journal:

A collision with the hearses seemed inevitable. However, the hearses in the lead were driven to one side of the road and the runaway horses with the fifth hearse attached dashed wildly down the road. The driver could not hold the frightened animals and when alongside the third hearse, the hearse to which the runaways were attached upset with a crash and was smashed to pieces. The horses finally broke loose … and ran into the woods, where they were caught. The driver was thrown from the hearse … and badly hurt. Eventually the casket containing the body of the one of the victims of the explosion was placed in a wagon and in this manner was conveyed to the cemetery.

Not all horses were cut out to be funeral horses. A horse named The Los Angeles Del Sur Wonder was known, for short, as the "hearse horse."

Bred by an undertaker, he was used for a while to pull the hearse, but was found to be faster than was needed to keep at the head of the procession. During his training to switch professions, he trotted a 2.20 mile and paced in 2.18.

—*Los Angeles Herald, Los Angeles, California April 5 1892*

It's unclear whether the Del Sur Wonder was ever successful as a racehorse, but he certainly seemed better suited to that than pulling a hearse.

Many long-term funeral horses were known and loved by members of the communities they served.

A local celebrity recently died after a kind, useful life of thirty-eight years, says the Indianapolis Journal. His name was Jesse, and the one act which entitled him to mention was participation in the funeral cortege of the martyred Lincoln. He was the last of the six white horses which drew the hearse containing the honored body along the streets of Indianapolis. His mate in the proud but sorrowful lead of the team died eight years ago.

—*The McCook Tribune July 3, 1891*

A similar horse, Dan, worked twenty years for Thomas O'Brien, an undertaker in New Jersey. O'Brien arranged for a farmer to take care of Dan in the horse's retirement. Dan was not to do any more work, and he was always to have good food.

> *Twice, on the way to the railroad station to be shipped to his retirement home, the horse balked. Each time he stopped it was in front of a house with a crape, a symbol of mourning, hanging on the door. When the driver whispered in Dan's ear that his boss already had the jobs, the intelligent animal moved on.*
>
> —*The York Daily, York, Pennsylvania February 10, 1909*

Old Bob, a large, white funeral horse that served the Sanford, Florida community for twenty-eight years, was honored by being buried in the Lakeview Cemetery. The horse that had carried most of the people to that cemetery is the only non-human buried there. Old Bob could find his way to the cemetery without a driver. Born in 1877, the horse faithfully pulled hearses until he was retired to pasture in 1913. He died the following year at the age of thirty-seven.

20

Horses Making House Calls

In the 1800s, most country doctors traveled on horseback to their patients' homes. Even though medical practices were limited and sometimes even questionable, doctors performed vital services such as attending to the births of children, stitching wounds, setting broken bones, treating ailments, and even pulling teeth.

In many areas, roads were limited and often muddy, rutted, and impassable by carriage. A trustworthy riding horse was vital to the doctor's practice. Riding horseback meant the doctor was limited in the amount of medical equipment he could bring along. Everything had to fit into a medical case or the horse's saddlebags. The bags or cases were made of oiled canvas or leather to withstand all kinds of weather.

Distances of fifteen or more miles a day were common, requiring a strong, dependable horse. Doctor's horses were known to find their way back home at night after a long day's work while the doctor slept in the saddle.

Nineteenth century doctors weren't always paid with cash. They might receive garden produce, cheese, chickens, or be compensated with a service the patient was skilled in, such as shoeing the doctor's horse.

Horses were also used by those who sold "quack" tonics or medications. The men selling these products became known as "snake oil peddlers" or "snake oil salesmen." At the time, traditional medicine often could not cure physical problems, so the astonishing claims of the snake oil salesmen about their products' ability to improve health or cure a variety of ailments created an audience of eager buyers.

These salesmen often traveled the countryside in horse-drawn wagons covered in advertisements promoting their miraculous cures. Often their products were said to contain secret ingredients. At best, the concoctions were harmless. But in the worst cases, they included harmful ingredients such as arsenic, cocaine, or mercury. After making their sales, the snake oil peddlers skipped town before anyone discovered their medicine was either useless or even worse, dangerous or fatal.

Primitive two-wheeled ambulances were first used to transport wounded soldiers off the battlefield during America's Civil War. Where available, those were replaced or supplemented by the stronger, four-wheeled "Rucker" ambulance, named after Major General Rucker.

Dr. Edward L. Dalton, a Civil War surgeon, started one of the first hospital ambulance services in the United States in 1869 at Bellevue Hospital in New York City. The hospital had its own stable. The horse-drawn ambulances were equipped with medical supplies—splints, a stomach pump, morphine, and alcohol. The ambulance driver sounded a loud gong to signal people to move out of the way.

Getting to the patient quickly was important, but it can take a while to harness and hitch a horse. At first, the ambulance drivers kept the horse harnessed so he would be ready for a call. Later, a system was developed where the harness was suspended from the ceiling. When a call came in, the harness could be quickly lowered onto the horse. That way the ambulance was often ready to leave within thirty seconds. This same type of harnessing system was used by horses at fire departments.

England also began to use horse-drawn ambulances around the same time. It was reported that an ambulance in London,

> received 433 calls in 1899, all of which have been responded to… The distance traveled was 1,304 miles, or an average of three miles per journey.

> —Annual Report for 1899 of the St. John Ambulance Association

Some hospitals were still using horse-drawn ambulances as late as 1923, however horses began to be replaced by motorized vehicles in the early 1900s. The first mass-produced ambulance, the Model 774 Automobile Ambulance, was produced in New York in 1909. During World War One, the Red Cross began replacing horse-drawn vehicles on the battlefield with motorized ones.

As with other horse occupations, the automobile eventually put the horse out of work as the doctor's transportation. Generally, the automobile could run all day, wouldn't get sick, die, or run off with the doctor.

Beginning in 2008, while in his fifties, Doctor Roberto Anfosso adopted the old-fashioned practice of making house calls by horseback. Dr. Anfosso and his horse Ambra visited patients in rural La Morra in northwestern Italy. His patients ranged in age from 70 to 104. Dr. Anfosso preferred riding horseback for routine visits, such as medical checkups for his elderly patients. Ambra was a four-year-old filly when she was enlisted to serve as the doctor's transportation. Each week, the pair covered fifty to sixty miles together.

Not only did the doctor enjoy these excursions on horseback, his patients looked forward to seeing Ambra, providing the horse with treats when she arrived. Most felt they had a closer relationship with the doctor, believing that his visits were less rushed. Looking forward to the pair's next visit helped keep the elderly patients' focus off of their physical problems. Dr. Anfosso was still making house calls on horseback as of 2018.

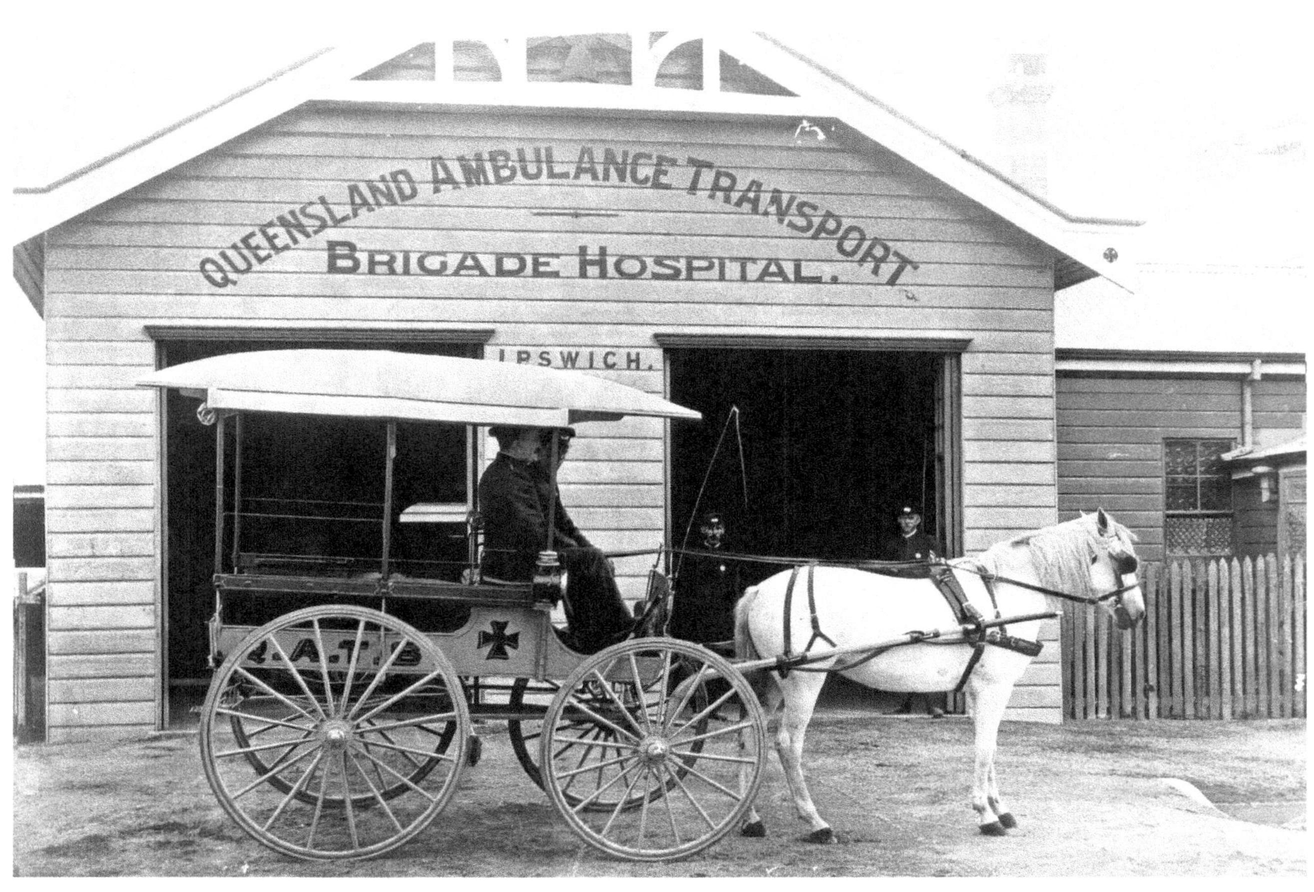
QUEENSLAND AMBULANCE TRANSPORT
BRIGADE HOSPITAL.
IPSWICH.
Q.A.T.B.

21

Special Delivery

The one-stop supermarkets of today didn't exist in the 1800s. Businesses were smaller and more specialized. The butcher was a separate shop from the baker, the dairy, and the produce market. Many things we purchase today or have delivered by truck or van were delivered in the past by horses. Depending upon your location, products such as coal, ice, milk, produce, and meat might be delivered to your home. Horses were well suited to the frequent stops and starts along these small town delivery routes.

Home deliveries sometimes turned dangerous if a horse or team became frightened. In this account, it was a delivery of baked goods.

An exciting race took place here this afternoon between a runaway horse owned by J. W. Willetts, a baker, and Ray Wells, a sixteen-year-old telegraph messenger. The horse had been left standing In front of the residence of Theodore H. Pettit by Mr. Willetts while he delivered some goods. His three-year-old child was left alone in the wagon. The animal became frightened and dashed down the street. The swaying and jolting of the wagon caused the child to cling to the end of the seat, and every moment the crowd that gave chase after the flying horse expected to see the child thrown out.

Wells was on his way to deliver a message when he heard the shouts of those pursuing the horse. He understood the situation at a glance, and, leaning over the handle bar of his wheel, started after the runaway. The boy is an expert bicyclist, and, after a race of nearly half a mile, he caught

up with the horse. He got a little ahead of the animal, and as the latter flew by him Wells sprang from his bicycle and managed to catch hold of the tailboard of the wagon. Two flour barrels prevented the boy from climbing into the wagon. But he held on with one hand and with the other tipped one of the barrels out into the roadway. Then he climbed into the wagon and, putting the child in the bottom of it, he seized the reins and, after a hard pull, succeeded in stopping the horse just as the animal was making a sharp turn Into Nostrand avenue.

When the panting crowd came up, young Wells was trying to soothe the crying child. He was showered with praise for his bravery. After handing the little one to its father, he remounted his bicycle, that had been brought up to where he had stopped the horse, and started to deliver his message.

—The Sun New York City, New York April 22, 1894

Ice

Since electric refrigerators weren't common until the 1930s, families relied on an icebox to keep perishable foods cool. As indicated by their name, the cooling mechanism of an icebox was a block of ice. Iceboxes made customers dependent on the regular delivery of ice harvested from frozen lakes or rivers. Companies stored the blocks of ice in insulated buildings and horses pulled the carts or wagons that delivered it to customers.

Coal

In Victorian England, coal was often used for heating.

Scrooge had a very small fire, but the clerk's fire was so very much smaller that it looked like one coal. But he couldn't replenish it, for Scrooge kept the coal-box in his own room; and so surely as the clerk came in with the shovel, the master predicted that it would be necessary for them to part. Wherefore the clerk put on his white comforter, and tried to warm himself at the candle; in which effort, not being a man of a strong imagination, he failed.

—A Christmas Carol, Charles Dickens

Strong horses were required to pull the heavy wagons loaded with sacks of coal. They were usually draft or part-draft animals. A single load of coal sometimes weighed as much as three tons. They avoided steep hills whenever possible. When they had to travel up a hill, they were harnessed in tandem, one horse lined up behind another, as that increased their pulling power.

Trash

A little-known service commonly provided by horses in the past is trash collection. In England, they were known as dust-cart horses. Today, a few areas are resuming the use of horses for this service. In Middlebury, Vermont, draft horses haul a cart twice a week through the neighborhoods to collect curbside garbage and recycling. Patrick Palmer alternates his two teams of dappled Percherons. The horses are named Jake and Jerry, and Pete and Paul.

Moving Companies

According to the United States Census Bureau, the average person in America will move eleven times over his lifetime. Today, we can do that easily by loading a U-Haul or having a moving company pack and move our items for us. Some of those businesses, such as Bekins Moving & Storage Co., currently one of the largest moving companies in the United States, started out using horse-drawn moving vans. Bekins was founded by brothers John and Martin Bekins in 1891 in Sioux City, Iowa. The company got its start with twelve employees and three horse-drawn vans.

These were primarily local moves within a limited area. By the mid-1800s, trains were used for long distance transfers, although horse-drawn vehicles transported people and items to and from the rail stations. From the 1920s on, horses were phased out of the moving industry by the increased use of motorized vehicles.

Not only did horses move the content of houses, they sometimes moved entire houses! In the late 1800s, horses moved fifty-five houses from the old location of the village of Katonah, New York to its new location a half mile away[1].

---

[1] *See Horsestory Volume II*

22

Milk Delivery

One of the longest-lasting equine delivery services was home milk delivery from a local dairy. Horse-drawn milk wagons were in use in some areas as late as the 1940s due to the gas rationing experienced during World War II. Milk delivery continued with motorized vehicles into the 1950s and 60s. In 1963, nearly 30 percent of American families still had milk delivered to their homes.

In the early days, milk delivery was directly from the cow to the customer, the "scoop and pail" method being used. When the milk wagon arrived with its large milk cans, the customer brought her own container to the wagon. The milk was then scooped out of the large container into the customer's.

Later, milk was packaged in glass bottles, using blocks of ice to keep it cold. Families left empty bottles on their front porch, and the delivery driver exchanged the empties for full ones.

The milkman's job often began before dawn, harnessing his horse and loading milk into the wagon. Horses quickly pick up repetitive things, and milk delivery routes were no exception. When the team arrived at the start of their route, an experienced horse stopped automatically at the location of the first delivery, and the driver jumped out with the milk.

The milk horse quickly learned whether the distance to the next stop was such that he should wait for the driver to climb back into the wagon or whether the man would walk there. If the latter, the horse started off, unattended, toward the next stop down the street.

Many newspaper stories of milk horses knowing their routes as well as their drivers indicate the horse's intelligence and reliability.

> *A newspaper man going home one morning followed such a milkman's wagon through several streets. He saw the horse jogging along with the reins lying loose across his back, and watched him stop a dozen times without a word from his driver. The milkman was running in and out of doorways, getting milk from his wagon and delivering it at the proper places. Not a word was uttered by the man at any time, and no sign was given to the horse when to stop and when to go ahead. After the milkman had delivered all his milk that morning, he got into his wagon and lay down to peaceful rest on a blanket thrown across the seat and let the horse start away for home. And the milkman didn't need to stay awake or to wake up until he struck the trail to his own barn door, content in the knowledge that his horse wouldn't loiter on the way or take a wrong road.*

> —*The Boston Globe Boston, Massachusetts October 9, 1898*

Jim was a farm horse who found his way into a milk delivery career. His good care and retirement were assured because of a young girl's love of the horse.

> *A little Reno county girl's love for a horse has ensured that "Jim" that's the horse's name will be well cared for the rest of his life. Last autumn Hazel, the twelve-year-old daughter of Mr. and Mrs. G. P. Lowe, of Valley township, was quite sick with pneumonia. On her recovery she was much disappointed to find, that during her illness her father had sold "Jim," one of the work horses on the farm.*

"Jim" was a patient, hard-working, plodding seven-year-old farm horse, who had grown up on the place, and Hazel was very much attached to the gentle animal. Hazel, finding that "Jim" had been sold, penciled a little note reading something like this:

"To the man who bought Jim: I want you to please take good care of Jim. He is good and gentle and never was whipped, and never runs away and he lets little girls ride him and I want you to see that he gets plenty of oats."

"Jim" was sold by Mr. Lowe to a local buyer, who shipped him to Iowa and sold him to a Dr. Bowen, of Sheridan, Iowa. Hazel Lowe's note was forwarded to Dr. Bowen. When the latter sold the horse to an eastern buyer, he sent along the Kansas girl's note.

Finally "Jim" was bought by the Gail Borden condensed milk concern in New York City, for service as a milk delivery horse in that city. The Kansas girl's note accompanied the horse and got into the hands of W. T. Irwin, manager of the big milk corporation. Mr. Irwin, touched by the

girl's interest in the horse, wrote her a letter, telling her that if she would reply he would send her something.

She made reply and Manager Irwin forwarded to her three large boxes of candy, and a large size photograph of "Jim", showing him togged up in his new city harness, with bright, brass tags and fittings, and hitched to a brand new milk wagon.

My how proudly Jim is stepping down the avenue in New York City, pulling his milk wagon. And accompanying the candy and photograph was a letter to the little girl from the New York manager, saying something like this:

"Dear Hazel: This is to advise you that Jim is well and hearty. He is in good hands, has good care and eats three times a day. I will see to it that Jim is never hurt or abused, and that when he gets too old to pull our milk wagons, we will not sell him but will retire him on a pension for the rest of his life on a blue grass pasture, just because there is somebody out in Kansas who cares for Jim."

—Hutchinson News The Hoisington Dispatch Hoisington, Kansas May 8, 1913

23

Down on the Farm

The most common picture of a work horse is the animal used on a farm. Before the invention of the tractor, horses or mules were used for every aspect of agriculture—clearing land, preparing the soil, planting, weeding, and harvesting.

Horses powered all manner of farm equipment including mowers, rakes, reapers, binders, seed drills, cultivators, plows, and manure spreaders. Early combines developed in the late 1800s to harvest grain required twenty or more horses to pull them.

Large families were vital to the success of a family farm. Children helped with farm chores from a very young age. Between 1854 and 1929, up to 200,000 orphaned or neglected children from New York were placed on trains to be adopted by families further west, many to help work on farms. These orphan trains were the idea of a minister, Charles Loring Brace.

Today, it is primarily the most conservative Amish groups that still farm with horses. Their work is done in much the same way it was practiced in the 1800s. Most horse-powered farms today are relatively small (under 200 acres).

There are advantages to farming with horses. Horses are cheaper than tractors and generally require fewer repairs. Horses are quiet. Tractors are loud. You can grow horses' food on the farm versus being reliant on outside sources for tractor fuel. Horses provide their own fertilizer. They compact the ground less than heavy mechanical farm equipment, resulting in better soil quality. And, they can do something the best tractor will never do—produce a replica of themselves!

But on the negative side, tractors don't usually run away with you as a team of horses might. And, they don't require the daily attention that horses do. Most of the non-Amish farmers that use horses today, do so because they enjoy working with the animals and appreciate the more self-sufficient lifestyle it provides.

24

Andrew Jackson

On May 30, 1806, Andrew Jackson faced Charles Dickinson, a Nashville attorney, in a duel. The two had squabbled over a horse race between Jackson's bay stallion Truxton and Dickinson's father-in-law's horse Ploughboy. Dickinson had also insulted Jackson's wife.

Dickinson fired first and hit Jackson in the chest. Jackson's gun misfired. Technically, this should have counted as a shot and ended the duel, but Jackson re-cocked his pistol and fired again, killing Dickinson. He was not prosecuted for murder. Jackson's wound wasn't fatal, but the bullet remained in his body, and he experienced pain from it for the remainder of his life.

Jackson's fighting began early. He was thirteen when he and his older brothers joined a local militia during the Revolutionary War. In 1781, they were captured by the British and held as prisoners of war. He fought the British again in the War of 1812.

When he wasn't fighting, Andrew Jackson was recognized as Tennessee's leading breeder and owner of racehorses at his Hermitage Farm. At this time, Tennessee rather than Kentucky, was the center for Thoroughbred racing. He was also part owner of the Clover Bottom race track.

Jackson became our seventh president, moving into the White House in 1829 with his best Thoroughbreds and his black jockeys. In addition to Truxton, some of Jackson's favorites were the fillies Emily, Lady Nashville, Busiris, and Bolivia *(shown on the following page)*.

Because it was considered inappropriate for the President of the United States to engage in horse racing, Jackson used the name of Andrew J. Donelson, his nephew and private secretary, to enter his horses.

After the British burned the White House in 1814, a wooden stable was built near the East Wing. But with Jackson's menagerie of horses, the small White House stable was overflowing. In 1834, Congress approved the construction of a brick stable east of the East Wing.

Jackson's favorite personal mount was Sam Patch, a gray stallion named after a daredevil who leaped 125-feet into the river at the base of Niagara Falls in October 1829. Unfortunately, the man was killed in a similar jump into the Genesee River the following month.

After serving two terms as President, Jackson retired to the Hermitage in 1837. He died in 1845 at 78, still carrying the bullet near his heart from the duel with Charles Dickinson.

25

Sea Rescues

Richard Hoodless farmed a small plot of land near the coast of Lincolnshire, England in the mid 1800s, but his true passion was rescuing shipwrecked sailors. Hoodless had an unorthodox technique for these rescues. His brave, faithful horse served as an equine life-boat when the usual variety was not available.

Although Hoodless' heroic rescues were mentioned in many newspaper articles, little was recorded about his horse. We don't know the animal's name, color, height, breed, or even whether it was male or female. Despite the animal's anonymity, Hoodless never could have saved people without the help of his horse.

When stormy weather threatened, Hoodless climbed to the highest point in his home, aimed his telescope out the window toward the sea, and watched intently as ships struggled against the crashing waves.

When a ship seemed to be losing the battle and all on board must have believed they were lost, Hoodless mounted his horse and plunged into the turbulent water. The horse, battered by the waves, had to continually right himself and battle on toward their goal. Hoodless' technique for maneuvering the waves was described as follows.

When meeting a particularly angry surf or swell, he would turn his horse's head, bend forward, and allow the wave to roll over them. Were the horse to face the larger billows, and attempt to pierce them, the water would enter his nostrils, and render him breathless, by which he would soon be exhausted.[1]

When they reached a ship, the pair would often bring two or three sailors at a time back to shore, then return to rescue more. In one rescue, Hoodless saved the ship's captain, his wife, and ten sailors—some on the back of the horse, others hanging on to the stirrups.

In another rescue, Hoodless was ready to head for shore with two sailors, but the horse wouldn't move. After several unsuccessful attempts to get the horse to leave the ship, Hoodless panicked, realizing the animal's legs were tangled in a rope under the water. The waves threatened to dash them all against the side of the ship. Fearing he might be washed away if he dismounted, Hoodless felt around frantically with his foot until he finally located the rope. He cut it with a knife, and they all made it safely to shore.

Hoodless is best remembered for his efforts during the wreck of the Hermione, a brig captained by Stephen Walton. The Hermione, carrying a load of coal, had gotten into trouble at Haile Sand Flat near Donna Nook. Hoodless and his horse saved four of the eight crew members. He was honored by the Royal Humane Society for this rescue.

It was resolved unanimously, that the noble courage and humanity displayed by Richard Hoodless for the preservation of the crew of the Hermione from drowning, when that vessel was wrecked near Donna Nook, on the coast of Lincolnshire, on the 31st of August, 1833, and the praiseworthy manner in which he risked his life on that occasion, by swimming his horse through a heavy sea to the wreck, when it was found impossible to launch the life-boat, has called forth the lively admiration of the special general court, and justly entitles him to the honorary medallion of the institution, which is hereby unanimously adjudged to be presented to him, at the ensuing anniversary festival.

That a horse could be trained to these unpleasant and hazardous enterprises may seem somewhat surprising. But it appears that in reality no training is necessary: all depends on the will and firmness of the rider. Hoodless declares he could manage the most unruly horse in the water; for that, as soon as the horse finds that he has lost his footing, and is obliged to swim, he becomes as obedient to the bridle as a boat is to its helm.

—*Chester Chronicle, and Cheshire and North Wales General Advertiser, February 2, 1849*

---

[1] *Horses can only breathe through their nose.*

26

Romanis

Gypsy is the common name for a member of an ethnic group officially called the Roma or the Romani. Their native language, based on Sanskrit, is also called Romani. They were called Gypsies because early Europeans believed they came from Egypt. It's now known they originated in northern India. The name "Gypsy" has been rejected by the Romani because it implies a stereotype of these people as thieves.

The Romani have traditionally been a nomadic people, traveling in brightly-colored, horse-drawn wagons. Their continual movement made school attendance and education difficult. The Romani practice a variety of religions including Christianity, Islam, Hinduism, or Buddhism. Some have retained the old superstitious beliefs, spells, and magical practices. Some superstitions include, "To see a white horse in the morning, means good luck all day." Or "If one of the bearers at a funeral stumbles during the procession, there will be another death."

The Romani began to immigrate to the United States in the 1860s. It's estimated one million Romani now live in the US, but most Romani today live in Europe. Some retain the nomadic lifestyle, using campers or RVs rather than horses and wagons. The official Romani flag, adopted in 1971, has a background of blue and green, representing the heavens and earth. In the center is a red cart wheel with sixteen spokes representing their traditional nomadic lifestyle.

The original Romani wagon or caravan, called a vardo, is unique among horse-drawn vehicles. These wagons were widely adopted around 1840. Prior to that, they had primarily lived in tents as they traveled. The use of the vardos continued until nearly disappearing around 1940. Those years were known as "the wagon time."

Since the family lived in it while traveling, the vardo could be compared to a modern day camper or tiny house on wheels. The highly ornate yet functional vardos took six months to a year to construct from a variety of woods, such as oak, ash, elm, cedar, and pine. Several varieties of vardos existed, but typically the wagons had a rounded top. Sides could be straight or curved. The exteriors were elaborately decorated with hand-carved or painted symbols. The lavishness of the decorations indicated the wealth of the family.

Charles Dickens described the interior of Mrs. Jarley's vardo in his novel, *The Old Curiosity Shop*, written from 1840 to 1841.

> *One half of it—that moiety[1] in which the comfortable proprietress was then seated—was carpeted, and so partitioned off at the further end as to accommodate a sleeping-place, constructed after the fashion of a berth on board ship, which was shaded, like the little windows, with fair white curtains, and looked comfortable enough, though by what kind of gymnastic exercise the lady of the caravan ever contrived to get into it, was an unfathomable mystery. The other half served for a kitchen, and was fitted up with a stove whose small chimney passed through the roof. It held also a closet or larder, several chests, a great pitcher of water, and a few cooking-utensils and articles of crockery. These latter necessaries hung upon the walls, which, in that portion of the establishment devoted to the lady of the caravan, were ornamented with such gayer and lighter decorations as a triangle and a couple of well-thumbed tambourines.*

To pull their vardos, the Romani needed strong, reliable horses. The desired type was a small, solidly built horse. The animals were often piebald (black and white) or skewbald (brown and white). They were known for long, thick manes, forelocks, and tails as well as feathering on their legs. Today they have a variety of names: Cob, Irish Cob, Gypsy Horse, Tinker Horse, or Gypsy Vanner. An official breed registry was established in 1996 with slightly varying requirements.

[1] *each of two parts into which a thing is or can be divided*

Although the original horses were not tall, today the horses range from 13 to 16 or more hands. A smaller horse was beneficial to the Romanis since it ate less and required smaller harness and equipment. The Dales and Fell Ponies along with the Shire and Clydesdale draft horses were instrumental in developing the Gypsy Vanner breed. A Gypsy horse's training began at an early age with the young horse tied to one of the horses in the team, so he could follow along as the horse pulled the vardo.

The Appleby Horse Fair is an annual gathering of Romani and Travellers in Cumbria, England. The fair is attended each year by 10,000 Romani and Travellers with approximately 1,000 caravans. The Travellers have a similar nomadic lifestyle but originated in Ireland and are not related genetically to the Romani.

Horses, harness, carriages, and other horse-related merchandise are sold at the fair. The event also attracts food vendors, fortune tellers, palm readers, and musicians.

During the Appleby Fair, the horses are washed in the Eden River. Spectators line the grassy river banks to watch the horses in the water. The horses are then trotted up and down the streets to show them off (known as flashing). Horses are not auctioned. Cash sales are arranged privately between a buyer and seller. The price usually includes extra for "luck money."

Luck money is an old tradition with the Romani and Irish Travellers. When a price was agreed upon, the two parties to the deal shook hands. The buyer handed cash to the seller, who counted it, then gave a small amount back to the purchaser, while saying, "I hope he's lucky for you."

Some say the superstition was that if the horse turned out bad or hurt the new owner, the luck money ensured the buyer couldn't curse the seller. Others indicate the good luck was intended for the buyer or the animal who was changing owners. Perhaps the good luck was extended to all three.

Modern Gypsy Vanner Horse

Bathing Machines

The saying "cleanliness is next to godliness" is not found in the Bible, but it's interesting that cleanliness is often a priority even in the animal world. The frequency of human bathing has varied over the years and in different locations. At times, people avoided full baths, fearing that removing the body's natural oils was harmful to one's health. But more often, it was the work required for bathing that caused its infrequent occurrence.

In the days before indoor plumbing, taking a bath was a strenuous and time-consuming process. Water had to be hauled in from a stream or well by the bucketful to fill a portable wood or metal tub. The tub was most often placed in a bedroom or kitchen as there were no "bath" rooms at the time. And if you wanted a warm or hot bath, a fire had to be started to heat the water. Because of the work involved, it was common for everyone to share the same bath water—father first, then mother, then each child in turn by age. By the time the youngest member of the family entered the tub, the water was so murky they could easily be lost in it, hence the saying, "Don't throw the baby out with the bath water."

Those who lived near a coast had the advantage of bathing in the sea. The sea not only cleansed one, sea water was thought to have health-giving powers. Some believed the colder the water, the better. Sea bathing became more widespread with the publication in 1753 of Dr. Richard Russell's *"A Dissertation Concerning The Use of Sea Water in Diseases of the Glands."* He claimed, "The sea washes away all the evils of mankind." Dr. Russell not only believed people should bathe in sea water, he recommended drinking it as well.

Public bathing was problematic for women. Standards of modesty were much higher in earlier days. Women's bathing suits of modern times would not only have been considered immodest but immoral.

The dilemma was "How could women bathe in the sea while preserving their modesty?" Surprisingly, horses helped provide the answer.

Bathing machines became quite popular in coastal areas in the 1800s. These machines date back at least to 1735 at Scarborough Beach in North Yorkshire, England. From their name, it sounds as if these "machines" might have mechanically scrubbed people until they were shiny and clean. In reality, a bathing machine was simply a specially designed cart or wagon used to transport bathers, primarily women, into the water so they could bathe in privacy.

And it was horses who pulled the machines into the sea.

Bathing machines resembled a miniature cabin on wheels with doors at each end. The carts averaged six feet in length, five feet wide, and eight feet high. Tall wheels lifted the cabin four feet off the ground. Holes were drilled into the flooring to allow water to drain out. A large number was

painted on the outside and advertisements or the name of the resort often covered the sides. Some had lavish interiors, but most bathing machines were fairly spartan.

The woman entered via steps at the back, closed the door behind her, and in the privacy of the cabin, changed into her bathing attire known as a bathing costume. This swim wear was made of wool and covered the body from neck to ankles. The bathing machine was towed by a horse into the water until the cabin floor was at sea level. The horse was unhooked from the sea end of the cart and reconnected to the opposite end in preparation for the return trip.

The bather then exited from the sea end, plunging into the cold water. If she couldn't swim or the waves were strong, a stout female attendant, known as a dipper, tied a rope around the woman's waist, attaching the other end to the bathing machine, so the bather would not be swept out to sea.

Fifteen minutes later, the dipper hoisted the bedraggled woman back into the cabin. The additional weight of the bulky, waterlogged swim wear is why dippers needed to be exceptionally strong women.

Once inside, the woman changed out of her wet bathing dress back into everyday attire. The horse then plodded to shore where a line of bathers awaited their turn in the machine.

Known as "The Venerable Priestess of the Bath," Martha Gunn was one of the most famous dippers, working at the Brighton, England resort from 1750 until poor health forced her to retire in 1814 at eighty-eight. Mrs. Gunn, mother of eight, most of whom she outlived, died one year after her retirement.

In 1773, author Frances Burney was tormented with a dreadful cold and was advised to try sea bathing to harden her constitution. She recorded her first experience in the water.

I was terribly frightened, and really thought I should never have recovered from the plunge. I had not breath enough to speak for a minute or two, the shock was beyond expression; but after I got back to the machine, I presently felt myself in a glow that was delightful—it is the finest feeling in the world, and will induce me to bathe as often as will be safe.

To ensure women's safety and privacy at the beach resorts, England's Baths and Washhouses Act of 1846 required men, and boys above eight years old, to bathe separately from women and children. Some communities expanded their regulations, specifying what was considered proper bathing attire and limiting the practice to certain times. In July 1888, Elgar Baynes, twelve, and Charles Roberts, thirteen, were charged with "unlawfully bathing from an open beach after the hour of seven in the morning without proper bathing dress." Both boys were fined for their infraction.

Even Queen Victoria joined in the craze with an ornate bathing machine built especially for her. It was painted a rich forest green with ivory trim and black wheels. A section of beach on the Isle of Wight was reserved exclusively for the queen's use. In July 1847, she noted in a journal,

A very fine morning, & the day became again very hot.... drove down to the beach with my maids & went into the bathing machine, where I undressed & bathed in the sea, (for the 1st time in my life) a very nice bathing woman attending me. I thought it delightful till I put my head under water, when I tough [thought] I should be stifled.

After Queen Victoria passed away, her ornate bathing machine suffered the indignity of being used as a chicken coop. But in the 1950s, it was restored and put on display at Osborne Beach on the Isle of Wight.

While the bathing machines were designed for the protection of women, at least two died using them. Mrs. Silvester, in 1871, in Dieppe, France experienced some type of difficulty in the water, and "was at once carried into the bathing machine. She gave a faint sigh and expired almost immediately."

A second victim that summer was Sarah Ball at Great Yarmouth, England. She also had difficulties, and exclaimed "Oh dear, oh dear, I shall die." She was helped back into the bathing machine but did indeed pass away. Both women were found to have died from natural causes rather than due to any fault with the bathing machines.

The practice of sea bathing lasted for nearly 150 years and created an entire industry, requiring the construction and maintenance of the specialized bathing machines, areas to store the vehicles, the acquisition, stabling, and care of the horses, the training of the animals to venture safely out into the water, and the employment of the strong "dippers" to assist the female bathers.

By the early 1900s, the regulations that segregated bathers by gender began to be relaxed. Men and women were allowed to "bathe" or swim at the same time. As a result, the use of bathing machines declined. They were almost totally abandoned by 1920. Some lived on as stationary beach changing huts or garden sheds.

28

The Woolly Horse

I am a showman by profession … and all the gilding shall make nothing else of me." P. T. Barnum's words described himself well. While in his twenties, he began promoting odd and unusual things including "human curiosities" some of which were later determined to be hoaxes. Barnum is credited with saying, "There's a sucker born every minute."

An early example of Barnum's belief that he could fool people was his exhibition of an elderly, blind slave woman, Joice Heth. Barnum began exhibiting her in 1835, claiming she was born in 1674 and had been the nanny of George Washington from his birth. Barnum claimed Heth was 161 years old. When Heth passed away the following year, an autopsy revealed her age to be closer to seventy-nine.

In 1841, Barnum purchased Scudder's American Museum in New York City, renaming it "Barnum's American Museum." This provided a permanent home for some of his exhibits.

Charles Sherwood Stratton was one of Barnum's most popular traveling "exhibits." Although Stratton weighed nine pounds and eight ounces at birth, he was only three feet four inches tall as an adult. In 1842, Barnum began including the boy in his exhibits. Stratton, only four years old at the time, was called General Tom Thumb.

It was while touring with General Tom Thumb, that Barnum encountered an equine oddity. Here is the truth of Barnum's discovery.

> In the summer of 1848, while in Cincinnati with General Tom Thumb, my attention was arrested by handbills announcing the exhibition of a "woolly horse." Being always on the qui vive for everything curious with which to amuse or astonish the public, I visited the exhibition, and found the animal to be a veritable curiosity. It was a well-formed horse of rather small size, without any manner or the slightest portion of hair upon his tail. The entire body and limbs were covered with a thick fine hair or wool curling tight to his skin. He was foaled in Indiana, was a mere freak of nature, and withal a very curious looking animal. I purchased him and sent him to Bridgeport, Ct., where he was placed quietly away in a retired barn, until such times as might have use for him.

Ever the showman, or should we say "stretcher of truth"? What follows is the account Barnum presented to the public of the discovery and capture of the woolly horse.

> The next mail was said to have brought intelligence that Col. Fremont and his hardy band of warriors had, after a three days' chase, succeeded in capturing, near the river Gila in California, a most extraordinary nondescript, which somewhat resembled a horse, but which had no mane nor tail, and was covered with a thick coat of wool. The account further added that the Colonel

had sent this wonderful animal as a present to the U.S. Quartermaster. Two days after this announcement, the following advertisement appeared in the New-York papers:

COL. FREMONT'S NONDESCRIPT OR WOOLLY HORSE will be exhibited for a few days at the corner of Broadway and Reade street, previous to his departure for London. Nature seems to have exerted all her ingenuity in the production of this astounding animal. He is extremely complex—made up of the Elephant, Deer, Horse, Buffalo, Camel, and Sheep. It is the full size of a Horse, has the haunches of the Deer, the tail of the Elephant, a fine curled wool of camel's hair color, and easily bounds twelve or fifteen feet high. Naturalists and the oldest trappers assured Col. Fremont that it was never known previous to his discovery. It is undoubtedly "Nature's last," and the richest specimen received from California. To be seen every day this week. Admittance 25 cents; children half price.

—The Life of P. T. Barnum, Phineas Taylor Barnum, 1855

Barnum was delighted with the success of his fantasy tale.

The community was absolutely famishing. They were ravenous. They could have swallowed anything, and like a good genius, I threw them, not a "bone," but a regular tit-bit, a bon-bon— and they swallowed it in a single gulp!

In reality, the horse had not been "captured at the risk of life and limb among the snow-capped impassable crags of the wildest mountains in America." The woolly horse was born on the farm of a Mr. Goodrich who sold him to John Stearns who used the animal to drive to and from the village. The animal was most likely related to today's breed known as the Bashkir Curly Horse.

At the age of sixty, Barnum joined with James Anthony Bailey to form the Barnum & Bailey Circus. Known as the Greatest Show on Earth, the traveling circus shows ran from 1871 to 2017.

COL. FREMONT'S
NONDESCRIPT

FROM CALIFORNIA.

This Animal Captured by

COL. FREMONT and HIS PARTY,

Near the River Gila, New Mexico, after a Chase of Three Days, has arrived in this City on its way to Europe, and is

TO BE SEEN ALIVE,

At 290 Broadway, corner of Reade st.

FOR A FEW DAYS ONLY.

It is beyond all question, the most astounding natural curiosity ever beheld by mortal Man. It appears to be a curious compound of parts of the

CAMEL, BUFFALO, HORSE, ELEPHANT,

DEER, &c. &c. &c.

AND IS COVERED WITH SILK,

FINE AND THICKLY MATTED.

In size, it is like the Horse, very fleet, clearing obstacles 12 or 15 feet high, with ease; has no mane, and swings the

TAIL OF THE ELEPHANT.

WOOLLY HORSE

Was sent by Col. Fremont to the Quarter-Master, stationed at Corpus-Christie, as a present, and by him sold to an English Gentleman, who designs it for the Zoological Gardens, London. It is thought by the purchaser to be more valuable, than even the GOLD OF CALIFORNIA.

The Oldest Trappers were unable to classify it, they never having heard of so curious an animal before. The papers throughout the City have noticed it, but to describe it accurately is impossible. It is the most wonderful Creature known, and astonishes the most curious.

The above Nondescript Animal may be seen

Every Day this Week, from 8 A. M. till 10 P. M.

AT 290 BROADWAY, CORNER OF READE STREET.

ADMITTANCE 25 CENTS, Children Half-Price.

Modern Bashkir Curly Horses

29

Hambletonian

In the world of horses, there have been several with some variation of the name Hambletonian. One famous Hambletonian was a bay Thoroughbred who lived from 1792 to 1818. He was an excellent racehorse, winning all of his starts except one. His sire was King Fergus and his pedigree shows Eclipse as a grandsire. That Hambletonian is not the subject of this section, however, and there doesn't appear to be any relation between the two horses. The famous Hambletonian of this chapter was officially known as Hambletonian 10 or Rysdyk's Hambletonian.

In early America, the need for fast horses was a practical one—to get people from place to place quickly. This often required extended travel over all types of terrain. Stallions were imported to improve the speed and quality of American horses.

As time went on, racing became a popular event at county fairs. Early trotting horses were raced under saddle, since the carts of that time were too awkward and bulky for speed. With the development of smaller, sleeker carts, harness racing increased in popularity with neighbors pitting their horses against each other. By the late 1860s, riding trotters had been abandoned for harness racing with a two-wheeled cart or sulky on a one-mile track.

Back in 1848, Jonas Seely of Sugar Loaf, New York was the owner of a horse known as the Kent mare. He'd owned the mare previously but had sold her to a butcher in New York City. When Seely learned the mare had been mistreated and one of her legs was permanently injured, he bought her back.

Seeley's brother, Ebenezer, just happened to be managing a twenty-five-year-old stallion named Abdallah 1. The horse was said to have a hollow back, a thin, skimpy, rat tail, and long, pointed ears. The stallion was rejected by many horsemen who claimed his temperament was as ugly as his appearance.

Whether Seely saw something in Abdallah that others didn't or he simply couldn't afford another stallion, the match between Abdallah and his crippled mare was made. The mating between these two misfits produced the dark bay colt Hambletonian 10, who became the foundation of the Standardbred horse breed. Hambletonian, foaled on Seely's farm on May 5, 1849, had a small star on his forehead and a white ankle on the off side. When full grown, he stood 15.3 hands tall.

Although Hambletonian's story is a happy one, his sire Abdallah was not as fortunate. The stallion, born in 1823, was a son of the Thoroughbred Messenger. Messenger, a gray Thoroughbred, was born in England in 1780 and imported to Pennsylvania as an eight-year-old. It's said when he was unloaded at the port of Philadelphia, the fiery Messenger charged down the ship's gangplank, dragging two grooms with him.

At the age of thirty-one, Abdallah was sold to a fish peddler in Long Island. Even at his advanced age, Abdallah retained his spirit. Pulling a smelly fish wagon didn't suit him. He threw a fit, demolished the cart, and freed himself. The old stallion ran to the beach, and no one cared to go after him. He fended for himself for a while, but in November 1854, the stallion was found dead in an old shack on Grave's End Beach.

But, returning to Abdallah's famous colt—a Dutchman named William Rysdyk, 1809-1870, (pronounced RYES-dick) worked for Jonas Seely, caring for the horses and doing farm chores. Seely allowed Rysdyk to name Abdallah's colt, since the farm hand was the first to see him after his birth.

A few potential buyers visited Seely's farm but decided not to purchase the colt, believing Hambletonian too closely resembled his father. They also didn't like that his hindquarters were higher than his withers. But from the start, Rysdyk believed in Hambletonian. He became very attached to the colt and was convinced he would someday be great. The farm hand convinced Seely to sell him the mare and her six month-old colt for $125.

Rysdyk first exhibited Hambletonian as a two-year-old at the nearby Orange County Fair. He'd purchased a white halter for the event. Hambletonian won his class and drew a lot of attention, some positive, some negative. But the following year, he was even more impressive. At the age of three, Rysdyk entered Hambletonian in a timed harness event at the Union Course on Long Island. The young stallion ran the mile in 2:48 ½. This was Hambletonian's only officially recorded race time.

After that public demonstration of his speed, Hambletonian's demand as a breeding stallion grew—and with it the price of his stud fees—from $25 to $500, making Rysdyk a rich man. The stallion earned nearly $200,000 for his owner even with Rysdyk sometimes turning away men who had sneered at Hambletonian when he was a young colt. Over his lifetime, Hambletonian produced about 1,335 foals.

In 1870, Rysdyk became ill and bedridden. He had his groom, Harmon Showers, walk Hambletonian in front of the house so he could see the horse from his bedroom window. William Rysdyk died on April 3 of that year. Hambletonian died six years later at the age of twenty-six. The horse and his owner are both buried in Chester, New York. Seventeen years after the horse's death, a tall, granite monument was erected in his honor on Hambletonian Avenue.

Approximately ninety-five percent of Standardbreds today trace their bloodlines back to Hambletonian. At least forty of his offspring trotted the mile in less than 2:30. The Hambletonian Stakes for three-year-olds is the first event in the Triple Crown of Harness Racing for Trotters.

Dexter, one of Hambletonian's sons, foaled in 1858, won forty-six of fifty races. In 1867, Dexter set a record for trotting the mile (2:17.1/4). After that race, he was purchased by Robert E. Bonner for $35,000 for his own private driving. Bonner didn't approve of horse racing or betting. It's not known if he could have gone any faster, for with Bonner's purchase, that was the end of Dexter's racing career.

30

Speedy Mares

After reading of Hambletonian, Ethan Allen, Dexter, and others like them, one might think the only speedy horses were colts. Actually, there were several mares who set speed records during the 1800s. What is striking about these horses is their longevity and their ability to continue racing at advanced ages. This may be due to the fact that many of them started racing later in life than horses do today. Not only did they race longer, the races in the early days were under saddle and consisted of multiple heats, sometimes as many as four or five heats to a race. Each heat might be anywhere from one to four miles.

Lady Blanche

Lady Blanche was a daughter of Abdallah. A gray mare, she stood 15.2 1/2 hands tall. Her best time for the mile was 2:43. At the age of twenty-four, she ran a race of four heats against two horses, Snowdrop and Beppo. She died in 1855 at the age of thirty-two.

Lady Suffolk

Lady Suffolk was foaled in Smithtown, Long Island, in 1833, a great-granddaughter of Messenger. A 15.2 hand gray, she was said to have an Arabian look with an arched neck and a small, refined head. David Bryan bought the four-year-old mare who was pulling an oyster cart at the time. He began racing her the following year.

Lady Suffolk won in her first outing at the age of five, a race of three heats. She was the first trotter to complete a mile race in less than 2:30, doing so at the age of twelve in 2:29.5. Lady Suffolk raced for fifteen years, trotting in an estimated one hundred sixty-two races over her career. She won eighty-nine times and was second fifty-six times, earning around $35,000[1].

---

[1] *Reports of the number of lifetime races and wins for these horses varied with different sources.*

Bryan and Lady Suffolk were so bonded that the mare seemed to become depressed when the man died in 1851. She competed both under saddle and in harness and was considered the "Queen of the Turf" until her death in 1855 at the age of twenty-two.

Some have claimed Lady Suffolk is the horse in the song, "The Old Gray Mare."

> *The old gray mare, she ain't what she used to be,*
> *Ain't what she used to be, ain't what she used to be,*
> *The old gray mare, she ain't what she used to be,*
> *Many long years ago.*

Flora Temple

The bay, Flora Temple, picked up where Lady Suffolk left off as a successful racing mare. She was foaled in 1845 in Oneida, New York. During her first five years, Flora changed hands many times because of her difficult temperament.

Flora set her first record (2:27) at the age of eight in 1853 and continued beating her own best times.

- 2.24 1/2 in 1856
- 2.23 1/2 on August 9, 1859 *(as a fourteen-year-old, and three more times that same year)*
- 2:22 on September 10
- 2.21 1/2 on October 7
- 2.19 3/4 on October 15

The celebrated trotting mare FLORA TEMPLE, driven by James D. McMann.
Best time in harness mile heat 2:19¾, two mile heats 4:50½ to wagon mile heat 2:25.

Flora Temple was the first trotter to break the 2:20 mark for the mile. She defeated the famous Morgan horse Ethan Allen in three heats on June 2, 1859. The mare was retired to a farm near Philadelphia at the age of sixteen after trotting one hundred and twelve races and winning ninety-five times. In her retirement, she produced two fillies and a colt, none of whom achieved the success Flora had.

One of the fillies, Kitty Temple, was a granddaughter of Hambletonian. Flora's only colt, Prince Imperial, never raced, but was sold to Robert Bonner, who used him as a driving horse. Bonner had also purchased the famous Hambletonian son Dexter.

Flora Temple died in 1877 at the age of thirty-two. It's claimed Flora was the "bob tail nag" of Stephen Foster's "Camptown Races" song.

> *Gonna run all night!*
> *Gonna run all day!*
> *I'll bet my money on the bob-tail nag—*
> *Somebody bet on the bay.*

Goldsmith Maid

Maid was foaled in 1857 on John Decker's farm in New Jersey. The bay filly was a granddaughter of Abdullah and inherited the stallion's disagreeable temperament. Decker kept Maid for seven years but was never able to harness her.

She was sold to a man who soon sold her again to Alden Goldsmith. It was not until 1865, at the age of eight, that trainer William Bodine was able to train Maid. The mare took on her new owner's name, becoming known as Goldsmith Maid. That same year, she won her first trotting race in 2:26. A few years later, her time had improved to 2:21 ½.

Alden Goldsmith believed Maid, at eleven, was nearing the end of her racing days. He sold her for $20,000 to Budd Doble in 1868. But Maid's popularity only increased. She was a favorite with the public, attracting thousands of spectators to specially arranged match races pitting the Maid against the fastest harness racers of the time. These proved to be so profitable that "The Maid" traveled to the matches in her own private rail car.

Maid would go on to race another six years for Doble. She was the top trotting horse in America for eight years. At seventeen, she set another record mile time of 2:17 which wasn't broken until 1878.

In 1874, Maid was sold to Henry Smith in New Jersey for $35,000. At the unbelievable age of sixteen, Maid came close to her mile record time, trotting 2:14 1/2. Her last race was in Toledo, Ohio, on September 27, 1877.

Over her career, Goldsmith Maid won ninety-two of one hundred and twenty-one races, earning $364,200.

At twenty, the great racing mare was retired to Smith's Fashion Farm in Trenton, New Jersey. She produced three colts, none of whom inherited her speed. She was a celebrity and attracted many tourists to Smith's farm. Goldsmith Maid died suddenly from pneumonia on September 23, 1885 at the age of twenty-eight. There was a period of national mourning after her death. A large monument stands in her memory at Smith's farm.

Whole villages used to gather at the depot for a glimpse of her as she passed through. No stall on a jolting boxcar was for The Maid. She had her own private car. It was always hooked on to passenger trains and in one end was a drawing room for her driver, Budd Doble.

Three times The Maid crossed the continent, racing on both coasts and throughout the Midwest, and never once did she miss a performance. An iron campaigner, she traveled some 130,000 miles by rail and made countless short jumps between towns under her own steam in her early days.

The Maid was ageless and her speed increased as she grew older. At the advanced age of 14, when most horses are finished, she stepped the fastest mile in trotting history: two minutes, 17 seconds. Unbelievably, she lowered her own mark six more times until she reached 2:14, the fastest of her career. That was in 1874 when she was 16, the equine equivalent of almost 50 years in a human.

—*Harper's Weekly, 1869*

Rosalind

Ben White, champion trainer of harness horses, raised Rosalind who was foaled on May 5, 1933. Ben's teen son, Gibson, was in the hospital with tuberculosis. Ben gave the filly to Gibson, hoping it would help the boy recover.

Gibson did recover. He helped as his father trained and began to race Rosalind. The mare became a champion trotter, winning the 1936 Hambletonian Stakes.

It was strictly a case of Rosalind first, and the rest nowhere, as Ben White moved his son's filly right to the top and held sway thereafter, the best mile in 2:01¾, a stake mark. Gib White smilingly joined his father in the winner's circle with the crowd wildly cheering the popular victory."

—*The Hambletonian Society archives*

Rosalind set a filly/mare record of 1:56¾ in 1938. In 1939, she was paired in harness with the great Greyhound, and the two set a team record of 1:58¼. Rosalind won twenty-four races during her career, with seven seconds, and one third. During her retirement, she produced six fillies. Rosalind died of cancer at the age of seventeen at Hanover Shoe Farms.

Several generations back in Rosalind's pedigree, you can find Hambletonian 10. Marguerite Henry intertwined the stories of Hambletonian, Gibson White, and Rosalind in her 1950 children's novel, *Born to Trot.*

Greyhound and Rosalind (Sep Palin) at Indianapolis, 1939

31

Horse Thieves

Punishment for a first offense was standing in a pillory for one hour, thirty-nine lashes on the back, and the thief's ears cut off. That sounds harsh, but in the past, horse theft was a big problem. People's transportation and survival often depended upon their horses, especially in the sparsely populated Midwest.

Stealing one or more horses was a serious offense that met with harsh consequences. Pennsylvania's "Act to Increase the Punishments of Horse Stealing," the source of the previously mentioned consequences, was passed in 1780 and remained in force until its repeal in 1860. According to that act, a second offense received the same whipping and pillory, but in addition, the person would be branded on the forehead with the letters "HT" for horse thief.

In order to deter thefts, recover stolen animals, and punish thieves, adult males formed anti-theft societies. These societies sometimes turned a thief over to the local legal system, but many enforced their own justice. Today, the anti-horse-theft societies would be considered vigilante groups as they often punished the thieves immediately without a trial. Many considered hanging the best punishment for a horse thief.

The Red Hook Society for the Apprehension and Detention of Horse Thieves claims to be the oldest of these groups in the United States. It was formed with sixty-three men in New York in 1796.

As police forces increased in the eastern cities, anti-theft societies focused on the sparsely populated Midwest and West. The National Horse Thief Detective Association (NHTDA) was formed in the 1840s in Indiana and oversaw the operation of similar groups in Indiana, Ohio, and Illinois. One such group was the Bentonville Anti-Horse Thief Society, formed in Bentonville, Ohio in March 1853.

The Society in Dedham for Apprehending Horse Thieves

FOUNDED JUNE 4, 1810

When a horse was stolen, the group was notified and provided identifying information about the animal (color, markings, breed, height, brand, and type of shoes). A group of men were selected to ride out and track the thief. Speed was of the essence. The longer the thief had to get away, the less chance he would ever be found. If a member refused to join the hunt when requested, he was fined.

Riders fanned out, notifying people in the area to be on the lookout for the thief. The men responsible for catching the thieves shared a ten-dollar reward.

Often a chase continued even when it cost the group more than the value of the horse or horses that were stolen. The groups intended to send a clear message to would-be thieves that the society was serious about capturing and punishing anyone who tried to steal horses in their area.

Horse thieves were often a man working single-handedly. George White, one of those thieves, would sometimes steal a horse, take it to the next town and sell it, then steal it again from the new owner of the horse. White might sell the horse a second time, then return it to its original farm before the horse was even missed.

James Middleton Riley known as Doc Middleton was one of the most notorious horse thieves. He stole his first horse in 1865 at the age of fourteen and would go on to steal as many as 2,000 horses from Native Americans and government herds in the Dakotas and Nebraska. He was imprisoned for murder at the age of nineteen but escaped. He later died in jail at the age of sixty-two.

> *One of the most unusual horse thieves was Jack Hall, known as No Arm Jack. As a child, Jack's arms were crushed in a sugar mill and amputated above the elbows. The loss of his arms didn't keep him from shooting a gun and working with horses . Not only could he manage horses, he was an expert at stealing them, for which he served ten years in jail.*
>
> —*The Marion Daily Star (Marion, Ohio) Aug 14, 1882*

Some thieves worked as part of a gang with each member serving a specific role. A spotter visited a farm or ranch, posing as a potential buyer. In reality he had no intention of buying. He would only scout out the place to see what type of horses were available, their location, and how best to access them. After allowing some time to elapse after the spotter's visit, so the theft wouldn't be connected to him, other members of the gang would steal the targeted horse or horses.

It was important to get a stolen horse out of the immediate area where he could be easily recognized. Relay stations were established so the gang's "runners" could ride the horse to the next station where another rider would cover the next leg of the journey. Relays allowed the horse to be quickly moved far away from its home.

It was the job of other experts in the gang to change a horse's appearance by dying his hair, adding facial or leg markings, cutting his mane or tail, or altering brands. Sometimes, the result was a horse so unrecognizable that he could even be sold in the same area where he'd been stolen.

Livery stables were an easy target for horse thieves. After surveying the stable's offerings, a man would hire the best team and

carriage for a drive and would never return. He would be well on his way to a relay station with the horses before the stable realized they'd been tricked.

Although men were, by far, the most common horse thieves, women were not above this crime. The modest style of dress for women in the 1800s presented a challenge for female horse thieves. Long, heavy, floor-length dresses made it difficult for women to ride. At the time, it was not socially acceptable for women to ride astride a horse. Racing off at high speed while riding sidesaddle would have been precarious at best, but female horse thieves did exist.

Belle Starr was born Myra Maybelle Shirley in 1848. Belle became more rebellious as she grew up. She joined a band of outlaws and began stealing horses with them. "The Bandit Queen" galloped away on her horse, always riding sidesaddle. But Belle's criminal ways and the bad company she kept finally caught up with her. She was murdered in 1889.

CLERMONT SOCIETY

FOR THE

DETECTION

—OF—

HORSE THIEVES

OFFICERS:

President--JOSHUA GARDNER.   Vice-President--PHILIP H. POTTS
Secretary--HAROLD WILSON.   Treasurer--URIAH FELLER.

RIDERS:

George Z. Foland,	Robert Dibblee,	Abram Coon,	Albert Potts,
George W. Feller,	Morgan Link,	Henry L. Rockefeller,	John H. Gardner.
Jacob H. Moore,	Robert Washburn,	Gilbert Rockefeller,	Wm. L. Fraleigh.

Another woman, Birdie McCarty, was a horse thief in Kansas. Convicted of her crime and facing a sentence of five years, the judge offered Birdie an interesting proposition. "Now if you will repeat the Lord's prayer I will knock off a year of this sentence." Birdie could not and had to serve her full punishment.

A few female horse thieves got around the bulky clothing and sidesaddle riding by dressing as a man. In Baltimore in 1838, a "youth" who said his name was George Wilson rode into the livestock marketplace one cold February morning. Wilson stated that the horse he rode was for sale. A horse of the animal's caliber would typically sell for $75, but Wilson quickly accepted $25 for it.

As the buyer handed over the money, a Mr. Magness arrived to interrupt the transaction. The horse had been stolen from his farm nearly twenty miles away early that morning.

Wilson was arrested, found guilty of horse theft, and was sentenced to two year's hard labor at the Maryland Penitentiary. The horse's true owner, Mr. Magness informed the prison warden that the footprints he discovered at his stable the morning of the theft appeared to be those of a woman.

An examination by a prison matron determined that Wilson was in fact a woman, and she was promptly moved to the women's section of the prison.

—Baltimore Gazette, May 18, 1838

Unfortunately, the theft of horses, although less common today, has never been totally eradicated. A sad, modern-day tale involves Fallon Blackwood, a third-year student at the Tuskegee University School of Veterinary Medicine in Alabama.

Fallon's technique was a scam rather than outright theft. She offered care and a retirement home for people's aging horses, claiming they would live as companions for one of her own animals. Sometimes she even signed a contract stating she would give the horse back if she could no longer care for it. But rather than caring for the horses, she sold them to be shipped to Mexico for horse meat.

Today, Stolen Horse International or Net Posse helps victims of horse theft attempt to track down their horses. The initial report on Fallon was for a horse named Willie. The owner missed her horse and requested that Fallon send her a photo of Willie, so she could see how he was doing. The photo never came, and the original owner suspected Blackwood had deceived her.

Soon reports involving nearly fifty horses were connected to Blackwood. She faced multiple charges in Alabama and North Carolina. The charges were not for theft, but for "felony obtaining property by false pretense."

A sad case of horse theft on November 3, 2011, involved Wendi Cox, a home health care nurse, and her daughter Jaci Rae Jackson. The two, with the help of two men—Billy Hamilton and George Berrish, stole five horses and a horse trailer from the Southern Arkansas University stable. The horses and trailer belonged to members of SAU's rodeo team. Ironically, Jaci was a freshman at the college and also a member of the team, competing as a barrel racer.

The men took the horses and trailer to Cox's home in Oklahoma. It seems the motive for the theft was to resell the horses, so Cox could afford to buy a more competitive barrel racing horse for her daughter. Jaci's younger sister, Jade, immediately recognized one of the horses, Credit Card, a fifteen-year-old, sorrel, roping horse gelding. Jade knew the horse would be recognized by anyone on the rodeo circuit if they tried to sell him. Credit Card, owned by team member Shaun Smith, had multiple brands that would be impossible to cover up.

Their plan began to unravel. Not wanting to be discovered with the easily recognizable horse, either Jaci or her mother ordered Billy Hamilton to kill Credit Card.

When someone spotted the stolen trailer on Cox's property, things really went haywire. The accomplices knew they had to get rid of the other horses fast. The remaining four animals were taken out and tied to pine trees where they went without food and water for nearly two weeks.

Realizing the gray mare owned by teammate Ty Lester would be easily visible, Wendi Cox purchased camouflage paint, which she and Jaci smeared over the horse, hoping it would help hide her.

The horses were finally found, malnourished and dehydrated. They had survived by eating pine needles and bark from the trees. All four fully recovered.

Wendi Cox, the mastermind of the plan, was tried, found guilty by a jury, and sentenced to sixty years in prison. Smiling for the television cameras after her sentencing, Wendy insisted she was innocent. She would serve at least ten years before being eligible for parole.

Jaci Rae received a ten-year sentence, however she was paroled after serving less than two years. Billy Hamilton was sentenced to twenty-five years and George Berrish to ten.

32

The Untamable Horse

The 16-hand, dark bay horse snorted, then bellowed fiercely and charged at the man who dared to open the heavy, solid oak stall door. The horse's British owner, Lord Dorchester, feared for John Rarey's life and advised him to stop. But, unlike everyone else who had encountered the animal, Rarey wasn't intimidated by Cruiser's vicious behavior. The stallion had spent the past three years in this brick stall, wearing an eight-pound iron muzzle with a bar in front of his mouth to keep him from biting anyone brave or ignorant enough to come near him.

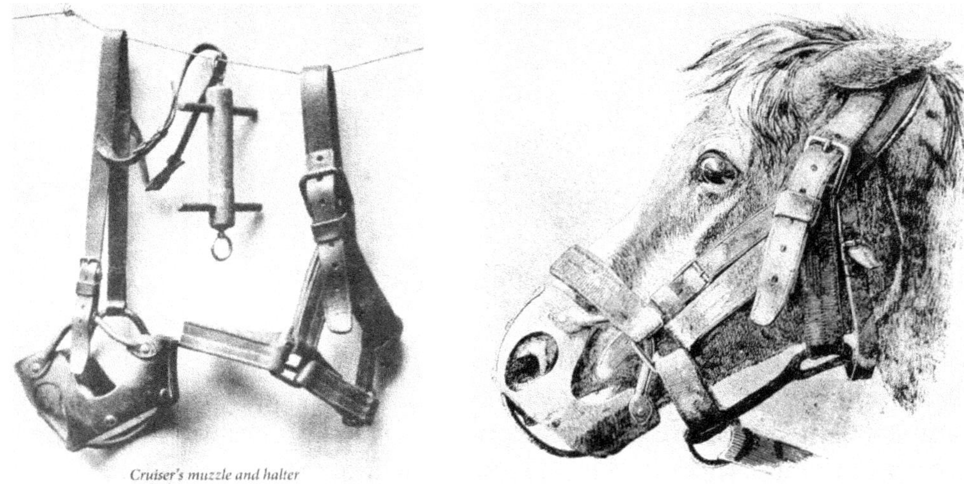

Cruiser's muzzle and halter

When his current handler needed to approach Cruiser, which was as rarely as possible, he carried a heavy club, ready to use it on the horse. In fact, some had suggested blinding the animal in order to protect those who had to deal with him. Others thought a bullet to the horse's head would be even better.

Mr. Rarey was not only confident, he was persistent. Soon, he had Cruiser tied to a rack in the stall. This enraged the horse, and for twenty minutes, he kicked and screamed, fighting against the restraint. Then, exhausted, the animal seemed to recognize this was a man he couldn't master.

After that, not only was Rarey able to enter the horse's stall unchallenged, within three hours, he rode Cruiser calmly around the stable yard.

Who was this vicious horse and the man with the amazing ability to tame him so quickly? First, we'll look at the man.

John Solomon Rarey (December 6, 1827 – October 4, 1866)

Three-year-old John Rarey rode the plow horse while his father or older brother worked the fields of their central Ohio farm. The youngest child in the family, John had few playmates, so he enjoyed the company of the farm animals, particularly the horses. At four, he received his own pony which he was able to scramble up on by himself. The pony quickly became his best friend, and the pair were often called upon to run errands and send messages throughout the community.

At the age of nine, John's horsemanship skills became the talk of the town after a rebellious horse took the boy on a perilous ride in which the animal raced across a narrow bridge, galloped madly through the village, and swam a deep ditch before finally reaching home with his rider still on board.

By twelve, Rarey was convinced many trainers were wrong with their approach of "breaking" horses. His father gave him a spirited, bay colt so the boy could try out his theories. The colt's progress was so amazing that young Rarey soon had a profitable training business. People not only brought their horses and mules for John to train, some came hundreds of miles to learn his methods.

In 1855, at twenty-eight, John traveled to Texas to study and train "wild" Mustangs. His techniques of kindness, firmness, and patience worked as well with these horses as they had with those at his family's Ohio farm. While in Texas, he owned and trained a team of elk. Driving the elk to town was guaranteed to draw attention!

By 1856, Rarey was back in Ohio. He published a book detailing his training methods and gave his first public demonstration in downtown Columbus. The following year, he took his training seminar to Canada where he impressed the cavalry officers.

Many people can train ordinary horses, but Rarey presented himself as an extraordinary trainer. Therefore, people were eager to offer their most challenging horses for him to work with—animals everyone else had given up on. In 1857, Queen Victoria invited John Rarey to England. An exhibition was arranged at Windsor Castle so the queen could see Rarey in action.

> *The riding master selected a horse belonging to Prince Albert, a wild, nervous animal. I was in a box stall alone with the horse for fifteen minutes. When Queen Victoria and Prince Albert entered, they found the animal lying down, and I lying beside him, with one of his hind feet under my head and the other over my chest. This so astonished them that they laughed. As the place was not large, all could not see; so after the Queen and Prince Consort had looked, they stepped back to let others of the royal party have a look. After that, the Queen and Prince Consort came back, talking to me about the horse, inquiring if I could make him rise. I answered "Yes," and commanded the animal to rise to his feet. They stood looking at the horse and said it was a wonderful performance, thanked me for the entertainment and departed.*

> —John Rarey

The queen was so amazed by Rarey's skill that a second exhibition was held, this time at Buckingham Palace, where Rarey worked with several horses previously considered untamable. The queen watched four of Rarey's exhibitions while he was in England and stated "for her there could be no better amusement."

But some who heard of Rarey's success were skeptical, including Lord Dorchester.

> *If Mr. Rarey would set criticism at naught, let him come down to Murrell's Green with a few of his aristocratic friends and try Cruiser. If he can ride him as a hack, I guarantee him immortality and an amount of ready money that would make a British bank director's mouth water.*

We've already seen that John Rarey's techniques were indeed successful with Cruiser as well. Lord Dorchester had given the trainer three months to tame Cruiser, but Rarey accomplished it in a mere three hours.

Now, more about the horse.

Cruiser's sire was named Venison and his dam, Little Red Rover. He was born in Lord Dorchester's stable in 1852, making him six years old when he met John Rarey.

Cruiser was considered vicious from a foal and had always been difficult to handle. He would sometimes lean against his stall wall and kick and scream for several minutes. He tore an iron bar in two with his teeth. Some sources claim he had killed two grooms. He'd worn an eight-pound, iron muzzle for the past three years and was kept confined to the brick stall. The muzzle barely allowed the horse to lick up his food. He was fed by two grooms, one who carried a club so he could kill the horse if Cruiser broke free and tried to attack him. Some had even proposed blinding the horse in order to keep his caretakers safe.

It makes one wonder why such a difficult horse was kept.

The answer is that he was of great racing bloodlines. Cruiser had only raced once himself, as a two-year-old, finishing second. After that, he was considered too vicious to race again, but he had sired six colts and seven fillies. The vision of the vicious horse producing the next racing phenomenon kept Cruiser alive.

Not only did Rarey ride Cruiser after three hours, Lord Dorchester was also able to ride the horse. The next day, Cruiser was taken to London where he became the most popular part of Rarey's exhibition.

Soon after, an attempt was made to have Cruiser perform in a circus. His handler, Mr. Cook, was not a skilled horseman, and his awkward manner made Cruiser nervous. When the horse became uncooperative, Cook applied the whip. That angered Cruiser, and teeth bared, he charged at the man. Mr. Cook fled the ring, Cruiser ran frantically back and forth, and the spectators clambered over their seats in a state of panic to reach the exits.

Fortunately for everyone, Mr. Rarey was in the audience. "Cruiser! Cruiser!"

Recognizing the voice, the frantic horse stopped and turned to face Rarey. Cruiser approached him slowly and extended his nose. Mr. Rarey stroked his face softly, and the horse calmed down. It was clear Rarey was the only human Cruiser fully trusted, and Lord Dorchester gave the stallion to him.

> *"I knew Rarey very well," said Uncle Claxton,— "the remarkable American horse-trainer who had a great name in England nearly forty years ago. He certainly did extraordinary things. I happened to have rooms in the same house with him, in London, when he was taming 'Cruiser.' Our lodging- house was kept by a nice old lady named Zanche—an Englishwoman with a Greek husband. We all liked her very much, and Rarey wanted her to visit the stables with him and be introduced to his reformed pupils; but she was afraid. One day, when she was sitting in her parlor, she heard a queer noise in the hall, and before she could look out to see what It was, the door opened, and Rarey rode in on his subjugated steed. 'Since you will not call on Cruiser, Mrs. Zanche,' he said, 'Cruiser has come to call on you.' The good lady was scared enough at first, but her four-footed visitor was on his best behavior, and went through a few tricks which Rarey had taught him, in the most affable manner. Mrs. Zauche was charmed, and considered herself highly complimented, for the conquered race-horse was a distinguished personage to entertain in those days."*
>
> *—The Daily Herald, Delphos, Ohio, April 4, 1899*

Rarey's success led to international fame. Over the next few years, he and Cruiser traveled to France, Sweden, Germany, Russia, Norway, Egypt, Turkey, and Arabia, giving performances that attracted large crowds. Rarey is thought to be one of the first to successfully tame a zebra. His training methods were adopted as the official training procedure of the U. S. Army.

A new word was created, "rareyfy" meaning "to tame a horse by kindness; to win by love; to mollify by the oil of kindness; to reclaim a badly broken horse; to cure madness by excessive kindness."

On his return to England in 1860, Rarey was presented with a gold medal by The Royal Society for the Prevention of Cruelty to Animals. He was invited to make England his new home, but in 1860, Rarey returned to America with Cruiser. In 1862, Rarey built Cedarlawn, a twenty-four room mansion in Groveport, Ohio, along with a stable and paddock for the horse who was nearly as famous as his trainer.

John Rarey suffered a stroke in 1865 and passed away the following year in the prime of his life at the age of thirty-eight. In his will, he left instructions for Cruiser's care.

> *The document [Rarey's will] is truly characteristic of the deceased, inasmuch as special bequests are made of several horses, whom he mentions by name, and bequeaths to various members of his family. The celebrated horse Cruiser by the taming of whom he mainly made his reputation, he leaves to his brother, Frederick but Cruiser is not to be used for any other purpose than as a stallion, nor for any purposes of exhibition, but he is to be kept and remain at the farm where he now is, and within the stable and enclosure now occupied by him, or similar ones, as long as he lives. The will proceeds: The said stallion Cruiser must be well taken care of by the said Frederick Rarey and his heirs, and must never be sold by either my said brother or any of his heirs. So long as Cruiser shall live, the enclosure and stable now occupied and, to be occupied by him on the said part of the farm shall be kept in good repair and comfortable and safe condition, and that Cruiser shall, as long as he lives, be furnished with suitable and sufficient food and other provisions for his comfort.*
>
> *—The Cincinnati Enquirer, Cincinnati, Ohio, September 6, 1867*

Unfortunately, upon the death of the only man Cruiser trusted, the horse's bad temper returned. Cruiser was cared for, but it must have been a lonely life for the horse as everyone was afraid to get too close to him. Cruiser lived another nine years, dying on July 4, 1875.

John Rarey and his exhibitions before the queen were instrumental in forming Nicholas Evans' idea for his book, *The Horse Whisperer* (1995). Rarey is briefly mentioned in Evans' book.

Rarey believed that "as the Creator intended the horse as the companion of human beings, he must necessarily have intellectual endowments in harmony with his destined purposes."

Some might be surprised by what Rarey considered gentle training techniques. He would often strap a horse's leg up and bring the horse down to lie on the ground. Powerless to object from this position, most horses accepted that the man was stronger and dominant over them. It's important to remember that Rarey usually dealt with vicious horses that most people considered untamable. Bringing a horse down to the ground was certainly more humane than having them euthanized.

> *You can do anything you wish with the horse in this condition, as when he becomes convinced of his incapacity to cope with man, he will abandon all antagonistic demonstrations, and become willing to obey, and generally docile. Operate on your horse in this manner as often as the occasion requires, and you will soon find him as gentle as his nature will permit him to be. By these means the most vicious, uneasy, unruly or fretful horse may be cured, though it depends upon the age and disposition of the animal how long it will take to make him amiable.[1]*

---

[1] *The full text of his book, Art of Taming Horses, is available at Project Gutenberg. http://www.gutenberg.org/e-books/28612*

Cruiser's memory lives on as well. In the 1920s, the horse became the official mascot for the Groveport, Ohio schools. The horse's strength and spirit provided an example that power with discipline brings success. The horse in various forms is featured on the logos of schools in the district. The school colors of red and black represent Cruiser's fiery temperament and the color of his coat. (He was apparently a dark bay, but must have looked nearly black.)

Illustrations from Rarey's book showing the progression of dealing with a severely difficult or vicious horse.

33

Livery Stables

In the days when horses served as the primary means of transportation, most towns had at least one livery stable. The word "livery" comes from the French "livere" meaning "to give or deliver." Of course, livery stables didn't give horses away, but for a fee, horses were rented for riding or carriage driving. The stables were often near or even attached to a hotel or boarding house for easy access. The livery often sold hay, grain, and other supplies. They sometimes included a blacksmith shop as well.

Strangers to the area were required to pay before receiving a horse. Since there was a greater risk that the horse would not be returned, they might also be charged more than the locals. Trusted local residents usually paid when they were finished with the animal. A one-way trip

with a horse was unheard of. The horse couldn't be left at another stable; it had to be returned to the livery from which it was rented.

In addition to renting mounts to the horseless, livery stables also offered boarding to horse owners. People who were passing through could store tack and leave their horse at the livery where he would be fed, watered, and bedded down for the night.

Charles W. Miller built and ran several livery stables in New York, beginning with seven horses and buggies in 1864. An enterprising businessman, in 1879, Miller's stable was the first business in Buffalo to have a telephone.

Always looking for ways to expand, Miller bought a former circus wagon to use as a moving van. By 1902, he'd added nine more wagons to his moving company. Horses were also used to pull hearses. Miller had nine of those available for use by funeral directors.

Due to the growth of his business and a fire that destroyed one of his stables, Miller needed more room. He bought property at a new location in Buffalo and began planning a multi-story stable. He soon ran into an unusual problem. Due to the flow of the nearby Buffalo River, there was quicksand in the area where he planned to build.

Miller consulted with architect William Lansing, who determined that multiple pilings driven deep into the ground would provide enough support for the stable. Additionally, a pumping system was installed to remove the water that continually pooled up from an underground spring.

In March, 1894, the six-story C.W. Miller Livery opened. The brick stable, 64 feet wide and 230 feet deep, received national attention. Although there were other multi-story liveries in the country, Miller's stable was considered the finest—"a palace for horses."

A blacksmith shop was located in the basement. Heavy wagons, vans, and buses were also stored on that level. The stable generated its own power to heat the building and had a sprinkler system for fire suppression. Three elevators were used to move grain, wagons, sleighs, coaches, and people between floors.

The first floor contained offices and living quarters for the carriage drivers. At the rear of the first floor,

were horses kept handy for customers who were in a hurry. These horses were hitched to vehicles, ready to go at a moment's notice.

Up to three hundred horses could be stabled on the second and third floors. The animals reached those levels by ramps. Generally, only sick horses were transported in the elevators. There were horse wash racks with hot and cold running water. Ventilation shafts from the roof provided fresh air. Hay and grain were dropped down other shafts from feed storage areas on the sixth floor. Carriages were stored on the fourth floor. The fifth was used for painting, varnishing, and repairing vehicles.

When automobiles began replacing horses after World War I, the Miller Livery was converted into a parking garage and was renamed the Huron Street Garage. Later, the building was owned by the Hertz car rental company. In 2000, the old livery building became vacant. As of 2017, it was slated to be turned into a school campus.

In 1906, the Palace Sales Stable in Charlottesville, Virginia boasted of being the only livery in the state to offer grooming services, using a new technology—electric clippers. The stable's ads promised to clip and clean a horse in less than fifteen minutes. That same year, the first automobile arrived in Charlottesville. In the coming years, more of the horseless carriages appeared. It was happening all over the country. In the United States, the horse and mule population reached its peak in 1920 at twenty-five million.

While most stables weren't as elaborate as the Miller Livery, they provided a vital service to American travelers. And, they all suffered a similar fate. As horses were replaced by automobiles, many of the old stables were converted to garages. You may have one in your hometown.

THE PALACE,
LIVERY FEED
& SALE STABLE

34

Horse Boats

A horse boat or horse ferry sounds like a type of watercraft designed to transport equines. But in the past, rather than carrying horses, some boats were actually powered by them. When multiple horses were used, the boats were known as team boats, a play on the word "steamboat."

Although records indicate they were in use as far back as Roman times, the boats were used as ferries in the United States from 1780 until they were replaced by steam engines in the late 1800s and early 1900s. The horse-powered ferries were popular for traveling short-distances across rivers or lakes.

They were used initially in the Northeast, on Lake Champlain and the Hudson River. Five horse ferries operated on Lake Champlain. The idea later spread to the Ohio, Mississippi, and Missouri Rivers.

The operation of the power mechanism varied. In the earliest days, the horses were attached to a whim. The setup was similar to a merry-go-round, with bars radiating out from the center to which one or more horses were attached.

The horses walked in a circle around a center post causing gears to rotate, which turned the boat's paddle wheel. The constant circular movement tended to make the horses dizzy, and the wheel and horses took up a lot of space on the boat. Sometimes multiple levels were built so the horses had their own deck.

A new design was invented by Barnabus and John C. Langdon of Troy, New York, a father and son team. In 1819, they patented a treadwheel, a horse-sized, wooden turntable. The circular, horizontal treadwheel was located under the deck with an opening above it large enough for one or two horses. The horses remained in place while a large treadwheel turned under their feet as the animals walked.

Treadwheels were used in boats for twenty or more years. Then, another improvement came along—the horse treadmill. Functionally, this was similar to an exercise treadmill for people. The equine version saved space over the

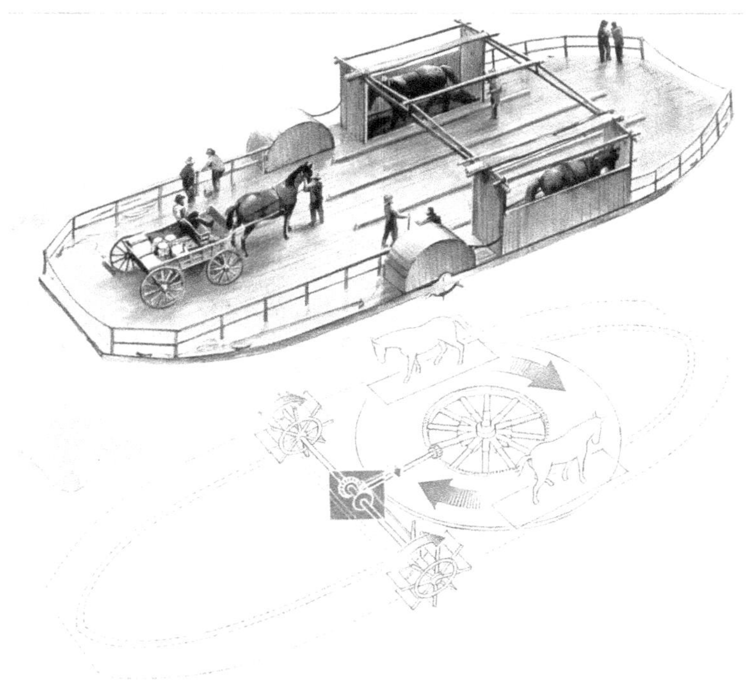

large treadwheel and was easier on the horses. It was common to use two horses, one at each side. Both horses needed to walk at the same pace or the boat traveled in a circle. Horse-powered treadmills were also used to run farming equipment, saws, and other devices as well as to pump water and churn butter.

In 1844, William M. Chick encountered some unusual passengers at his horse-powered ferry station on the Missouri River in Kansas City. Chick successfully ferried a traveling circus across the river. Mr. Chick stated that he had no trouble with any of the animals, except the elephant, which at first refused to come on board. After much coaxing, the elephant was finally induced to board the boat, causing the deck to creak in protest. The elephant was brought safely across, causing $10 in damages to the boat.

A "Horse Power Boat" created by Rufus Porter was featured in the American Mechanic magazine in 1842. Porter had high hopes for his invention.

We may see farmers harness their horses in a boat, to take a ride up or down a river, as they now do in a buggy or gig.

While Porter's expectations never became reality, the horse-powered ferries were used in some areas for more than a hundred years. The last horse ferry to operate in North America was a small, treadmill ferry powered by a blind horse who carried passengers across the Cumberland River in Rome, Tennessee until the 1920s.

In 1983, a sunken horse ferry was discovered fifty feet underwater in Lake Champlain at Burlington, Vermont. The boat apparently sank or was deliberately sunk in 1841. It used the treadwheel design, with the large turntable mounted below the main deck.

Boats weren't the only vehicles powered by horse treadmills. The first cyclopeds were created in the 1820s. The name sounds like a bicycle, however the first pedal bicycles weren't invented until the 1860s. The cycloped was a horse-powered treadmill mounted on a special rail car—the first equine locomotive. A cycloped called "The Flying Dutchman" was used by the South Carolina Canal and Railroad Company in 1829 and 1830.

In Italy, in 1850, Clemente Masserano built a cycloped called the Impulsoria. It was promoted as cheaper to purchase and run than a steam locomotive. Powered by two horses during a test run in London, England in 1850, the Impulsoria reached a speed of seven miles per hour. When used with four horses, it could achieve even faster speeds. The locomotive was able to pull up to thirty rail cars. However, as with the other cyclopeds, the horse-powered Impulsoria never caught on. Soon steam engines became the preferred source of power for the railroads.

35

Along the Tow Path

In 2012, Bilbo Baggins, a cob stallion, towed a canal boat from Leeds to Liverpool in England. The stocky, bay stallion pulled a 150-year-old, sixty-foot canal boat called the Elland. Riding in the boat was England's Horse Boating Society chairwoman, Sue Day. The 128-mile journey was taken at a leisurely pace over five months. Baggins and Day's trip was a reminder of a time, nearly forgotten, when travel by canal boat was common.

To understand when and why canal boats were popular requires a glimpse back in time. In the early days of the United States, people were primarily farmers or tradesmen with skills such as leatherworking, carpentry, blacksmithing, candlemaking, or printing. They worked for themselves or in small, local shops. The Industrial Revolution refers to the transformation of a society based on local businesses into one where goods are mass produced.

Equines played an important role in the Industrial Revolution, which ironically resulted in societal changes that nearly rendered them obsolete. To make mass production work, businessmen needed an efficient way to transport raw materials such as coal, wood, cotton, and wool from their source to a factory or mill. Once the products were made, they also needed a way to ship the items to people who wanted to buy them.

Pack animals couldn't carry that much weight. Even transport by horse-drawn wagons was limited. The wagons were slow and not suited for the large, heavy loads. Transportation by water was recognized as the most cost-effective way to ship goods. This wasn't a new concept as canals were used by ancient civilizations.

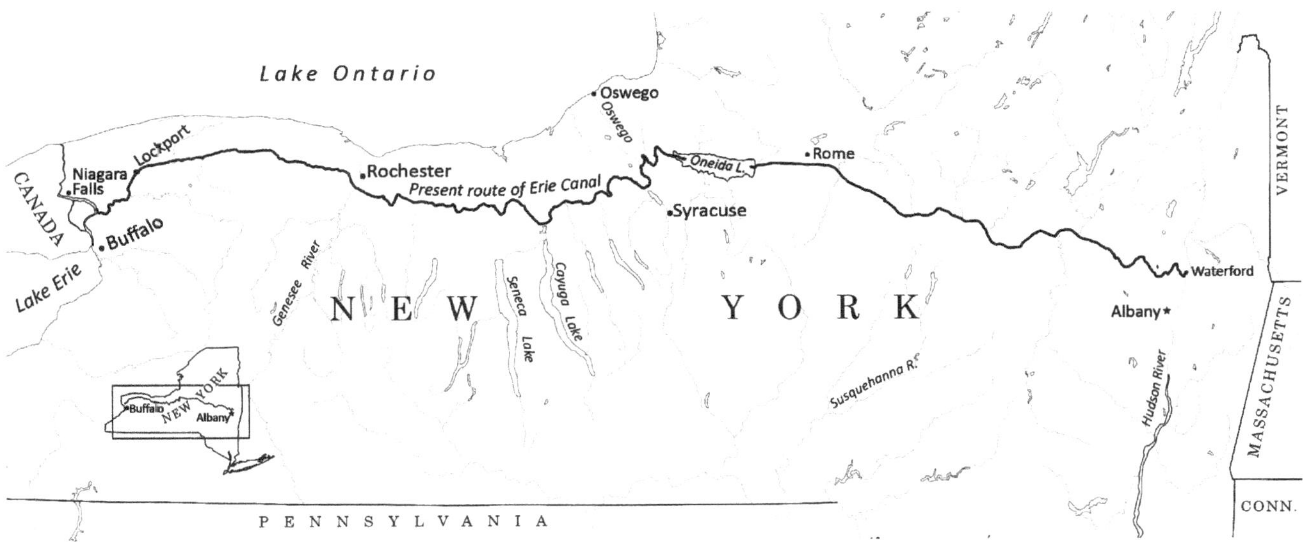

By the early 1800s, plans had been developed in the United States for a system of canals. One of the earliest and most famous was the Erie Canal. A second war with England was behind them (the War of 1812), and Americans were able to focus on improvements within their own country. Work on the Erie Canal began on July 4, 1817, near Rome, New York. Since machinery for digging didn't exist at the time, the canals were dug by hand, often using Irish immigrants.

Canals were forty feet wide at the top of the banks. Their sides sloped inward, making them twenty-eight feet wide at the bottom. Canal boats had flat bottoms, so the water didn't need to be very deep. Most canals had a depth of four feet. Clay was packed along the bottom of the canal bed to form a watertight seal.

The first fifteen miles of the Erie Canal opened for use in 1819. Eight years later, on October 26, 1825, the canal was finished. Stretching 363 miles across the state of New York, it linked the Hudson River to Lake Erie.

Where there was a significant difference in elevation along the canal route, locks were built. These large stone enclosures had gates at each end. Water was added to or released from the lock to raise or lower the boat as needed. Once the required level had been reached, the gate was opened and the boat continued on.

Canal boats were approximately eighty feet long and fourteen feet wide. The boats weren't used only for transporting raw materials and finished products. People enjoyed traveling on the canals as well.

Packet boats were designed to carry passengers—up to one hundred at a time. Each boat was given a name. When the name was registered with the state, no other boat could use it. Each boat typically had a crew of three people. The captain was often the owner. The boats had living quarters for the captain's family who would ride up and down the canal from spring through fall. Young children who traveled with their families were often tied or chained to the boat, so they wouldn't fall into the canal.

A bowsman or helmsmen steered the boat by the rudder. His job was to keep the boat traveling straight, away from the sides of the canal. That was challenging at night when the only light came from two kerosene lamps at the front of the boat.

The third crew member was the teamster or hoggee. His job was to care for the horses or mules. President James A. Garfield, from Ohio, worked as a hoggee on the canals in his youth.

The boats weren't powered by engines as those hadn't been invented yet. Along one side of the canal, a ten-foot-wide path was constructed—the towpath. That's where the horses came in. A team of two or three were attached to the boat by a tow rope, typically ninety feet long. Horses, mules, and even a few donkeys were used. Mules were the most popular towing animals as they tended to live longer and were more sure-footed than horses. A mule's towing career could last twenty years.

Walter Conley, in his article "Life on the Canal", from the Syracuse Star, April 29, 1850, describes an incident with one mule.

> *We had one very stubborn mule, her name was Janie. When a fly landed on her side she would lie down, harness and all. One time she rolled right into the canal and we had all we could do to get her unfastened from the other two beside her.*

With some animals, the hoggee had to walk alongside the team to keep them moving. It was a great temptation for the animals to stop to graze at the side of the towpath. The hoggees, often barefoot, might walk twenty miles a day beside the horses or mules. Other animals, accustomed to the routine of their job, didn't require the hoggee's supervision.

One hoggee, J. P. Mose, recalled his experience.

> *I was kicked by a mule. He was a young mule; we hadn't had him very long, and I scared him. I'm telling you he caught me right in the hip. He knocked me clean across the towpath. It sort of knocked the ball out of the hip socket. He didn't mean to do it. I just scared him.*

It might sound like hard work for animals to pull a boat, but horses can pull nearly fifty times as much weight in a boat as they can when pulling a wagon on land.

A canal isn't the same as a river. The water is still, without any current. The nearly friction-less motion of the boat makes it much easier to pull—so easy that even a person was capable of pulling an unloaded canal boat a short distance. The hardest part for the tow animals was getting the boat started. Once moving, they could easily pull loads of thirty to sixty tons.

The tow animals learned to lean into their harness collars to keep the tow rope taut. The boat moved ahead at a steady speed of approximately three to four miles per hour. Each team of horses or mules pulled for six hours. Then, another team would take their place. The additional team was either stabled on the boat while they rested or housed in a stable along the route.

At its peak in 1855, 33,000 shipments were made on the Erie Canal, and the Erie was only one of many canals in operation at the time. Nearly 3,000 miles of canals were constructed in the United States, requiring large numbers of horses and mules to transport the cargo.

All that walking quickly wore out horseshoes. Teams of blacksmiths were employed to keep the horses shod. An industry also existed to provide the enormous quantities of food the animals consumed along the way.

Since canal boats don't have brakes, a way to slow or stop the boats was needed. Vertical posts of wood or iron, known as strapping posts, were set in the ground along the side of the canal where a boat needed to slow down, for example to enter a lock or stop at a wharf. The boatman would wrap one end of a rope around the post. By altering the tension on the strapped rope, the boatman could vary the speed or gradually bring his boat to a stop.

Boat traffic traveled both ways on the canals, but there was only one towpath. When two boats approached each other, one of the parties had to unhook their animals and lower their tow rope into the water. The other boat would then float over the rope, and the animals passed each other on the path.

Because the shallow water in the canal froze easily, the Erie Canal was closed in cold weather. During the winter months, it was partially drained and any necessary repairs made. The frozen canals provided an opportunity for winter recreation such as sledding and ice skating.

In the late 1800s, steam-powered canal boats began to be used in addition to those drawn by equines. In 1869, railroad construction workers from the East and West met at Promontory Summit in Utah Territory where a golden spike was driven to celebrate the completion of the transcontinental railroad. However, the railroad's celebration led to the end of the canal era. Although some canal boats were used into the 1950s, the railroads increasingly took over the transportation of people and goods.

A song about mules on the Erie Canal, "Low Bridge, Everybody Down" was written in 1905 by Thomas S. Allen. The lyrics begin:

> *I've got a mule and her name is Sal*
> *Fifteen years (miles) on the Erie Canal*
> *She's a good old worker and a good old pal*
> *Fifteen years (miles) on the Erie Canal*

Some canals or portions of them have been preserved and are still in limited use today, primarily in parks and historic villages The parks may offer horse-drawn canal boat rides, allowing visitors to experience for themselves the peaceful, leisurely pace of the canal era.

36

More Powerful Than a Locomotive?

While not more powerful, at one point in our past the horse was faster than a locomotive! Rather than steel rails, the earliest railways were made of wood and were called wagonways. The use of wagonways goes back as far as the mid-1500s.

Rail cars with sails powered by the wind were used in England from World War I until the 1950s. The cars were called sail bogeys or sail trolleys.

Railroad handcars were typically powered by four or more men operating a see-saw lever with handles at each end. These handcars could reach speeds of eight to fifteen miles per hour.

The Baltimore and Ohio Railroad, the oldest rail line in the United States, was built to compete with the Erie Canal. Eventually, it was extended to connect Baltimore, Maryland with the Ohio River. The first thirteen miles, running from Baltimore to Elicott Mill, Maryland opened on May 24th, 1828.

The Baltimore and Ohio (B&O) hoped to be the first to utilize steam rather than horses for its rail line. Directors approached inventor Peter Cooper with their idea. Cooper was eager to take on the challenge. "I told the directors that I believed I could knock together a locomotive."

If anyone could "knock together" a steam locomotive, the enterprising Peter Cooper probably could. He was a thirty-nine-year-old, self-educated inventor from New York City. One of his inventions, a self-rocking cradle, was equipped with a fan to shoo flies away as well as a musical element that played a lullaby.

Cooper constructed the locomotive for B&O using an old brass engine, discarded wheels from a railroad shop, and the barrels of two muskets for the boiler tubes. His creation was known as the Tom Thumb.

On August 28, 1830, with Cooper at the controls, the locomotive built up steam in preparation for its first journey. The passengers were thrilled when the new locomotive reached a speed of eighteen miles per hour. Although a galloping horse can run at thirty or more miles per hour, he can't sustain that speed for long.

Two tracks paralleled each other along the line between Baltimore and Elicott. Reports differ as to the date of the legendary race. But whether on Tom Thumb's maiden voyage or another time, a driver for a local stagecoach company pulled up in a horse-drawn rail car alongside the locomotive and challenged Cooper to a race.

John H.B. Latrobe one of the B&O leaders aboard the Tom Thumb, reported the event.

> *The race was neck and neck, nose and nose. But soon, the engine passed the horse and a great 'hurrah' heralded the victory. Just as the horse cart was about to concede, a pulley slipped on Tom Thumb, causing the locomotive to lose steam. As the machine cruised to a stop, the horse burst back into the lead. Cooper was able to get the locomotive fixed and regain much of the lost ground, but in the end, nature won out over machine.*

The identity of the horse who won this famous race is unknown. Some said he was a gray. Peter Cooper still believed in his engine. "Although the race is lost, steam has won. The iron horse will work better than the real horse."

The Tom Thumb, though never designed for regular service, is considered the first successful American steam locomotive. Despite its loss to the unnamed horse, the Tom Thumb had demonstrated the capabilities of steam locomotion. From that time on, the railroad focused on the development of "Iron orses" powered by steam.

By 1836, the B&O Railroad no longer used horses to pull their trains. They kept a few horses to pull cars through the city until the 1880s. In 1974, B&O held a re-enactment of Tom Thumb's race against a horse, using a replica of the original locomotive. The horse won again.

THE HORSE WINS THE RACE

On August 25, 1830, Peter Cooper had his "Tom Thumb," first American-built locomotive, out for a trial run on the thirteen-mile stretch of Baltimore and Ohio track between Baltimore and Ellicott's Mills. Here he was challenged to a speed trial by the stage coach owners of the day.

It was a spirited race, the horse ahead first, then nip and tuck, then the "Tom Thumb" steaming into the lead. But a belt on the engine slipped off, and by the time Cooper had replaced it, the horse had won. The race proved, however, that steam was destined to power the railroad. Baltimore and Ohio Railroad At "A Century Of Progress," Chicago, 1933

37

Mass Transportation

It might seem that in the days before motorized vehicles, everyone was an experienced horseman, able to mount his horse and ride wherever he needed to go. But then, as now, not everyone could afford a horse, had a place to keep one, or enjoyed riding. In fact, some people in those days, even though they relied on horses for transportation, were afraid of them.

Stagecoaches were used for long-distance travel in sparsely populated areas. Within towns or cities, the most common way to get around was simply by walking. Some form of horse-drawn transportation was the other option, although not everyone could afford to ride. Two basic types of vehicles were used—the omnibus and the horse streetcar.

The Omnibus

The horse-drawn omnibus first appeared in the 1820s. Omnibus was eventually shortened to "bus." The horse bus was similar to a stagecoach, only larger with more seating, some carrying up to twenty-five passengers. Most had three steps at the back and allowed passengers to enter through a rear door. The horse-drawn omnibus had wooden wheels and was pulled over the rough, unpaved roads which were often muddy and rutted, producing a rough ride.

Often the driver of the bus was also its owner. Passengers signaled the driver when they wished to exit by pulling a leather strap which ran along the inside roof of the bus. The front end of the strap wrapped around the driver's leg—a sure way to get his attention.

When the passenger paid the fare, the driver opened the door so he could exit. Omnibuses provided the first mass public transportation in many towns, following a regular schedule and fixed routes.

The Horse Streetcar

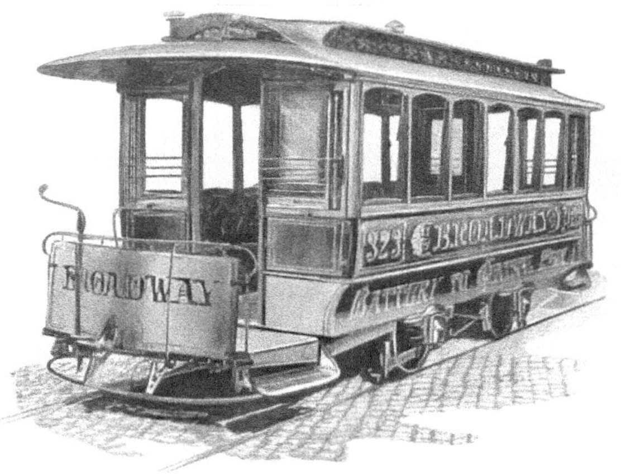

While an improvement over walking, the omnibuses had some disadvantages that horse-drawn streetcars improved upon. Street cars rode on a rail system set up within towns. Flanges were added to the car wheels to keep them from sliding off the rails. This new system provided a smooth ride. The reduction in friction made it easier for the horses to pull, allowing them to carry more passengers at a faster speed. The John Mason was the first horse car to operate in the U.S.

Built by carriage builder John Stephenson, the John Mason opened in November, 1832, operating on Fourth Avenue in New York City. The car was divided into three compartments, each of which could hold ten passengers. Additional cars built for this line were named the President, the Mentor, and the Forget-Me-Not.

Although steam engines were beginning to be used by railroads, they weren't used to pull streetcars within towns and cities. Noisy steam engines were known to spook the many horses still working in the cities. The streetcars primarily used a team of two horses or mules.

John Stephenson invented a reversible horse car design in 1859. The body of the carriage could be rotated, allowing a horse car to reverse direction at the end of the line without requiring additional space for a turnaround. The body was rotated, and the horse re-hitched to the car.

Horse-drawn streetcars became so popular that the idea spread to other large cities across the country and to Europe. Horse cars were used in Boston for nearly forty years, the first opening in March 1856. By the 1860s, streetcars had replaced omnibuses in many cities. The service was typically closed on Sundays. African Americans might be prohibited from riding the cars or were only permitted to ride segregated cars.

In Chicago, the horse rail system opened in 1858 and was called the State Street Horse Railroad. According to the Chicago Tribune, "Horse railroads have become to the cities what the steam railroad is to the country at large."

In 1872, Chicago had 188 horse cars. Passengers were charged five cents per ride. By 1880, there were 18,000 horse cars running in the United States. Streetcar companies owned hundreds of horses, which they kept in small stables around the city or in large, multi-story stables.

An interesting variation of the horse car operated in Englewood, Colorado from 1892 to 1910. The unique Cherrelyn horse car was known as the "Gravity and Bronco Railroad." A horse pulled the car a mile uphill. At the top, the animal was unhitched and led up a ramp onto a platform at the back of the car. Then, the car and its passengers, human and equine, coasted back down the hill. The car, no longer in use, is on display in the Englewood Civic Center.

It was reported that when horses who retired from the Cherrelyn line were sold to farmers, they would pull plows uphill but not down.

Carville, California

In 1895, the Market Street Railway Company in San Francisco, California discontinued its horse-drawn transportation service. The company offered its horse cars for sale at twenty dollars per car—or ten dollars without the seats.

Area residents purchased the cars and used them as residences or commercial buildings. Some used the cars individually while others combined several to make both single and multi-storied structures in

a variety of layouts. The old cars became homes, beach houses, coffee shops, and business offices. A church was even created from them. The area became known as Carville.

As San Francisco grew and expanded into Carville, the Oceanside Improvement Club was formed. Their catchy motto was "Make clean today by sweeping and burning up the debris of yesterday." In 1913, a ceremony was held to burn four of the horse cars. Most of the remaining cars had disappeared by the 1920s.

Horse cars were the forerunners of trolleys and trams that were later powered by steam, cable, and electricity. Eventually, many large cities developed subway systems that helped ease traffic congestion by moving much of the transportation underground.

38

Ponies in the Pits

Coal is a sedimentary rock formed from dead plant matter under pressure. In the past, people burned coal in stoves and furnaces to heat their homes and for cooking. When steam engines were invented, coal was used to power them. Coal also fueled the blast furnaces which produced steel from iron ore.

In 1882, Thomas Edison developed the first power station to generate electricity from coal. Throughout recent history, there has been a huge demand for this natural resource. At its peak in 1968, 60% of America's electricity was generated from coal. In 2016, for the first time, natural gas passed coal as the top resource for generating electric power in the United States. World-wide, coal still fuels 37% of electricity production.

Until the Middle Ages, coal was dug out from just below the ground's surface. When those coal outcroppings were exhausted, pits were dug to access coal deeper underground. When those supplies dwindled, a mine shaft was dug hundreds of feet into the ground. Horizontal passages branched off from the deep shaft to access multiple coal seams.

At the working edge of those seams, called the face, miners chipped off chunks of coal with a pick ax and tossed them into coal cars. Coal mining was dangerous work. Breathing in coal dust caused Black Lung Disease, resulting in the early deaths of many miners. The buildup of gases in the mines sometimes caused explosions and cave-ins. Although coal is mined in many countries, including the United States, this section focuses primarily on the mining operations in Great Britain where ponies were often used.

In the early 1800s, it was common for children to work long hours at physically-demanding and dangerous jobs such as in factories, lumber and textile mills, and mining. In the earliest days, coal was carried by hand in baskets. An improvement upon that was hauling coal in small carts or wagons. In the early days of mining, this job was often performed by women and children.

A woman attached a chain to her waist which connected to a coal cart. As the "hurrier,"[1] she pulled the heavy cart, sometimes on her hands and knees through passageways that

---

[1] *See the mining terminology section at the end of the chapter.*

might only be three feet high. One or more children, the "thrusters" would help by pushing the cart from behind. The children's small size allowed them to move more easily through the tight mine passages. With no restrictions on child labor, there was nothing to prevent children as young as five or six from working all day in the mines. Many children worked as hurriers or thrusters. The youngest worked as trappers, sitting all day in a dark tunnel where their job was to open or close a door when needed.

Huskar Pit Disaster

The Huskar coal mine is located near the village of Silkstone Common in South Yorkshire, England. On July 4, 1838, a tragedy occurred at the mine. Heavy rainfall extinguished the fire on the steam engine which powered a winding machine that lifted miners up the shaft. The workers stranded at the bottom were instructed to remain there until the equipment could be restarted.

Some of the child miners, confused or frightened, tried to escape through a flooded ventilation shaft. Twenty-six children drowned, the youngest a seven-year-old boy. When the Huskar tragedy came to the attention of Queen Victoria, she demanded an inquiry which became the Ashley Mines Commission Investigation of 1842.

Several children testified of their experience working in the mines. Sarah Gooder began working as a trapper at the age of eight.

> *I'm a trapper in the Gawber pit. It does not tire me, but I have to trap without a light and I'm scared. I go at four and sometimes half past three in the morning, and come out at five and half past. I never go to sleep. Sometimes I sing when I've light, but not in the dark; I dare not sing then. I don't like being in the pit. I am very sleepy when I go sometimes in the morning. ... I would like to be at school far better than in the pit.*

Mary Davis also worked as a trapper, at just six years of age.

> *I went to sleep because my lamp had gone out for want of oil. I was frightened for someone had stolen my bread and cheese. I think it was the rats.*

Patience Kershaw, seventeen, also testified.

> *My father has been dead about a year; my mother is living and has ten children, five lads and five lasses; the oldest is about thirty, the youngest is four; three lasses go to mill; all the lads are colliers, two getters and three hurriers; one lives at home and does nothing; mother does nought but look after home.*
>
> *All my sisters have been hurriers, but three went to the mill. Alice went because her legs swelled from hurrying in cold water when she was hot. I never went to day-school; I go to Sunday-school, but I cannot read or write; I go to pit at five o'clock in the morning and come out at five in the evening; I hurry in the clothes I have now got on, trousers and ragged jacket; the bald place upon my head is made by thrusting the corves; my legs have never swelled, but sisters did when they went to mill; I hurry the corves a mile and more under ground and back; they weigh 300 cwt.; I hurry 11 a-day; I wear a belt and chain at the workings, to get the corves out...*

After hearing these, and other, testimonies, the British Parliament passed the Mines and Collieries Act of 1842. This prohibited all females from working underground in the mines and required boys to be ten or older. Women were permitted to work at mining jobs but only above ground.

The mines were to be inspected periodically to ensure they were in compliance with the new regulations. But, initially, there was only one mining inspector for all of Britain. Because he was unable to keep up with all the work, women and children continued working in the mines. When the number of inspectors was increased, most had no desire to actually go down into the mines. To do so meant facing the wrath of the miners and mine owners.

In 1854, Commissioner of Mines, Hugh Seymour Tremenheere reported two instances where persons attempted inspections and were "maltreated, and very nearly lost their lives."

In 1872, the legal age for boys to work in the mines was raised to twelve; and in 1903, it increased to thirteen. Since births weren't scrupulously recorded, it was common for the boys or their parents to lie about a child's age so they could work.

Pit Ponies

While the Mining Act of 1842 protected women and children, it had the opposite effect for ponies. After its enactment, mine operators were desperate for cheap replacements to do the work women and young children were no longer permitted to perform.

Strong ponies were in demand to haul coal in the mines. Equine mine workers varied in size depending on the job they were required to do. Taller horses were used above ground or in the large roads near the main shaft. As the tunnels became smaller near the coal face, shorter animals were needed, typically averaging 12 hands in height. Nearly all pit ponies were geldings. Mares and stallions would cause too many behavioral problems in the confined quarters of the mine.

Shetland was the most common breed. The small, stocky ponies were particularly suited for mining. The breed originated in the Shetland Isles northeast of Scotland. Due to the harsh climate and scarcity of food, the ponies were quite hardy. For their size, Shetlands are considered the strongest of all horse and pony breeds. They are also long-lived, often living more than thirty years.

In addition to the Shetland pony, other breeds used in the mines included Welsh, Dartmoor, Dale, Icelandic, and Russian or Asiatic. Mining ponies needed to be even-tempered, brave, strong, and sure-footed. A low head carriage was important because of the low height of the tunnels. A pony might be injured by banging his head on the ceiling or even worse cause a rock fall.

Some legal protection came with the British Coal Mines Act of 1911, which required ponies to be four years old before working in the mines. Teeth were inspected to determine the ponies' approximate age.

During World War I, British coal operators exhausted the pony supply within their country and began importing them from Scotland, Wales, Iceland, Belgium, and the United States. Ponies arriving by train or ship were unloaded,

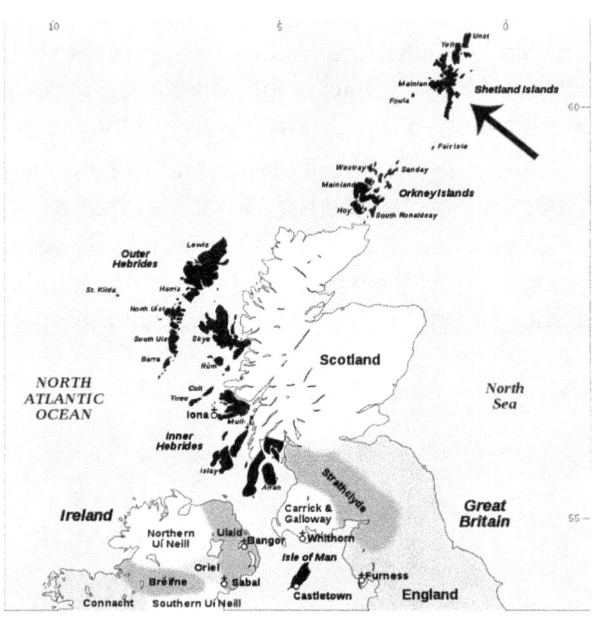

130

then herded through the streets of the town to the dealer's lot. From there, they were purchased by mine representatives.

Training generally occurred when the pony arrived at the colliery (coal mine). But no amount of training could prepare the animals for what they would experience in the mines.

Before the invention of safety lamps, miners used candles. The open flames caused disastrous explosions when gases seeped from the coal seams. Safety lamps were developed in which the flame was contained inside a glass enclosure.

Beginning in 1911, canaries were taken into the mines to detect dangerous levels of carbon monoxide and other gases. John Scott Haldane, a Scottish scientist, originally came up with the idea to use the birds.

Carbon monoxide is odorless, so it could reach deadly levels before people were aware of its presence. Since birds take in oxygen when both inhaling and exhaling, they're more sensitive to lower levels of oxygen. The tiny birds were easily carried in small cages into the mines. If the canary acted faint or stopped chirping or singing, the men were alerted and quickly returned to the surface until the buildup of gases was alleviated.

The miners sometimes carried small oxygen vials to revive the canaries. The birds were used in mines until 1986 when they were replaced by modern carbon monoxide detectors.

Mining Terminology

After Damp - Gasses resulting from underground combustion, normally carbon monoxide. Gasses in a mine could cause an explosion or fire (other gases were known as firedamp, blackdamp, chokedamp, whitedamp, and stinkdamp).

Air Shaft - An opening into a mine for the passage of air.

Boom - A horizontal wooden support in the mine roof.

Breaker boys - Children, usually boys, who sat above a conveyor belt that carried freshly-mined coal. The children picked out rocks and other debris from the coal as it passed by.

Cage - The elevator that carried the men from the surface down into the mine and back out.

Coal Seam or Bed - A stratum (layer) of coal.

Collier - A worker in a coal mine.

Colliery - A coal mine including the buildings on the surface and the underground shafts and tunnels.

Corf/Corves - The cart, tub, or basket used to transport coal from the face to a shaft where it would be taken to the surface. The coal carts deep in the mines were pulled on steel rails, like a railroad track, usually on flat areas, so heavy carts could be pulled even by children. The ponies often pulled several carts connected together.

CWT - Hundredweight (about 112 pounds, so 3 CWT would be 336 pounds).

Drift - A horizontal passage leading into or out of a mine.

Driver - A workman, usually a boy, who drives an underground work horse, also known as ganging.

Face/Workings - The active part of a coal seam where coal is currently being extracted.

Gearing Up - Harnessing the horse or pony.

Getter/Hewer/Loader - A coal face worker who digs out the coal. In the early days, this was done with a pick, working by candlelight. Candles were replaced by safety lamps, then by electric lights. This was one of the few jobs that wasn't done in nearly total darkness. The job was held by the strongest boys and men. A hewer was paid based on the amount of coal he produced. Explosives, black powder or dynamite, were later used to loosen the coal at the face. And more recently coal-cutting machinery has been developed.

Hoist - An engine with a winding drum and rope which hauls people, horses, or materials up or down a shaft.

Hurrier/Drawer - One who pulled a coal car by means of a belt attached to his/her waist, sometimes assisted by thrusters pushing the car from behind. In the early days of mining, hurriers were frequently women or children due to the limited height of the passages.

In-bye - Going toward the coal face away from the main shaft, opposite of out-bye.

Loader - A hewer's assistant who loads the coal chipped from the face into the carts.

Out-bye - Going away from the coal face toward the main shaft, opposite of in-bye.

Putter - A worker who moved the coal from the face to the main underground road or tunnel, often by driving a pony.

Seam - A layer of coal between rock layers.

Shaft - A vertical tunnel which provided access to the horizontal passages in the mine.

Thruster - One who assisted a hurrier/drawer by pushing a coal cart from behind. This was frequently the job of children, some of whom used their heads to push against the cart, causing bald spots.

Trapper - Usually a young child who wasn't strong enough to do any other job. The child was stationed by an underground door, to open and close it in order to allow carts through and to provide fresh air in the tunnels. The child was alone and in total darkness for most of their shift of twelve or more hours each day.

39

Pit Pony Care and Training

Most of the ponies purchased by the mines had little training. While still on the surface, a quick training program accustomed the ponies to wearing harness and pulling a cart. Some collieries had a training area with wagons that traveled on rails as they did in the mine. During training, the ponies were initially led around the track, pulling an empty cart, then heavier weight was added. A few mines simulated the underground conditions by covering a frame with canvas, creating a dark tunnel for the ponies to pass through.

If the colliery was a drift mine that could be entered through a horizontal tunnel, the ponies would be led into that to gradually accustom them to the darkness and close quarters of the mine. Ponies also needed to adjust to the clanging and clattering noises which echoed through the shafts.

A few ponies never made it past this preliminary training. For the more nervous ones, it was soon obvious they were unsuited for mining. Those ponies were returned to the dealer from whom they'd been purchased.

When the brief training was complete, the day came for the pony to begin real work. In a deep-shaft mine, that meant a trip to the bottom. This was often done at night, so the darkness of the mine wouldn't be quite as alarming. Smaller ponies traveled down in a cage-like elevator similar to the one used to transport the miners. Larger ponies and horses were lowered down the shaft in a sling.

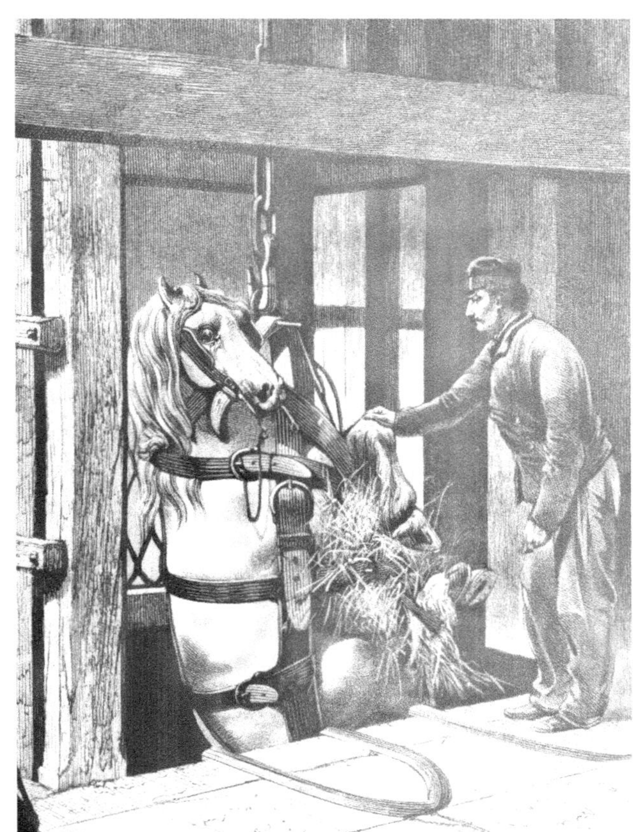

The horses which draw the wagons on the underground railways are sometimes sent down into the mine fastened to a rope, but generally in the English collieries on a properly constructed platform and cage, either in nets or baskets. When the former mode is adopted the horses do not make the slightest movement, being paralysed with fear and to all appearances dead, but when they reach the bottom of the pit they gradually recover their senses.

—*Pit Ponies, Bright, p. 33*

As he began his work underground, the pony pulled empty tubs behind an experienced animal. The narrowest passages left at most a foot, sometimes only inches, on either side of the coal cars. The driver often had to stoop to avoid banging his head on the low roof. If the inexperienced pony became frightened, he couldn't run away—there was no place to go.

It didn't take most ponies long to adapt to the routine in the mine. When traveling away from the coal face, the pony opened the door by pushing it with his head. On the return trip, he stopped and waited for a trapper or the driver to pull the door open.

Some ponies wore a bit in their mouths, but others never did. There was usually a single lead strap on one side, but never a set of driving reins that the pony or cart might get caught up in. The ponies were trained to respond to voice commands telling them when to stop, go, and turn left or right. Eventually, the ponies knew their jobs so well, they performed without any commands at all.

> *Ideally, after ponies were broken, you didn't have to give orders. You unhooked them off full tubs and they crossed the way and backed up to chummins (empty tubs).*
>
> —*Bright, p. 37*

The Stables

In deep mines, the ponies didn't return to the surface after each shift, but were housed in an underground stable, which might contain up to 100 animals. Some ponies spent their entire working lives underground, while others were given a two-week holiday each year. Those that had the luxury of that vacation ran about in a pasture at the mine and, for a short time, enjoyed the life of a normal horse.

The quality of the underground stables varied, but in general the conditions were good. The stables were required to be lit and well-ventilated. They usually consisted of stalls lining one side of a long corridor with an aisle running behind the stalls. Areas were reserved for horse feed, harnesses, and other equipment.

The stable was located at a distance from the main tunnels to provide a quiet area for the ponies to rest. Roofs had to be high enough for the ponies to raise their heads when stalled, since they had to constantly keep them low when traveling through the tunnels. As little wood as possible was used in

the stable to reduce the risk of fire. Walls were typically rock or brick. Most stables were white to improve the lighting, but the Langwith Mine stable, in Derbyshire, had green walls, perhaps an attempt to simulate grassy fields.

Each pony had his own stall, often with his nameplate at the front, and his own feed manger. The ponies were led to a community water trough for drinking. The stall floor sloped toward the aisle for drainage. Bedding consisted of shavings or peat moss. The stalls were narrow tie stalls rather than box ones. The ponies were generally exhausted after working and didn't move around much anyway.

A horse keeper or ostler was in charge of the stable. The stables were kept exceptionally clean to reduce odors and ensure the ponies' health. Some miners believed the operators were more concerned with the condition of the ponies than that of the men and boys. Glanders, a deadly equine disease caused by bacteria, is one of the few diseases that can be passed from horses to people. One ostler was known to have died of the disease.

Pit ponies were shod using a cold shoeing technique, since a fired blacksmith forge would be too dangerous to operate in the mine.

Darkness didn't cause the ponies to go blind any more than it caused blindness in the human miners. Blindness that occurred in the ponies was usually a result of injury. The use of blind ponies in the mines was forbidden.

The ponies' coats were clipped to prevent overheating as they performed their strenuous work. A short, clipped coat allowed them to cool down quickly. The horse keepers not only clipped the ponies, they were also known to give haircuts to the drivers.

Most ponies had their mane and tail shaved also. Long, flowing hair might become entangled in equipment. Shorter hair was safer and easier to keep clean. There were few if any flies in the mines, so the lack of a tail wasn't as bad as it would be for a pony on the surface. While flies weren't a problem underground, cockroaches were. Thousands of the pests crawled around the ponies' stalls, feed, and on the harnesses. The grain fed to the ponies also attracted rats and mice. Rats climbed right into the ponies' mangers and ate with them.

A mine pony was fed a mixture that might include chopped hay, oats, beans, peas, and corn. Sometimes, straw was added to the feed in order to slow the hungry ponies down and prevent them from gorging themselves after their strenuous work shift.

Since horses are designed to eat almost continually, the pit ponies needed some food during their long work shifts. Mangers were placed in wider tunnels, allowing the ponies to eat while waiting for carts to be filled.

Because of the multitude of rodents in the mines, the workers carried their food in a rat-proof, metal container called a snap tin. The twenty-minute lunch break was called snap time. Water was stored in a thermos-like container called a dudley.

The pony driver brought along a feed bag when he left the stables in the morning for his pony's snap time, but he often shared his own food also. One boy quickly learned that his equine partner loved bread with jam. The pony preferred plum to strawberry.

Some of the ponies enjoyed Jelly Babies, a British candy created in 1919 to mark the end of World War I. Each of the named, baby-shaped candies had a particular color and flavor. Of course, the ponies enjoyed the more traditional treats of fresh grass, carrots, and apples as well.

When the ponies returned to the stable after a work shift, the horse keeper led them to a wash stall to clean the dirty coal residue from their legs and bellies. Each pony was groomed and examined for injuries. If anything was wrong, the ostler could refuse to permit the pony to be used until it recovered. Notations of injury or illness were kept in the Pony Records Book which was available to the Mines Inspector of Horses.

40

Pit Ponies at Work

If the ponies received mostly on-the-job training, that was even more true for the young drivers. Often, they were assigned a pony and sent into the mine to figure things out on their own. A pit pony driver's day began early. He rose before sunup, ate a quick breakfast, then set off for the mine in order to have his pony ready when the miners arrived. Former driver, Tony Banks, recalled one of his ponies.

> *I used to have a pony called Ted. He was a great pony to drive. I used to give him a nice brush down before we left the stable before I fitted his collar and mobs. Then the next job was his nose bag for snap [lunch] time. He would get a mint or spangle [a boiled candy] just before we set off on our way. I used to whistle on my way up to his stall and he knew it was me. It was a sad time when I had to give him up when I went coal face training.*

After grooming his pony, the driver harnessed him, in some places this was called "gearing up." The mining harness was similar to a regular horse harness with a few exceptions. The ponies were fitted with a leather helmet or skull pad that protected the top of their head. The helmet had guards over the top and sides of the eyes to protect them. There were various designs, some of which contained a metal grid over the pony's eyes.

The leather harness was kept on a hook near his stall in the mine stable, but the limbers (shafts) remained at the coal face. The harnessed pony was led from the stable to the coal face, sometimes a distance of several miles. The only light in the roadways came from the small lamp attached to the driver's helmet. If that went out, they walked in total darkness.

For a modern pony cart, the shafts are permanently connected to the cart. In the mines, the limbers or limmers were not part of the wagon. Instead, they were

attached to the pony's harness. That allowed the pony to quickly be detached from one wagon and hooked to another.

The limbers were connected at the back forming a u-shape. Generally, the portion of the limber at the sides was made of wood, while the connecting piece at the back was metal. Some limbers were joined in the front as well, making a fully-enclosed oval. The advantage of the oval style was that there were no shaft ends to become stuck on the timbers at the sides of the tunnels.

To hook the pony to a tub, the animal stepped over the limbers placed on the ground. When the pony was in position, the driver lifted the limbers and attached them to chains hanging down from the harness on each of the animal's sides.

The pulling weight of the cart was concentrated on a thick, padded collar fitted around the pony's neck—similar to the collars worn by farm workhorses. At the center back of the limber, a steel bar extended out with a pin to connect to the coal car. The limber harness contained a breaching which served as a brake, preventing the cart from slamming into the back of the pony.

An alternative harness style used chains rather than limbers. This worked only in flat areas or where the pony pulled uphill. When using chains, there was no breaching to stop the cart. The only way a cart pulled with chains could be stopped was to insert pieces of wood called lockers into the spokes of the wheels.

Once the limbers were attached, the pony and driver continued to the entry shaft to pick up empty coal cars. In some mines, they would meet the men arriving for work in the morning. The miners might climb into the tubs for a ride to the working face of the coal seam.

Pit ponies pulled the tubs full of coal from the mine face to a point near the main roadway where they would be left for a horse or machine to complete the coal's journey to the surface. After the filled carts were delivered, the pony would be turned around and

hooked to empty ones to return to the coal face. Ponies developed unique ways of turning themselves around in the narrow passages.

> —Eright, p. 40

Pony drivers were supposed to lead their charges from the front. Although it was forbidden, the driver often rode inside the car or perched on the limbers at the pony's side. In a typical day, a pit pony might haul thirty tons of coal. The size and strength of the pony determined how many cars they could pull at a time. Some of the drivers insisted their ponies could count, refusing to budge if too many carts were connected.

When working, ponies pulled drams or tubs of coal. These tubs were on rails a little like railway carriages. They listened for the click as each tub was attached. Three was acceptable, four was not. The pony would not move until the fourth was taken off.

> —Wendy Priest, Horse Keeper Supervisor at The National Coal Mining Museum

Although the work was hard, the ponies were rarely mistreated. Everyone's income depended on getting as much coal out of the mine as possible, so it made sense to treat the ponies well. It was common for the drivers, whether men or boys, to form a strong bond with their equine partner. They often bragged of the intelligence, strength, or heroic deeds of their pony.

Miners respected the sixth sense the ponies seemed to have that allowed them to detect danger before the men were aware of it. The workers were sometimes saved from death or injury because of this ability. Young miner, Eric Squires, relates such an incident with his pony, Ben.

He backed off, then darted forward to within five or six yards of me before spinning and moving quickly away again… He was acting like a dog asking his master to follow. Suddenly as he turned to face me again, he screamed… I recall the icy shiver that went through me, something I had never experienced before, and I came slowly to my feet. This move brought a strong reaction from Ben…

Once again he screamed and I knew then that he wanted me to follow him. I did, dropping my snap-tin, snatching up my lamp instinctively and racing towards him… The moment I started running there was a vicious crack above the junction, with thunderous rollings and boomings coming from above. The junction collapsed with a roar that shook the ground and gave me strength to run harder.

Hundreds of tons of hard grey rock crashed down on the place where the junction had been, mangling my snap-tin and dudley into flat pieces of useless metal. Had I been still seated with my back to that prop I would have been crushed.

> —Squires p. 47

Ponies in the deep shaft mines returned to their underground stable after their long shift for a well-deserved rest and meal. In fact, some ponies had an inner timer that seemed to go off when it was quitting time, and they refused to work any longer. If they got loose, they would even find their way back through the dark tunnels, often several miles, to their stall by themselves.

Horses and ponies who worked in drift mines had an easier life. The horizontal tunnels of these mines opened out on the side of a hill. Ponies working in that type of mine were taken to the surface and turned out in a pasture or housed in an above-ground stable after each shift.

Although ponies are generally long-lived, because of the difficult work they performed and the potential for serious injury, a pit pony might work anywhere from four to fifteen years. In the early years of mining, when the ponies were no longer able to work, many were sold to slaughterhouses.

As the public became aware of that practice, several pit pony retirement facilities were created to rescue the ponies. In 1876, the Royal Society for the Prevention of Cruelty to Animals (RSPCA) began working to have legislation passed to protect the mining ponies. Their efforts resulted in the Coal Mines Regulations Act of 1887 which provided protection for equines in the mines.

In 1913, at their peak use, 70,000 pit ponies worked underground. Mechanized techniques for cutting coal increased production to quantities that ponies could no longer keep up with. Conveyor-like machines were developed to transport the coal. By the end of the 1930s, pit pony numbers had been cut by more than half, to 32,000. Over the years, the number continued to decline.

- 1947 - 21,000
- 1952 - 15,500
- 1962 - 6,400
- 1973 - 490
- 1984 - 55

Depending upon the location, the use of mining ponies continued into the 1970s to 1990s. As the use of ponies diminished, the British Coal Board worked with the RSPCA to find qualified homes to adopt nearly 1500 of the ponies. One such equine miner was Fred, who was adopted by the Bell family. Fred enjoyed his well-earned retirement and was known to march right into the kitchen of the Bell's home.

Two ponies, Carl and Sparky, retired from the Ellington Colliery in 1994. The pair spent their retirement years at the National Coal Mining Museum in Overton, Wakefield, England.

The last two horses from Welsh mines, Patch and Robbie, retired in 1999. They also went to the National Museum. Still relatively young, the two were trained for driving and were used in exhibits at the museum.

Pip, another retired pony, passed away in 2009 at the age of thirty-five. He had worked at Blackburn Drift, Marley Hill Colliery, near Sunniside, Gateshead, England until it closed when he was five. Pip then moved to Sacriston Colliery where he worked until 1985. He remained there another year to help with salvage work before being given to the Beamish Open Air Museum near Stanley. His successor at the museum, Flash, was trained to wear Pip's mining harness.

41

Mining in Other Areas

Coal wasn't mined only in the UK. Some of the other top-producing mines were located in Canada, Australia, and the United States. The earliest coal mines in Canada were on Cape Breton Island in Nova Scotia. Mining also took place on Vancouver Island and in the interior of British Columbia, Alberta, and Saskatchewan. Many of the ponies used in the Canadian mines came from Sable Island, east of Nova Scotia. These mines used ponies until the 1960s.

In Australia, the pony handlers or drivers were called wheelers. The Australian mines typically used larger horses, often Clydesdales or other draft types, which pulled larger coal tubs than the British ponies, however they were still called pit ponies.

Collinsville, Queensland, Australia was known as the pit pony capital of Australia. On October 13, 1954, one wheeler, Raymond Brunker, of Collinsville survived a mine explosion because of a fluke accident that happened with his horse. As they were making their way deeper into the mine, a chain from the horse's harness got caught on a piece of machinery, bringing both of them to a sudden halt.

While working to free the horse, there was an explosion further down in the mine. If the horse hadn't become stuck, Brunker would have walked right into the explosion.

The last pit ponies (Clydesdales) used in Australia, Wharrier and Mr Ed, of the Collinsville Coal's No 2 Mine in Queensland were retired in 1990. The two Clydesdales were made honorary members of the miners' union and were cared for in their retirement by their previous handler.

The Penallta Colliery near Hengoed in the South Wales Valley closed in 1991. Reclamation of the land began a few years later. Now, the area contains bicycle and hiking trails, fishing lakes, and a business park.

The most famous attraction is one of the largest earthwork sculptures in the UK. An enormous pony was created by Welsh artist, Mick Petts, using 60,000 tons of coal shale, dirt, and stone. Locals named the earthen pony, Sultan, after a pit pony who worked in the mine. The sculpture is so large, it's best viewed from the air. A park trail allows visitors to walk right over Sultan's body.

The story of one mining mule, Bess, at the Pacific Coast Coal Co. in Franklin, Washington came to light after the account of a cave-in appeared in a 1914 issue of The Seattle Star newspaper. The deaths of two miners, Andrew Chernick and Mike Babcanik, were reported by the paper. Chernick and Babcanik were trapped in the No. 11 chute, an area known by the company to be dangerous.

"Hard luck," said Superintendent of Mines, William Hann.

"It is not my business to fix the responsibility," said State Mine Inspector, James Bagley.

Seven days later, Mike Babcanik was found alive. But this heartless attitude of the officials toward the miners was an indication of how their animals were also treated.

Fred L. Boalt, a reporter for the Seattle Star discovered a mule, Bess, while covering the tragedy at the mine. He learned that the coal company considered mules cheap, hard to kill, and easily replaceable. Their policy was to work one as long and hard as possible. While alive, the company would get the work of three mules from the one.

Bess was worked nearly continuously, only catching ten-minute naps between trips into the mine. Her condition was brought to the attention of the local humane society. Mrs. S. C. Griggs, the society's secretary, visited the mine with two officers.

"The mule had worked two weeks without a rest," Fred reported.

Griggs immediately ordered Bess to the barn. It seems Bess remained at the mine, however one can hope that she received better care after her abuse was exposed.

Coal Miner Unions

The mountains of West Virginia are the source of some of the word's highest-quality coal. It wasn't until the late 1800s that equipment was created to extract the coal and railroads were available to transport it. Wealthy businessmen from outside the state purchased tracts of land in West Virginia to

142

gain access to the coal fields. The owners often leased the land to a coal operator.

Because of its sparse population, workers from outside West Virginia were brought in to work the mines, including African Americans from the South and many European immigrants.

Unlike the ponies used in Britain, mules were the preferred mine animal in the United States, perhaps because they were more readily available than in Europe. In 1913, the price of a mule was about two hundred dollars. Boys often drove the mules used to cart the coal to the surface.

The remote location of the West Virginia mines meant the workers had limited access to the outside world. Coal companies created what was known as the company town. Cheap houses were built close together in rows and rented to the miners. Rent was taken out of their pay automatically.

The miners were forced to buy supplies from the company store where they were often overcharged. Some companies didn't pay the workers with money, but used what was known as scrip, which could only be used in the company store.

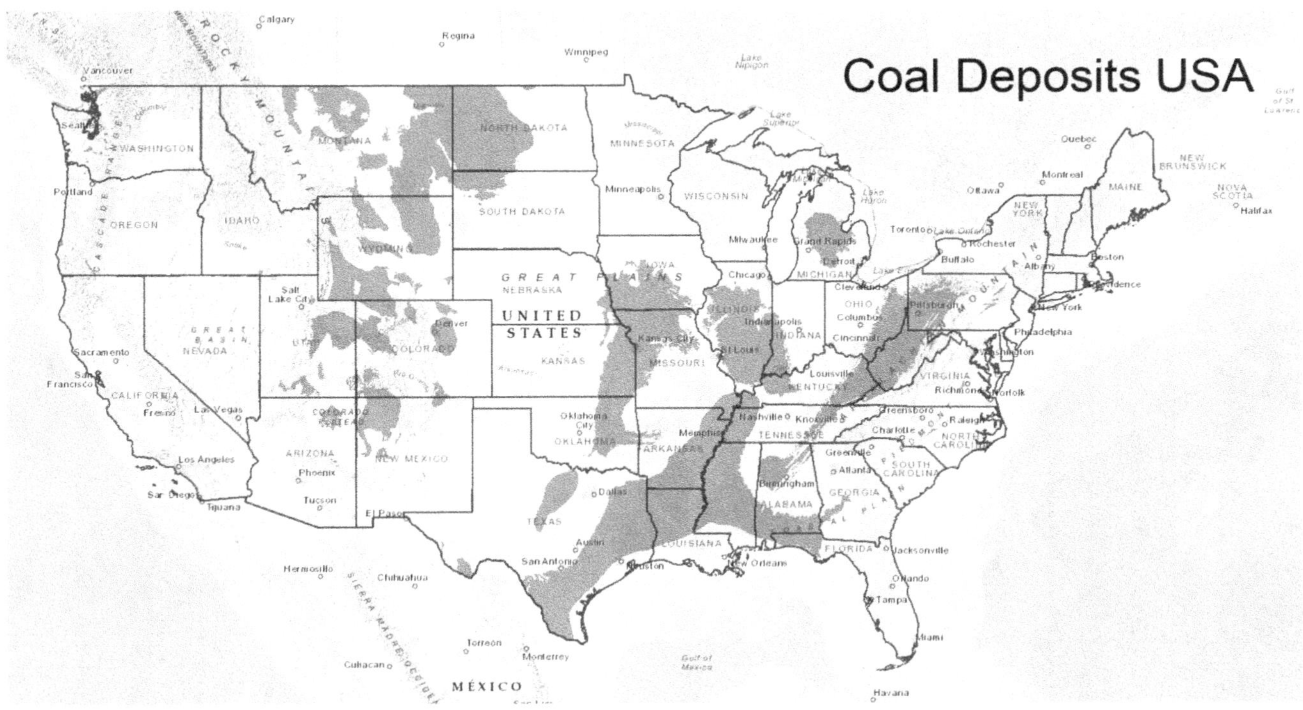

Company towns also included a school, church, and medical facilities. The coal company operators hired the school teachers and ministers. This gave the owners and operators nearly complete control over the miners' lives, leaving them not much better off than slaves.

Due to the poor working and living conditions, miners formed the United Mine Workers Union in 1890. Mary Harris Jones (Mother Jones) was one of the early organizers of the union. Members came from Pennsylvania, Ohio, Indiana, and Illinois. One of the union's first achievements was a nine-hour work day.

West Virginia miners were forbidden to join the union. Feeling threatened by the United Mine Workers, the West Virginia coal operators hired men from the Baldwin–Felts Detective Agency to patrol the railroad station to keep union organizers out of the company towns.

When the West Virginia miners decided to go on strike, refusing to work, the coal operators fired them and forcibly removed the families from the company houses. Then, they brought in new workers to take their places.

Ultimately, the miners took up arms against the owners, which resulted in martial law being declared by the governor. The years from 1912 to 1921 were known as the West Virginia Coal Wars. On May 19, 1920, seven detectives and two miners were killed in the Battle of Matewan. Even more men were killed that August in the Battle of Blair Mountain. Similar labor disputes and violence occurred in other coal mining areas such as Kentucky.

42

The Whitman Mission

The route that became the Oregon Trail was first traveled by fur trappers, explorers, and missionaries. Doctor Marcus Whitman was one of the first missionaries to reach the area, crossing the trail to Montana and Idaho in 1835. Whitman earned respect on that first trip when he stopped in Wyoming at the annual rendezvous of mountain men. While there, the doctor treated an outbreak of cholera. He also operated on mountain man, James Bridger, to remove a three-inch arrowhead that had been embedded in the man's back for three years.

Dr. Whitman returned East, and the following year married Narcissa Prentiss. Two months later, the newlyweds were headed west, traveling with a group of ten including fellow missionaries Henry and Eliza Spalding, Mr. Dulin a driver, sixteen-year-old Miles Goodyear, three Nez Perce Indians (Richard, John, and Samuel), and William Gray. Fourteen horses, six mules, and fifteen head of cattle traveled with the group.

> *We have two wagons in our company. Mr. and Mrs. S., husband and myself ride in one, Mr. Gray and the baggage in the other. Our Indian boys drive the cows and Dulin the horses. Young Miles leads our forward horses, four in each team.*
>
> —*Narcissa Whitman*

Each night, they assembled a tent to sleep in. Narcissa didn't always ride in the wagon. At times, she rode one of the horses alongside her husband.

> *We take plenty of Mackinaw blankets, which answer for our bed and bedding, and when we journey place them over our saddles and ride on them.*
>
> —*Narcissa Whitman*

As they entered the Rocky Mountains, it became more difficult to travel by wagon.

> *Husband has had a tedious time with the waggon today. Got set in the creek this morning while crossing, was obliged to wade considerably in getting it out. After that in going between two mountains, on the side so steep that it was difficult for horses to pass the*

waggon was upset twice. Did not wonder at this at all. It was a greater wonder that it was not turning a somerset continually.

    —Narcissa Whitman, July 25

One of the axle trees of the waggon broke today. Was a little rejoiced, for we were in hopes they would leave it & have no more trouble with it. Our rejoicing was in vain however for they are making a cart of the hind wheels this afternoon & lashing the forward wheels to it, intending to take it through in some shape or other.

    —Narcissa Whitman, July 28

Perhaps you have wondered why we have left the waggon at the fort, & I have nothing to say about it this time crossing. Our animals were failing & the route in crossing the Blue Mountains is said to be impassable. We regret now to loose the use of [the wagon] when we have been at so much labour in getting it thus far.

    —Narcissa Whitman, August 22, Fort Boise, Idaho

From this point on, there were no trails that were passable for wagons, and they were forced to continue on foot or horseback. Toward the end of the journey, they followed a narrow Indian trail.

Before noon we began to descend one of the most terrible mountains for steepness & length I have yet seen. It was like winding stairs in its descent & in some places almost perpendicular. We did a long time descending it The horses appeared to dread the hill as much as we did. They would turn & wind in a zigzag manner all the way down. The men usually walked, but I could not get permission to, neither did I desire it much. We had no sooner gained the foot of this mountain, when another more steep & dreadful was before us. Our ride this afternoon exceeded everything we have had yet, & what rendered it the most aggravating the path all the way was very stony resembling a newly McAdamized road.

While upon this elevation, we had a view of the valley of the Columbia River. It was beautiful. Just as we gained the highest elevation & began to descend the sun was dipping his disk behind the western horizon. Beyond the valley, we could see two distant Mountains. Mount Hood & Mount St. Helens. We had yet to descend a hill as long but not as steep or stoney as the others. By this [time] our horses were in haste to see camp as well as ourselves, & mine made such lengthy strides in descending that it shook my sides surprisingly.

    —Narcissa Whitman, August 29

On September 1, the Whitmans and company arrived at Fort Nez Perce.

If you could have seen us now you would have been surprised, for both man and beast appeared alike propelled by the same force The whole company galloped almost all the way to the Fort. The first appearance of civilization we saw was the garden, two miles this side of the Fort. The fatigues of the long journey seemed to be forgotten in the excitement of being so near the close. Soon the Fort appeared in sight, & when it was announced that we were near Mr. MacLeod Mr. Pambrun…sallied forth to meet us After the usual introduction & salutation, we entered the fort & were comfortably seated in cushioned armed chairs.

    —Narcissa Whitman

Narcissa Whitman and Eliza Spalding were the first white women to cross the Rocky Mountains, proving women were not too fragile to make the journey. Five years later, an increasingly large migration of settlers would begin.

The Whitmans set up a mission at nearby Waiilatpu to introduce the Cayuse to Christianity. Initially, the Native Americans were welcoming and receptive to Dr. Whitman's message, although there were communication issues, since neither fully understood the other's language.

On March 14, 1837, Alice Clarissa Whitman became the first white child born in Oregon Territory. Alice and her mother shared the same birthday. Narcissa wrote to relatives that Alice was "a treasure invaluable."

The infant was a curiosity to the Cayuse, since their babies were strapped to a cradleboard and carried on the mother's back, often until the child was six months old. As Alice began to talk, she picked up some of the native language as well as English.

On Sunday morning, June 23, 1839, Alice asked her mother to sing the hymn, "Rock of Ages." When Narcissa stopped after the first verse, Alice prompted her for the second, saying, "Mama, should my tears forever flow."

Later that morning, Alice accompanied her parents to a worship service Marcus conducted for the Native Americans. The same hymn was sung there.

As her parents were reading that afternoon, Alice took two cups from the table. "Mama, supper is almost ready; let Alice get some water."

By the time they realized she was gone, their only child had drowned in the Walla Walla River. Although the Whitmans had no more children, over the next few years they cared for several others. Narcissa wrote to her sister, Jane.

The Lord has taken our own dear child away, so that we may care for the poor outcasts of the country and suffering children.

In 1840, Joe Meek, a mountain man, left Helen, his two-year-old daughter, at the Whitmans' mission for them to raise and educate. Helen was the daughter of Meek and a Nez Perce woman. The girl died of measles at the age of nine. Jim Bridger, the man Dr. Whitman had removed the arrowhead from, left Mary Ann, age five, with the Whitmans. This girl was also half Native American. She died at age eleven. David Malin was the third child accepted by the Whitmans. They also took in Marcus' thirteen-year-old nephew, Perrin Whitman.

In 1843, the Oregon Legislature passed a law that gave 640-acre plots of land to each pioneer family. The already-increasing numbers of travelers grew even larger. In 1844, the family of Henry and Naomi Sager started west with their six children. A seventh child, Henrietta, was born along the trail. John Sager, the oldest at thirteen, was followed by Francis/Frank (eleven), Catherine (nine), Elizabeth (seven), Matilda Jane (five), and Hannah Louise (three). The Sagers were part of a group of 300 people traveling in seventy-two covered wagons.

Just before reaching Wyoming, Catherine Sager's dress caught on an ax handle as she was getting out of the moving wagon. She fell under a wheel and broke her leg. A Dutch doctor in the wagon train, Dr. Dagan, set the girl's leg. Catherine was confined to the wagon for the rest of the journey, but her leg healed with only a slight limp.

When Henry Sager became sick and died in Wyoming, Dr. Dagan and Captain Shaw, leader of the wagon train, assisted Mrs. Sager. But just twenty-six days after her husband's death, Naomi Sager passed away in Idaho. Her dying request of Dagan was that he take her children to the Whitman Mission.

The seven orphaned Sager children arrived at the Whitman's on October 17, 1844, after a seven-month journey on the Oregon Trail. Narcissa wanted to take in only the girls, but Marcus insisted they would keep all seven children.

As an adult, Matilda Sager remembered droves of Indian horses passing through Waiilatpu, the "place of the rye grass." The grass was so tall, all she could see were the horses' manes and tails. During the long winters, she saw wolves come right up to the mission's door in search of food.

Although not on the Oregon Trail, the Whitman Mission was close enough that some travelers diverted from the trail to stop there to rest or receive medical treatment. The settlers brought diseases with them—influenza, whooping cough, and measles. The Cayuse had no immunity to these illnesses that were unknown in their land prior to the arrival of the pioneers. While Dr. Whitman successfully treated many of the settlers, large numbers of the Cayuse died.

The natives started to believe Marcus Whitman was deliberately poisoning them in order to take their land. The Cayuse stopped attending his services. They, along with the Nez Perce and Walla Walla Indians, advised the Whitmans to leave. In retrospect, Marcus should have heeded that advice, but he was determined to stay. To return to the East would mean having to admit he had failed as a missionary.

In 1847, seventy-five travelers stopped to winter at the Whitman Mission. That fall, a measles outbreak killed half of the Cayuse, mainly children. On November 29, 1847, the Cayuse chiefs Tiloukaikt and Tomahas led a group of warriors that killed thirteen at the mission.

Narcissa Whitman was the only woman killed. John and Francis Sager, then seventeen and fifteen, were among the dead. Forty-nine of the remaining people were held captive for a month. A few months later, the Cayuse returned to the mission and set fire to all the buildings. In 1850, five Cayuse men were tried and hanged for the massacre.

In 1855, the Cayuse, Walla Walla, and Umatilla tribes reluctantly accepted a treaty with the U.S. government which required them to surrender over ninety percent of their land. They were restricted to a small area in Oregon Territory, the Umatilla Indian Reservation.

Henrietta Sager died at twenty-six. Just three of the Sager children lived to old age —Catherine, Elizabeth, and Matilda.

43

Trail Preparations

In 1836, Narcissa Whitman and Eliza Spalding proved that women were capable of completing the Oregon Trail journey, leading the way to larger numbers of people heading west. In 1842, the first organized wagon train of 100 pioneers set off on the Oregon Trail. The following year, that number increased to 1,000. But it was the discovery of gold in 1848 at Sutters Mill in California and the promise of 640 acres of fertile farmland for settlers in the Oregon Territory that caused westward migration to explode.

Men with the pioneer spirit were determined to make a better life for themselves, and they brought their families along for the five-month, 2,000-mile journey. Families didn't travel alone. The pioneers banded together to form parties or companies. They elected leaders and had rules everyone in the company agreed to abide by. Exact numbers aren't known, but it's estimated that 400,000 people traveled the Oregon Trail and other trails bound for the West and Southwest.

The limited wagon space was reserved for vital items. An empty wagon typically weighed 1,200 pounds. The goal was to keep it under a ton, 2,000 pounds, when fully loaded. This meant many of the settlers' treasured possessions had to be left behind.

Here are the recommendations for clothing and personal supplies from Randolph Marcy's guidebook, *The Prairie Traveler*.

A suitable dress for prairie traveling is of great import to health and comfort. Cotton or linen fabrics do not sufficiently protect the body against the direct rays of the sun at midday, nor against rains or sudden changes of temperature. Wool, being a non-conductor, is the best material for this mode of locomotion, and should always be adopted for the plains. The coat should be short and stout, the shirt of red or blue flannel, such as can be found in almost all the shops on the frontier: this, in warm weather, answers for an outside garment.

The pants should be of thick and soft woolen material, and it is well to have them re-enforced on the inside, where they come in contact with the saddle, with soft buckskin, which makes them more durable and comfortable. Woolen socks and stout boots, coming up well at the knees, and made large, so as to admit the pants, will be found the best for horsemen, and they guard against rattlesnake bites.

The following list of articles is deemed a sufficient outfit for one man upon a three months' expedition,

2 blue or red flannel overshirts, open in front, with buttons.
2 woolen undershirts.
2 pairs thick cotton drawers.
4 pairs woolen socks.
2 pairs cotton socks.
4 colored silk handkerchiefs.
2 pairs stout shoes, for footmen.
1 pair boots, for horsemen.
1 pair shoes, for horsemen.
3 towels.
1 gutta percha poncho.

150

The Wagons

The older Conestoga wagons used in the East were too heavy to make the long trip. The wagon preferred by settlers when traveling west was known as a prairie schooner. The smaller, lighter wagons fitted with white canvas covers looked like ships sailing across the prairie. Some Native Americans called them horse canoes.

Two of the best-known wagon makers were Murphy and Studebaker. Each wagon was about four feet wide and nine to eleven feet long. Its sidewalls were lower and the ends didn't angle out as the freight-hauling Conestogas did. The front wheels, about forty-four inches in diameter, were smaller than the rear ones to facilitate turning. All four wheels were made of wood and the rims fitted with iron bands for durability. Without any kind of suspension system, traveling over the rough terrain provided a jolting, uncomfortable ride. The wagon was coated with tar to make it waterproof for fording streams and rivers. The canvas covers were oiled to keep out rain.

Early trail travelers created guidebooks for subsequent pioneers. One of the most popular was *The Prairie Traveler* by U.S. Army officer, Randolph Marcy.

> *The allowance of provisions for each grown person, to make the journey from the Missouri River to California, should suffice for 110 days.*
>
> *The following is deemed requisite, viz.: 150 lbs. of flour, or its equivalent in hard bread; 25 lbs. of bacon or pork, and enough fresh beef to be driven on the hoof to make up the meat component of the ration; 15 lbs. of coffee, and 25 lbs. Of sugar; also a quantity of saleratus[1] or yeast powders for making bread, and salt and pepper.*
>
> *These are the chief articles of subsistence necessary for the trip, and they should be used with economy, reserving a good portion for the western half of the journey.*

Kitchenware included a cooking kettle, frying pan, coffee pot, tin plates, cups, knives, and forks. When fully loaded, there typically wasn't any room for passengers. The wagons weren't designed for riding in and often had no seats. Most settlers preferred to walk or ride if they had saddle horses.

---

[1] *Saleratus is similar to baking soda and makes bread rise.*

44

Horses, Mules, or Oxen?

Although horses and mules pulled the Conestoga freight wagons in the East, they were not commonly used for westward migration. Oxen were the favored animals on the Oregon Trail. It's estimated that anywhere from one-half to three-quarters of pioneer wagons were pulled by oxen. Pound for pound they weren't necessarily stronger than horses or mules, but they offered several advantages.

Randolph Marcy addressed this issue in his guide, *The Prairie Traveler*.

> *There has been much discussion regarding the relative merits of mules and oxen for prairie traveling, and the question is yet far from being settled. Upon good firm roads, in a populated country, where grain can be procured, I should unquestionably give the preference to mules, as they travel faster, and endure the heat of summer much better than oxen; and if the journey be not over 1000 miles, and the grass abundant, even without grain, I think mules would be preferable. But when the march is to extend 1500 or 2000 miles, or over a rough sandy or muddy road, I believe young oxen will endure better than mules; they will, if properly managed, keep in better condition, and perform the journey in an equally brief space of time.*
>
> *Besides, they are much more economical, a team of six mules costing six hundred dollars, while an eight-ox team only costs upon the frontier about two hundred dollars. Oxen are much less liable to be stampeded and driven off by Indians, and can be pursued and overtaken by horsemen; and, finally, they can, if necessary, be used for beef.*

The advantages of using oxen:

- They were cheaper, both for the animals and their yokes
- Oxen were generally calmer, less likely to stampede
- If they did stray, they were slow and could be rounded up by horsemen
- They could survive on less food than horses and would eat food horses wouldn't
- In desperate times, they became food for the pioneers

The disadvantages of using oxen:

- They were slow, averaging about two miles per hour
- The working life of a horse or mule is longer than that of an ox
- Oxen couldn't handle heat and dust as well as horses or mules

- Pairs of oxen had to be matched more closely in size than teams of horses or mules, so the yoke would fit
- Oxen typically preferred to work from one side or the other

What exactly is an ox? Some have the misconception that these beasts of burden are a unique species. They're not. Oxen are simply domesticated cattle, primarily steers four years or older. The main distinction between cattle and oxen is training. A fully-trained steer earned the right to be called an ox.

No specific breed was required, although popular ones at the time were the Red Durham and Devon. Cattle breeds of today—Jersey, Hereford, Brown Swiss, and Holstein hadn't been imported to America at the time.

Rather than wearing harness, oxen wore a yoke, a curved wood beam, about four feet long, fitted over their necks. The yoke was connected loosely from under the ox's neck with a u-shaped wooden bow. The yoke, weighing forty to eighty pounds, suited the conformation of the ox better than a harness, making it easier for the animals to pull. A chain hooked to a ring in the center of the yoke connected to the wagon tongue or to the next pair of oxen.

Because of the shape and function of the yoke, oxen that pulled wagons needed to have horns. This was particularly important for the wheel oxen, the pair closest to the wagon. To back a wagon or slow it on a descent, the yoke moved forward, pressing against the horns. Without the horns to stop it, the yoke could slip right over the animal's head.

Oxen weren't bridled and driven with reins like horses or mules. With time and patience, they were trained to respond to voice commands—gee (turn right) and haw (go left), go easy, whoa, and come up. During the training, ropes were used to reinforce the commands until the animals responded to the driver's voice alone.

Wagons were pulled by two to eight oxen. A team of six was common. In such a team, the two smartest, bravest, and most obedient animals would

be hitched at the front in the lead. The lead ox, the one on the front left was the most important as he received commands from the driver who walked alongside him, and through his responses, communicated to the other oxen.

Two short, stocky, strong oxen were placed at the back, closest to the wagon in the wheeler position. These animals pulled more weight than the others. The younger or less well-trained pair were used in the middle where it was difficult for them to do anything but obey.

Sometimes, when six oxen were available, only four were hitched at a time with the additional pair following behind the wagon. The animals would be rotated daily, giving each pair time to rest.

Not all pioneers were knowledgeable about oxen, and some sellers had no qualms about taking advantage of their inexperience. The unsuspecting traveler might end up with oxen that were poorly trained or not trained at all. Catherine Sager Pringle, who traveled the Oregon Trail in 1844, described her father's experience with their team.

> *We had one wagon, two steady yoke of old cattle, and several of young and not well-broken ones. Father was no ox driver, and had trouble with these until one day he called on Captain Shaw for assistance. It was furnished by the good captain pelting the refractory steers with stones until they were glad to come to terms.*

Although generally calm, oxen weren't totally stampede-proof. J. Henry Brown, an 1847 traveler on the Oregon Trail, described a stampede of oxen that began when a spooked horse ran between a wagon and its wheel oxen, startling the pair.

> *The animals started on the run, bellowing as they went. Within moments, the whole train was dashing over the plains, damaging the wagons and injuring those riding inside. It is astonishing with what speed a yoke of four oxen can run.*

Brown described another stampede in Nebraska that occurred in a different party but reached his own wagon eight miles away.

> *The Blue Wagon Train party had just brought its cattle inside the circle for the night when the accidental pop of a pistol's firing-cap startled an ox. The ox gave a jump and bellowed, then the whole herd became panic stricken, making a general rush for the opposite side of the circle of wagons or corrall, entirely going over the same, and it was said, that some of the animals actually went over the wagons, crushing everything beneath them. All of the company's loose stock, including milk cows, horses, and sheep, joined the rampaging oxen and thundered into the night.*

> —*J. Henry Brown Autobiography, 1938*

Oxen weren't particular about what they ate. In her 1852 trail diary, Cecelia Adams wrote.

> *Last night my clothes got out of the wagon and the oxen ate them up and I consider I have met with a great loss as it was my woolen dress.*

The oxen apparently suffered no ill effects from their unusual meal.

Oxen have split hooves. A journey of 2,000 miles meant a lot of wear on their feet. Some pioneers fitted their animals with boots made of buffalo hide. A mixture of tar and resin could also be applied to protect the soles of their feet.

Others used special steel shoes. Given that each foot of an ox has two toes, eight shoes were required for each animal. Since oxen can't stand on three legs for very long, they were typically placed in a wooden cage or stock, sometimes with a sling to help them stand. Stocks weren't available on the trail, so ox shoes were applied when the animal was lying down with his feet tied to prevent him from struggling.

Unlike horses and mules, cows have very few sweat glands. Their primary means of cooling is through their breath. Although they don't pant unless near death, their cooling system is similar to the way a dog pants when hot. Cattle can breathe through their nostrils, but do not do so unless they are overheated.

A big problem for oxen on the trail was the continual dust. When dust began to coat their nostrils, the oxens' cooling mechanism became less effective. On hot, dusty days, boys wiped the animals' nostrils to keep them clear, otherwise they might suddenly die. Randolph Marcy, in his *Prairie Traveler*, stressed the importance of not allowing the oxen to become overheated.

> *In traveling with ox teams in the summer season, great benefit will be derived from making early marches; starting with the dawn, and making a "nooning" during the heat of the day, as oxen suffer much from the heat of the sun in midsummer. These noon halts should, if possible, be so arranged as to be near grass and water, where the animals can improve their time in grazing.*

Many oxen died along the way. You'd think the ones that made it the entire length of the trail would have been rewarded for their faithful service, but that was often not the case. The fortunate ones went on to work on farms or in the mining or logging camps. The unfortunate ones were fattened for slaughter.

Mules and Horses

As Randolph Marcy advised, for shorter distances with good footing and adequate food supplies, mules were the preferred draft animals. But, given the length of the Oregon Trail, horses and mules were not commonly used. A saddle horse might be brought along, tied to the back of the wagon or ridden. The extra horses were useful for hunting and rounding up stray livestock.

In addition to being more expensive to purchase, the problem with both mules and horses was that they required more food than oxen did. The extra grain was an additional expense, and it took up too much space in the already jam-packed wagons.

Marcy notes in his guide that when mules were used, a common technique to keep them from straying was the use of a bell-mare. Mules often have a love for horse mares, since their mother was a horse.

> *In herding mules, it is customary among prairie travelers to have a bell-mare, to which the mules soon become so attached that they will follow her wherever she goes. By keeping her in charge of*

one of the herdsmen, the herds are easily controlled; and during a stampede, if the herdsman mounts her, and rushes ahead toward camp, they will generally follow.

In crossing rivers, the bell-mare should pass first, after which the mules are easily induced to take to the water and pass over, even if they have to swim. If a man leads or rides a bell animal in advance, the mules follow, like so many dogs, in the most orderly procession.

The instincts of the mulish heart form an interesting study to the traveler in the mountains. I would (were the comparison not too ungallant) liken it to a woman's, for it is quite as uncertain in its sympathies, bestowing its affections when least expected, and, when bestowed, quite as constant, so long as the object is not taken away.

Marcy also tells of an incident when a whole train of mules galloped off, ran for half a mile, then stopped suddenly.

The cause of their freak was found to be a buffalo calf which had strayed from the herd. They were frisking around it in the greatest delight, rubbing their noses against it, throwing up their heels, and making themselves ridiculous by abortive attempts to neigh and bray, while the calf, unconscious of its attractive qualities, stood trembling in their midst.

Handcarts

Horses, mules, and oxen weren't the only ones to pull wagons over the westward-bound trails—some people did also. From 1856 to 1860, ten different companies, consisting of nearly 3,000 Mormons, made the trip to Utah. Many of these converts came from England by ship, then took a train to the Mormon base camp at Iowa City, Iowa. Their goal was Salt Lake City, Utah, which the Mormons founded as their new Zion in 1847.

Too poor to afford horses or oxen, they walked to Utah, pulling two-wheeled handcarts a distance of more than 1,000 miles. Each cart carried from 250 to 500 pounds of supplies. Five people were

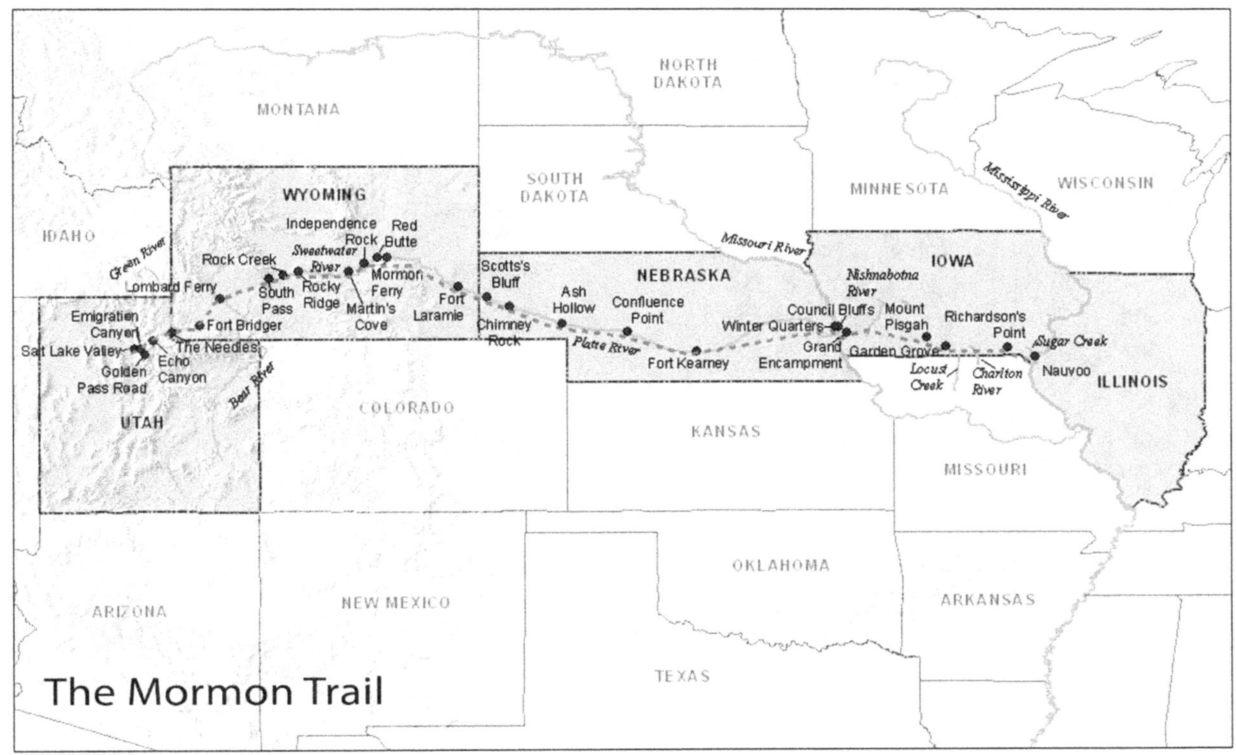

assigned to a cart. A wagon pulled
by oxen accompanied each handcart
company to carry food and tents.

Two of those ten companies, led
by Martin and Willie, left late in the
season, in August 1856. They
encountered extreme weather and
ran low on supplies, resulting in the
deaths of 250 of their 900 members.
Unwilling to accept responsibility
for the poor planning of those
expeditions, the Mormon leaders
transformed the tragedy into an act
of faith on the level of the pilgrims'
passage to America on the
Mayflower.

45

Seeing the Elephant

The "jumping off" point for emigrants was normally Independence, Missouri. It became a popular trading post, providing most of the supplies pioneers needed for their journey. Saint Joseph, Missouri and Council Bluffs, Iowa were also common starting points.

The complete trail ran to Oregon City near present-day Portland, passing through the current states of Missouri, Kansas, Nebraska, Wyoming, Idaho, and Oregon. Some families decided to take branches off of the main trail or stopped to homestead somewhere along the way rather than travel all the way to Oregon.

It was crucial to leave at the right time of year in order to successfully complete the five to seven month journey. If the pioneers set out too early in the spring, draft animals and wagons might become stuck in the mud. Early departures also meant there wouldn't be an adequate supply of grass to support the livestock along the way. Starting too late had its own problems. The pioneers might encounter severe winter weather as they crossed the Rocky Mountains at the western end of the trail. The optimal departure time, dependent upon the weather, was mid-April to early May.

Once their journey began, the pioneers gauged their progress by landmarks described by earlier travelers in the trail guides, such as Courthouse Rock, Jailhouse Rock, Chimney Rock, and Scott's Bluff. The travelers knew they were making good time if they reached Independence Rock by the Fourth of July.

Wagons traveled between ten and twenty miles per day, depending on weather, terrain, and the type of draft animals used. Some wagon trains didn't travel at all on Sundays, reserving a full day for rest and worship. The policy regarding Sabbath observance was one of the rules set by the wagon train leader and agreed upon by all parties who joined him. Some families deserted their company rather than sit idly all day Sunday when they had the entire country to cross.

In 1853, Phoebe Judson and her husband joined a wagon train bound for Oregon. Their captain, Reverend Gustavus Hines, insisted on stopping to rest on Sundays. The first Sunday, Phoebe impatiently watched as wagons from other groups passed them by. She and her husband, Holden, didn't agree with Hines' policy, but they remained with his group. In the coming weeks, Phoebe began to notice a distressing number of dead oxen, mules, and horses along the trail—overworked to the point of death. Later, the wagon train led by Hines passed some of the companies that had earlier passed them on a Sunday.

Phoebe concluded that the Sabbath day of rest had not only been good for their animals but lifted the spirits of all the members of their party.

The pioneers' day started before dawn with breakfast, which usually consisted of coffee, bacon, and dry bread. The wagons were packed, the animals yoked or harnessed, and the group set off by seven o'clock.

The wagons stopped at noon to allow the animals to rest during the heat of the day. The travelers' midday meal would typically be something that didn't require starting a fire, perhaps leftovers from the previous day or that morning. After an hour, they'd hit the trail again, traveling until five or six o'clock when they stopped for the night.

The wagons were formed into a circle each evening with the wagon tongues and chains connecting them together. Animals were corralled inside this area, and the circle provided a form of protection against attack. The men cared for the animals and made any needed wagon repairs. The women cooked a hot meal over an open fire. Keeping bugs and dirt out of the food was a challenge.

There was little to no wood on the prairies. It was often the job of pioneer children to gather dried buffalo manure, known as buffalo chips, to use for their fires. The chips burned rapidly, so it took two to three bushels to keep a fire going long enough to cook a meal.

> *Dry bread and bacon consisted our breakfast, dinner and supper. The bacon we cooked when we could obtain wood for fire; but when nothing but green grass could be seen, we ate our bacon without cooking.*
>
> —*Emigrant Rev. Samuel Parker*

During the evening, the travelers sang, danced, or told stories around the campfire. By nine p.m., they bedded down in tents or directly on the ground.

At the most difficult parts of the trail, the emigrants sometimes had to leave prized possessions behind to lighten the load. The items abandoned along the trail became known as "leeverites." The travelers had to "leave 'er right here" to lighten their wagons. Other settlers might pick up the best of these items to use or sell.

Pulling a loaded wagon uphill in the mountainous sections of the trail was difficult for the draft animals, but going down the steep hills was even more treacherous. On steep descents, emigrants inserted a chain or piece of wood through the wheels to lock them and slow the wagon. Another option was to attach one end of a rope to the wagon and wrap the other end around a strong tree at the top of the hill to gradually lower the wagon.

Not everyone who started out on the trail kept going. Difficulties caused about one in ten to change their mind and turn around. They were known as "turnarounds" or "go-backs."

In 1852, Ezra Meeker met eleven wagons heading East as his wagon traveled West. The returning wagons were driven by women whose husbands had died near Fort Laramie, Wyoming. Rather than starting a new life by themselves in an unknown area, the women agreed to return to relatives in the East.

Nearly one out of ten pioneers didn't survive the journey. A conservative estimate of 20,000 deaths on the Oregon Trail meant ten graves per mile. The most common cause of death was disease. The leading killers were cholera, dysentery, and typhoid fever—all caused by unsanitary conditions.

Settlers couldn't carry enough water for the entire journey. Water was collected from the rivers and streams along the trail which had been contaminated by human and animal waste, garbage, and dead animals.

The most terrifying disease was cholera because of its sudden onset and rapid progression. A person could feel fine in the morning, by midday be in severe pain, and be dead by evening. Cholera wasn't a problem only on the Oregon Trail; it was an epidemic across the United States at that time.

Accidents were the second-most-common cause of death, including:

- Being run over by a wagon
- Accidental gunshots
- Stampeding livestock

- Drownings during river crossings
- Attack by Native Americans

It's ironic that a man named John Shotwell was the first person to die on the Oregon Trail from a firearm accident. John Bidwell reported the event which occurred on May 13, 1841.

> *A mournful accident… a young man by the name of Shotwell while in the act of taking a gun out of the wagon, drew it with the muzzle towards him in such a manner that it went off and shot him near the heart—he lived about an hour and died in full possession of his senses.*

Crossing rivers was also dangerous. Rivers swollen with spring rains could tip a wagon over, drowning both the passengers and the draft animals. Even when lives weren't lost, valuable supplies and equipment might float away or be ruined. In 1850, it was reported that thirty-seven people drowned trying to cross the Green River.

An alternative to fording a river was for the wagon, animals, and people to be ferried across. Operating a ferry was a lucrative business. With little competition, the ferrymen sometimes charged as much as the price of an ox for a journey across the river. Riding a ferry came with its dangers as well.

> *The ferryman allowed too many passengers to get in the boat, and the water came within two inches of the gunwale. He ordered every man to stand steady as the boat was liable to swamp. When we were nearly across, the edge of the boat dipped; I thought the boat would be swamped instantly and drowned the last one of us.*
>
> *—Emigrant John B. Hill*

While relatively rare, attacks by Native Americans sometimes happened. One such attack occurred near Soda Springs, Idaho. When their company started out one morning, a family of seven stayed behind to look for their lost horses. The next day, three trappers found the entire family murdered. The trappers removed the wheels and cover from the family's wagon and buried the father, mother and five children inside it, marking the location of the grave. The Wagon Box Grave headstone still marks the burial site in the Soda Springs Cemetery.

"I have seen the elephant" was a common statement in journals and letters of the pioneers traveling the westward trails. A possible origin for the expression traces back to the story of a farmer who heard a circus was in town. He harnessed his team to a wagon and headed out to get a glimpse of this animal he'd never seen before. Along the way, he encountered the circus parade. Sure enough, it was led by an elephant The farmer was thrilled to see the exotic animal, but his horses experienced a different emotion. They were terrified and bolted, dumping the farmer, and overturning the wagon. Despite what it had cost him, the farmer was satisfied, "for I have seen the elephant."

"Seeing the elephant" became an expression that symbolized both the difficulty and adventure of the long Oregon Trail journey.

Travel on the Trail peaked in the 1850s and rapidly decreased with the completion of the transcontinental railroad in 1869.

<h1 style="text-align:center">46</h1>

Four-time Trail Traveler

Ezra Meeker was born in Huntsville, Ohio on December 29, 1830. He first traveled west, with his parents, at nine when they moved to Indianapolis, Indiana. He attended school there four months, the only formal education he received. At twenty-one, he married Eliza Sumner and moved to Iowa. The following year, on May 28, 1852, Ezra, Eliza, and their seven-week-old son, Marion, joined a company heading west on the Oregon Trail. The Meekers had a wagon, two yoke of oxen, and three cows.

Upon arrival in Oregon Territory, they claimed land in Kalama, Washington where they lived ten years before moving to the Puyallup Valley. Meeker founded the city of Puyallup and became its first mayor. The Meekers became wealthy growing hops used to brew beer. Between 1887 and 1890, he and his wife built a mansion in Puyallup. Over the next few years, a bug infestation destroyed the crops and much of their wealth.

Ezra Meeker's next venture was selling canned goods and produce in the mining camps of northwestern Canada during the Klondike gold rush days. On his first trip in 1898, at the age of sixty-six, he transported 30,000 pounds of dried produce. The following year, he and a son-in-law opened a store, the Log Cabin Grocery in Dawson City. Meeker returned to the Klondike for the next two years, but he lost most of the money he earned from the grocery in failed gold mining attempts.

Dedicating Monument at the Dalles, Oregon.

Ezra returned to Puyallup where he wrote books and served as president of the Washington State Historical Society. Meeker was concerned the Oregon Trail would be forgotten as towns and cities grew up all around it and the land was plowed for farms. His new passion was to preserve the trail by adding markers and monuments along its route.

To bring public attention to the disappearing trail, Meeker decided to retrace the route with an oxen team, this time traveling in reverse—from West to East. It had been fifty-four years since his first trip, and in 1906, oxen and covered wagons weren't readily available. When he couldn't locate a complete, authentic wagon, Meeker had one constructed from new materials and parts of other wagons.

He purchased two oxen—Twist and Dave. A dog hadn't been along on his original journey, but this time, Meeker acquired one named Jim.

Most people did not support his idea. Meeker's own daughter thought everyone would laugh at him. A local minister stated, "It's cruel to let this aged man start on this journey only to perish by exposure in the mountains."

Undaunted by the skeptics, at seventy-six, Ezra Meeker set out from Puyallup on January 29, 1906. Since he didn't have an oxen driver yet, the wagon was pulled to Tenino, Washington by horses, with the oxen following along behind. The first stone trail monument was dedicated in Tenino a few days later.

Meeker finally located a driver, William Mardon, who was paid thirty dollars per month. Mardon also served as the cook and remained with Meeker for several years. As they traveled along the route, Meeker stopped to give lectures about the Oregon Trail. To raise funds, he sold a book he'd written as well as postcards of the journey. He met with local leaders to designate areas where monuments could be located. The slight, elderly man with his long, white beard and dusty clothing looked as if he had stepped out of the pages of a history book.

164

Near Brady, Nebraska,Twist ate some poisonous weeds and died. Meeker used a local farmer's horses to pull the wagon to Omaha, where he purchased Dave's new teammate, Dandy.

Meeker didn't stop when he reached Independence, Missouri, the usual starting point of the Oregon Trail. He continued on to the East to increase awareness for his project. When he arrived in New York City, the driver, Mardon, was arrested for driving cattle on the street. Meeker refused to move his team, and the police had no idea how to make the oxen move. Finally, the authorities released Mardon.

Meeker's oxen and wagon were photographed at the New York Stock Exchange and crossing the Brooklyn Bridge. Meeker met President Teddy Roosevelt in Washington, D.C. on November 29, 1907.

Ezra traveled the Oregon Trail a second time by wagon with Jim, Dave, and Dandy from 1910 to 1912. In 1916, he covered the route by car, and made a fourth trip in 1923 by airplane.

At ninety-seven, Meeker arranged with Henry Ford to cover the route a fifth time. This trip would be in a Model A Ford, but Meeker became ill and returned to Washington state by train. He passed away a few days later, on December 3, 1928, a few weeks shy of his ninety-eighth birthday.

Ezra Meeker founded the Oregon Trail Association, which was succeeded by the Oregon-California Trails Association. The Meeker mansion in Puyallup is now a historical museum.

166

47

Forty-Niners

In 1834, at the age of thirty-one, John Sutter left his wife and five children in Switzerland and traveled to America. He dreamed of building a large agricultural empire. Over the years, Sutter found his way to California, which then belonged to Mexico. He began constructing a complex he called New Helvetia (New Switzerland). By becoming a Mexican citizen and living on his land for one year, Sutter received title from Mexico to 48,827 acres in 1841. The area where Sutter settled is now Sacramento.

In order to build additional buildings at New Helvetia, Sutter needed lumber. In 1847, he hired carpenter James Marshall to construct a sawmill in the Colluma Valley on the South Fork of the American River.

> *I was very much in need of a new sawmill, to get lumber to finish my large flouring mill, of four run of stones, at Brighton, which was commenced at the same time, and was rapidly progressing; likewise for other buildings, fences, etc., for the small village of Yerba Buena.*
>
> —*John Sutter*

On January 24, 1848, James Marshall checked the tail race where water flowed out the back of the completed sawmill. He spotted something glittering in the water. This glittery substance forever changed the two men's lives.

> *It was a rainy afternoon when Mr. Marshall arrived at my office in the Fort, very wet. He told me then that he had some important and interesting news which he wished to communicate secretly to me, and wished me to go with him to a place where we should not be disturbed, and where no listeners could come and hear what we had to say. Mr. Marshall began to show me this metal, which consisted of small pieces and specimens, some of them worth a few dollars.*
>
> —*John Sutter*

Sutter immediately sensed this discovery would ruin his plans for the agricultural community, New Helvetia. Although he and Marshall attempted to keep the discovery quiet, too many of Sutter's workmen had seen the gold. Word soon got out.

When President James K. Polk announced the discovery in his December 1848 State of the Union address, many Americans contracted a serious case of gold fever. Some borrowed money, mortgaged homes, or spent their life savings to travel to California, in hopes of making their fortune.

Sutter's employees abandoned their work to search for gold.

So soon as the secret was out my laborers began to leave me, in small parties first, but then all left, from the clerk to the cook, and I was in great distress; only a few mechanics remained to finish some very necessary work which they had commenced.

—John Sutter

Because the largest influx of fortune-seekers arrived in 1849, they became known as the Forty-Niners. The miners destroyed Sutter's sawmill, so they could search below it. His cattle were stolen and butchered. The miners turned their animals loose to graze on Sutters' farm land. The men even took the giant stones from his flour mills to crush rocks that might contain gold.

It's estimated that as much as two billion dollars worth of gold (in today's value) was found in California in the highest-reported year, 1852. While it's impossible to give exact numbers, a fortunate miner might have earned $20 a day in 1848. That dropped to $3 per day by 1856.

While a few struck it rich, most did not. Poor diets and unsanitary conditions in the camps left the miners susceptible to disease. Cholera and smallpox killed many. A letter from Sheldon Shufelt describes the reality of a miner's life in 1850.

Many, very many, that come here meet with bad success & thousands will leave their bones here. Others will lose their health, contract diseases that they will carry to their graves with them. Some will have to beg their way home, & probably one half that come here will never make enough to carry them back.

There is a good deal of sin & wickedness going on here, stealing, lying, swearing, drinking, gambling & murdering. There is a great deal of gambling carried on here. Almost every public house is a place for gambling, & this appears to be the greatest evil that prevails here. Men make & lose thousands in a night.

—Sheldon Shufelt, Library of Congress, letter from a gold miner, Placerville, California, March, 1850

California's first millionaire wasn't a gold miner but a store owner. Samuel Brannan realized men couldn't mine for gold unless they had the right equipment.

Brannan filled his store with mining supplies: tents, shovels, pick axes, buckets, pans, food, and clothing. Then, he marched up and down the streets of San Francisco waving a bottle of gold flakes over his head and shouting "Gold, gold, gold in the American River!"

It's estimated that at the height of the gold rush, Brannan made $2,000 per day.

Store owners charged high prices because the miners had no other options. A single egg or one slice of bread might sell for $1.00 ($92 today). Pans that sold for $0.20 before the rush, now sold for $8 ($246). Boots cost $6 ($185).

Earlier, Henry Wells, William Fargo, and John Butterfield had formed the American Express company and were successful hauling freight in the East. With the discovery of gold in California, Wells and Fargo proposed expanding their service to the Pacific Coast. Butterfield rejected the idea, but undeterred, Wells and Fargo formed their own business. The Wells Fargo stagecoaches served the mining communities in California.

A common misconception is that Levi Strauss came up with the idea for blue jeans for the gold miners in California. But it wasn't until 1873, that he and Jacob Davis, a tailor, were awarded a patent for their denim jeans with copper rivets. The jeans became popular anyway, but if they had invented them twenty-five years earlier, they would have certainly been a big hit with the miners. In 1886, Levi Strauss & Co. introduced their two-horse trademark which depicts horses pulling in opposite directions, attempting to rip apart a pair of Levi's jeans, demonstrating the strength of the copper rivets.

The Gold Rush created significant changes in California. Before gold was discovered, the entire population of the area was roughly 157,000, including a large percentage of Native Americans. In 1849, an additional 90,000 people found their way to California. By the mid-1850s, a total of 300,000 had arrived.

Over 90% of the new arrivals were men. It was said that women in California were more rare than gold. The immigrants didn't come just from the United States either; 25,000 were from China. Others came from Hawaii, Mexico, and Central and South America. As the non-native population increased, the number of Native Americans decreased. Some died of diseases brought by the immigrants. Others were murdered.

When the Mexican-American War ended with the signing of the Treaty of Guadalupe Hidalgo in February 1848, California became the property of the United States. Its rapid increase in population led to California being admitted as a state in 1850.

When the supply of surface gold was exhausted, large mining companies began using a technique called hydraulic mining. Water at high elevations was diverted into flumes, from which it was channeled through a pipe and out a narrow metal nozzle. The high-pressure water blasted craters in the hillsides, devastating California's environment. A court ruling brought the practice to an end in 1884.

By 1857, the California gold supply had dwindled to such an extent that miners took up other professions or searched for gold elsewhere.

- New Mexico—1820s and 1858
- Nevada—Comstock Lode (silver) near Carson City in 1857
- Pike's Peak or Colorado Gold Rush—1858
- Klondike or Yukon Gold Rush—1896

Sutter and Marshall, the two men who indirectly started it all, never profited from the gold they discovered. In 1850, after sixteen years of separation, Sutter's wife and several of his grown children left Switzerland to join him in California. Sutter's land grant from Mexico wasn't recognized by the United States, and he was in financial trouble. He moved his family to Pennsylvania in 1871. They were granted a pension of $250 a month for the loss of his property out west. John Sutter died in 1880. James Marshall received a pension from 1872 to 1878, but he lived his last years in poverty, dying in 1885.

Horses never played a major role in the gold rush. With hundreds of thousands of prospectors traveling west, undoubtedly a few horses pulled wagons or carried their riders over the Oregon Trail. Horses were used to pull the Wells Fargo stagecoaches to and from many of the mining towns. They also delivered supplies to the mining stores as well as the timbers used to prop up mine shafts. When mining moved underground, horses and mules hauled ore out of the gold and silver mines.

A horse-drawn arrastre functioned much like a grist mill. Horses or mules were hooked to large spokes. As they walked in a circle, turning the spokes, rocks were crushed, making it easier to extract veins of gold or silver.

But the most frequently used equine for miners was the burro or donkey. Serving as a pack animal and partner in the mining adventure, the burro became nearly synonymous with gold prospecting.

48

Fifty-Niners

According to folklore around the mining camps, a wandering burro was thought to have the ability to lead a prospector to gold. No record exists of that ever happening, however gold and silver prospectors in rugged areas found that a trusty burro was invaluable as a pack animal.

A burro is a member of the equine family, also known as a donkey. Some use the word "burro" to refer to the untamed animal and "donkey" for the tame version. Like the horse, burros first arrived in America in the 1500s with the early Spanish explorers.

The hardy burro is strong, sure-footed, and not easily frightened. When afraid, he will often stand his ground and survey the situation rather than bolting as a horse is prone to do. When overloaded, a burro may lay down and refuse to work at all.

The most common coloring is gray with a light-colored muzzle and belly, but burros also come in brown, black, red, white, and spotted. They average eleven hands or forty-four inches in height and weigh about 400 pounds. When well-cared for, burros may live thirty to forty years. They are protective animals and will attack coyotes or other predators that threaten livestock.

Burros are well suited to life in the dry, barren Southwest. Although their digestive systems are nearly identical to horses and mules, burros can survive on lower quantities and quality of food. And more importantly, burros require less water.

Their distinctive voices led to burros being given nicknames such as the Arizona Nightingale or Mountain Canary. If you're familiar with the sound of a donkey's bray, you'll see the humor in that. The donkey's unique voice is due to his ability to make a sound while breathing both in and out.

It was said that after a few months of working with a prospector, a burro was able to understand everything his master said and read his mind, but no man could ever read the mind of a burro.

As the gold rush in California died down, miners moved on to Colorado. Nearly 100,000 men swarmed into the area. The Colorado Gold Rush was also

known as the Pike's Peak Gold Rush. Its biggest year was 1859. The slogan of the hopeful prospectors was "Pike's Peak or Bust!"

Coming a decade after California's Forty-Niners, the Colorado miners were known as Fifty-Niners. Due to the rapid population growth, Colorado was organized as a territory in 1861 and became a U.S. state in 1876.

The town of Fairplay in Park County, Colorado, at an elevation of 10,000 feet, was founded in 1859 as a mining settlement where everyone would be treated fairly. Its current population is 700. Located at the junction of Beaver Creek and the South Platte River, the original name of the town was two words—Fair Play. The name was changed to South Park City in 1869, then changed back to Fairplay (one word) in 1874. Two Park County burros are typical of the animals used by prospectors.

Prunes

Rupert M. Sherwood, a trapper and fur trader, arrived in Colorado in 1862. In 1889, he was lured to the gold fields. Sherwood purchased a burro named Prunes for $10 from two retired prospectors. Already seasoned with years of mining experience, Prunes became Sherwood's constant companion.

The burro cheerfully carried supplies such as a gold pan, shovel, frying pan, coffee pot, pick, rope, blankets, flour, bacon, sugar, and oats. When Sherwood was too busy to go to town, the miner pinned a shopping list to Prunes' pack and sent the burro off by himself. When Prunes arrived in town, the shopkeeper filled the order and sent the burro back up the trail to return to Sherwood's camp.

After several years of mining, Sherwood became ill. His doctor advised him to leave the high elevation of Fairplay. Sherwood reluctantly complied, leaving Prunes in the care of the townspeople. The trusty little burro died in the spring of 1930 at the advanced age of sixty-three.

172

A stone monument in the center of Fairplay honors Prunes. The monument contains shadow boxes with the burro's harness and other mementos from his life. Sherwood returned for the dedication ceremony. Through tears, he said, "Lord I hate to see him go. I would trust him ahead of any man."

The old miner read a poem he'd written, "Me and Prunes." When Sherwood passed away the following year, his ashes were placed in the monument alongside Prunes, as the miner had requested.

Prunes' monument marks the starting and ending point for a pack burro race currently held in Fairplay each July.

Shorty

Shorty was another well-known Fairplay burro who worked as a pack animal for various prospectors. When the last miner no longer needed him, Shorty was abandoned to fend for himself.

In 1949, the burro made a friend—a stray dog named Bum. The two became inseparable. When they couldn't find a meal elsewhere, the pair wandered through town, begging. It didn't take them long to figure out which places provided the best chance for a tasty handout.

Bum led Shorty to the door, then it was the burro's job to bray the announcement of their arrival. The local hotel was a favorite stop. The cook almost always had a stack of warm pancakes or biscuits ready for the pair. When Bum was given food, he dropped it at Shorty's feet. After the burro had eaten his fill, then Bum ate.

When Shorty became blind, the burro relied on Bum more than ever. During the summer months, the dog led his friend to grassy areas at the edge of town and waited as Shorty grazed.

During the coldest weather, the courthouse janitor, Johnnie Capelli, allowed Shorty and Bum to sleep in his garage on a bed of hay. One bitterly cold night, Capelli brought them into the courthouse, and the animals slept in the jail.

In 1951, Shorty was struck by a car and died at the age of forty-five. Grief-stricken, Bum refused to leave the dead burro's side. Fairplay residents were touched by his devotion. They buried Shorty's ashes on the courthouse lawn and added a small marble tombstone to mark the grave site. Bum died four months after the burro, and the dog's ashes were buried next to his friend.

Brighty of the Grand Canyon

In 1890, a small, gray burro served as a pack animal for two miners on their journey from Flagstaff, Arizona to the Grand Canyon. The burro was later found at the men's abandoned camp at the junction of the Colorado River and Bright Angel Creek. The two miners were never found. Authorities presumed they had drowned in the river. The burro was named Bright Angel after the creek where he'd been found, but everyone called him Brighty.

In 1917, Thomas and Elizabeth McKee founded a tourist camp consisting of ten cabins on the North Rim of the canyon at a point called Wylie Way. By this time, Brighty had lived in the area nearly thirty years. The McKees spent their winters in California, returning to the Grand Canyon each summer. Brighty had a seasonal living arrangement as well. His habit was to spend summers up at the rim where the grazing was better and winters further down in the canyon.

It was the job of the McKee's son, Robert or Bobby, to haul water up to the family's camp from a spring 200 feet below the canyon rim. Each morning, Bobby called out, "Pancakes, Brighty!"

The burro came running, eager to get to work—or more likely—to enjoy his favorite breakfast!

Before the McKee's arrival, Brighty hung out mostly with Jim Owens, a game warden known as Uncle Jim. Along with the McKee family, Uncle Jim remained one of Brighty's favorites. The burro was never penned up or tied. He enjoyed wandering freely around the camp.

While working with Bobby, Brighty wore a pack saddle with two ten-gallon metal cans, one on each side. Bobby led Brighty up and down the trail to haul water several times a day. When full, the tanks weighed more than 150 pounds. Brighty, already up in years, took his time, stopping to rest when he was tired. Sometimes, Bobby went ahead, knowing the trusty burro would continue when he was ready. At the end of each trip, Brighty was rewarded with the pancakes he dearly loved.

The young women who worked at the camp teased Bobby, asking the boy who was the boss of their water operation—him or Brighty. Bobby replied, "Neither. We are pardners."

Brighty and Bobby were indeed partners, but the sly burro wasn't so willing to work for other people. For those who tried to use him as a pack animal, Brighty was known to "sneak away from his kidnappers; then rub the pack against trees until the lashings loosened and the load fell off."

Brighty allowed smaller children at the camp to ride him, but when older boys tried, he would pitch them off.

In 1921, a construction crew arrived to build the first footbridge across the Colorado River. Brighty, curious about this new project, wandered over to offer his assistance. When the bridge was finished, Brighty made the first official crossing.

The burro lived and worked in the Grand Canyon from 1890 to 1922, until he

met a tragic end. During the winter of 1921-22, a thief captured Brighty for use as a pack animal. In December, the burro was taken to a cabin on the North Rim used by ranch cowboys during the summer months.

Soon after that, a former Marine traveling on foot from Utah to southern Arizona, happened to find his way to the same cabin. The soldier had underestimated the distance of his journey and the severity of the weather. Now, his feet were frostbitten, and he was in desperate need of shelter.

The thief, however was in no mood for hospitality. He opened the cabin door and threatened the unwelcome visitor with an ax. When the Marine flashed a Bowie knife, he was reluctantly allowed to enter, and the two men established an uneasy truce. They were trapped together in the cabin with almost no food and three months of impassable winter weather ahead of them. When they exhausted their meager food supply, the men agreed to sacrifice poor Brighty to keep them alive.

By March, several feet of snow remained on the ground. The men left the cabin anyway and made it to Jim Owen's home ten miles away. The Marine lost both of his feet to frostbite. The thief, after leaving Owen's place, was never heard from again.

A life-size, bronze statue of Brighty was donated to the Grand Canyon.

As if Brighty's sad end wasn't bad enough, many park rangers considered the burros a nuisance and a hazard to the environment. Between 1924 and 1931, it's estimated rangers shot and killed nearly 1500 burros. In the 1960s, the park service flew helicopters into the canyon, so rangers could more easily shoot them.

By the late 1970s, the number of burros was once again increasing, but the practice of shooting the animals had prompted public protest. In 1978, hoping to avoid calling unnecessary attention to the burro issue, park officials moved the Brighty statue into storage. Its removal only increased the public outcry.

Cleveland Amory's rescue group, The Fund for Animals, raised money to airlift the remaining burros by helicopter to the Black Beauty Ranch in Texas. In 1979, the two-year project began. Over 500 burros were removed by helicopter from the Grand Canyon. After the burros were removed, a fence was erected along the park's boundary to prevent them from returning.

Marguerite Henry made Brighty's story famous with the publication in 1953 of her fictionalized account, *Brighty of the Grand Canyon*. The book was made into a movie in 1965. Portions of it were filmed in the Grand Canyon. Henry's own donkey, Jiggs, played the part of Brighty.

In 1980, Brighty's statue was moved to the lobby of the Grand Canyon Lodge on the North Rim. Hikers consider it good luck to rub Brighty's nose before heading out on the trail.

50

Jack Packer

In Colorado, as in California, there was often more money to be made selling supplies to the miners than in mining. That was true for the storekeepers who sold the supplies, but also for those who transported materials to the mining camps. The supplies were usually carried by trains of pack burros. Those who drove them were called jack packers.

Olga Schaaf was one of the most successful packers in Colorado. Born in Germany in 1883, Olga immigrated to America with her family. By the age of fourteen, she and her brother were training horses for ranchers. Olga also drove horses to make deliveries or to carry tourists into the mountains.

Flooding in 1909 made it difficult for wagons to get through to deliver supplies. A mine owner asked Olga if she would lead a pack string to make the deliveries. She was reluctant, having never used pack animals before. Although later she used burros exclusively, Olga began her packing career with horse and mule teams. On one of those early trips, her saddle horse fell on an icy trail, breaking one of Olga's legs. She managed to get back on the horse and rode the rest of the way to the mine. A doctor later arrived to set her leg, and she was brought home on a sled.

Between 1909 and the mid-1940s, Olga packed supplies into and out of the gold and silver mines of the La Plata Mountains near Durango, Colorado. Olga married Scottish immigrant and miner Bill Little in 1913.

She never whipped or cussed at her burros. In fact, according to True West Magazine, she never cursed at all.

Dressed in men's clothing to withstand the rigors of mountain life, full of good humor, unlike her fellow pack-train drivers, she never spoke a cuss word in her life.

Olga owned forty burros and often used a string of twenty at a time to navigate the steep, treacherous trails at elevations of 11,000 feet. Each burro carried no more than 200 pounds. Ten burros could pack a ton of supplies. Olga charged $5 a ton.

In addition to the more common items like food, medicine, and mail, Olga's burros packed lumber, coal, steel rails, tools, cook and heating stoves, and explosives. On one trip, her burros carried wooden crates full of dynamite. Three of the burros slipped over a cliff on the Eagle Pass Trail. The burros died, but the dynamite didn't explode.

When packing coal or ore, she divided it into seventy-pound bags which she loaded herself—one on each side of the burro and the third on top of his back. The ore the burros carried from the mines was then loaded onto railroad cars.

Olga is best remembered for saving the lives of seventeen men who were snowbound at the Neglected Mine in La Plata County, Colorado during the winter of 1912. With ten feet of snow on the ground, thirty below zero temperatures, and a meager supply of food, the men and burros would soon have starved.

Olga's job was to get them all to Transfer Camp, seven miles away. She tied the men and animals together, so no one would get lost. At 7:30 a.m., the group set out, trudging through drifts as snow continued to fall. They arrived at their destination fifteen and a half hours later. Some of the miners suffered frostbite, but Olga hadn't lost a man or burro.

Lots of people thought my job was awful, but I never gave it a thought. There's nothing dangerous about it.

—Olga Little

Olga has a mountain named for her—Olga Little Mountain, an 11,426-foot-tall peak east of Kennebec Pass in the La Platas.

51

Faster Than a Speeding Burro

Many of the burros roaming public lands in the West and Southwest are descendants of animals abandoned by the gold and silver prospectors. Today, there's not much demand for burros as pack animals in the United States, but that hasn't kept their numbers from increasing.

Arizona is home to more wild burros than any other state, over 6,000 in 2024. The recommended number for Arizona is about 1,700. Wildlife officials are concerned the burros will destroy the habitat for native species.

The Wild Free-Roaming Horses and Burros Act of 1971 established herd management areas (HMAs) for burros as well as for Mustang horses. The Bureau of Land Management (BLM) attempts to regulate the burro population through roundups and adoptions.

In Oatman, Arizona, the burros have become a tourist attraction. The town has a herd totaling nearly 150 burros, twenty-five of which are comfortable wandering into town each morning from the nearby hills. They roam the streets and sidewalks, begging for food from the locals and tourists. Sometimes, they stretch out on the sidewalk for a nap. The first local to spot a newborn burro gets to name it. The animals have names such as Tornado, Ida, Elmo, Libby, Jackie, and Summer.

The shops sell hay cubes, the only food people are allowed to feed the animals. Young burros wear stickers on their foreheads warning tourists not to feed them at all. The burros are not tame. Some visitors have been bitten or kicked. Around 5:00 p.m., when the shops close and the tourists leave, the burros head back to the hills for the evening.

Pack Burro Races

Colorado holds several pack burro races each year. The races serve as a reminder of the important role burros played in mining. According to legend, this type of race was inspired by two miners who struck gold in the same area, then raced to town to be the first to file the claim.

In 2012, the Colorado legislature designated pack burro racing the state's "summer heritage sport."

You'll never see a burro in the Kentucky Derby, but that's okay because they have their own "Triple Crown" with races at Fairplay, Leadville, and Buena Vista.

There's a big difference between burro races and the Kentucky Derby—no horses, no mules, not even any jockeys. The burros aren't ridden; their human partner runs alongside the animal.

The Fairplay race, held annually on the last weekend of July, began in 1949. This race isn't for the faint of heart. The course covers twenty-nine miles, beginning in the center of Fairplay, running up to the 13,186-foot Mosquito Pass Summit, then back to the starting point.

A team consists of one man or woman and a burro. Each burro carries a pack which includes a pick, shovel, and gold pan. The equipment must weigh at least thirty-three pounds. The human team member walks or runs alongside the animal. Riding is forbidden, but runners are allowed to push, pull, drag or carry their burro. The lead rope attached to the burro must be fifteen feet long or less.

The human runner's speed doesn't always determine the winner. Since the winning team must cross the finish line together, cooperation between human and burro is a critical factor.

The age range of the human runners at the 2018 Fairplay race was fifteen to seventy. Kirt Courkamp and his donkey, Mary Margaret, won that race with a time of six hours, six minutes, and thirty-eight seconds. The first place prize was $1,000. Karen Thorpe was the first woman to win the race in 2011 with a time of five hours and forty-one minutes.

Burros competing in past events had names such as Buckwheat, Hershey, Sweet Pea, BonBon, Cream Puff, and ReDONKulous. In the nearly seventy-year history of the Fairplay race, no burros have died or been seriously injured. The burros are willing participants in the races. As anyone who knows donkeys can attest, it's virtually impossible to force them to do anything they don't want to do![1]

---

[1] *For more information and photos, visit the Western Pack Burro Association site, packburroracing.com.*

52

Old Whitey

Captain George McCall at Fort Smith, Arkansas was an expert horseman and enjoyed the challenge of riding a spirited horse. Whitey would have been the last choice as a war horse for most soldiers. He wasn't exactly spirited. In fact, McCall used him as a buggy horse. In addition to being lethargic, the horse was a faded gray, so light he would stand out on the battlefield.

When General Zachary Taylor visited Captain McCall in search of a horse, the general's companions urged him to pick any of the horses but Whitey. But the general was impressed with the buggy horse's laid-back temperament, believing Whitey would be calm and steady in battle.

Old Whitey lived up to Taylor's expectations. The general rode the horse in the Mexican-American War from 1844 to 1847. His soldiers came to respect the brave horse and gave him the name Old Whitey. Taylor always called him Billy or Old Billy.

His light color made Whitey a special target in battle. The horse received two bullet wounds—one on his neck and another on his right hip, but Old Whitey carried the general safely to the end of the war.

General Taylor was given the nickname "Old Rough and Ready" due to his disheveled appearance and his willingness to fight alongside his men. Oddly enough, the Rough and Ready general could sometimes be seen riding sidesaddle into battle. It's said that Taylor's legs were so short he found it easier to mount quickly that way.

The following account hardly seems possible, but Samuel McNeil, an Ohio shoemaker, recalled an incident involving General Taylor in The Battle of Buena Vista on February 23, 1847.

After the Mexican-American War, Taylor was surprised when his supporters suggested he run for president. He immediately declined, saying running for president "never entered my head… nor is it likely to enter the head of any sane person." Taylor had been a military man for nearly forty years and wasn't interested in politics. He'd never held a political office and, in fact, had never voted.

At their convention, the Whig party nominated him anyway, without Taylor's knowledge or presence. In 1848, General Taylor ran as a Whig against Democrat Lewis Cass and Free Soil candidate Martin Van Buren.

During the 1848 presidential campaign, the Whigs wanted to avoid conflict over the issues of slavery and states' rights. They portrayed Taylor as a military hero, an appealing leader regardless of party. Originally from Virginia, Zachary Taylor grew up in Kentucky in a slave-holding family. Taylor himself at one time owned as many as 200 slaves with estates in Louisiana, Kentucky, and Mississippi. But, he opposed secession and the extension of slavery into new territories.

The issues dividing the country were evident in Taylor's own family. One of his daughters married Jefferson Davis, the future president of the Confederacy, and a son, Richard, would later fight in the Confederate Army.

During the campaign, the Whigs capitalized on Taylor's war hero status. Images of the general on Old Whitey were printed on leaflets and in newspapers. Old Whitey became nearly as much a hero to the people as General Taylor. Poems and music featured the brave horse.

The 1848 election was the first time all states voted on the same day. When the votes were counted, Zachary Taylor had won, becoming the United States' twelfth president. There was probably no one more surprised at this victory than Taylor. He hadn't voted in that election either.

Given his bravery on the battlefield, Whitey had earned a nice retirement. The horse was about eighteen when Taylor was elected. But, the public had fallen in love with him, and Taylor made plans to bring Old Whitey along to Washington, D.C. As it turned out, Whitey would have a companion.

Before the election, the Taylors received an unexpected gift. A family friend had purchased a former circus pony named Apollo for his own daughter. Unfortunately, the girl was killed in a carriage accident (Apollo wasn't involved). The grieving father gave Apollo to Taylor's daughter, knowing Mary Elizabeth (Betty) would take good care of the pony.

Whitey and Apollo were shipped by boat and train from Taylor's Louisiana plantation to Washington, D.C. At each stop along the way, people gathered to see the general's horse. If close enough, they plucked a hair from his tail as a souvenir. Upon their arrival in Washington, the horse and pony were made comfortable in the White House Stable.

Whitey grazed on the White House grounds. When he saw people gather at the fence, he wandered over to see whether they had an apple, carrot or other treat for him. Visitors loved to pet the war horse and feel the indentations from his bullet wounds.

A description of Taylor's war horse was given in an old history book.

Old Whitey is a compact, hardy, well-proportioned animal, less of a battle-steed in appearance, than of the style usually defined by the phrase 'family horse,' slightly knock-kneed, and with a tail very much thinned by the numerous applications for a hair of 'him for memory.' But remembering the beatings of the great heart he had borne upon his back—the anxieties, the energies, the defiances of danger, the iron impulses to danger, it was impossible to look upon him without a throb in the throat.

—N.P. Willis in Esther Singleton, *The Story of the White House*, 1907

Taylor served just sixteen months as president. On July 4, 1850, he became severely ill after eating cherries and iced milk. His last words were:

I have always done my duty. I am prepared to die. My only regret is in leaving behind me, the friends I love.

President Taylor died on July 9, 1850. Although some suspected foul play, the cause of death was officially declared to be cholera. Millard Fillmore, the vice president, assumed the office in Taylor's place. Taylor was the second president to die in office. The first being William Henry Harrison, who died of an illness in 1841 on the 31st day of his presidency.

On July 13, Whitey was called to serve Taylor one last time. The old horse marched riderless behind the hearse pulled by eight white horses. Whitey wore Taylor's military saddle with the general's boots turned backwards in the stirrups, symbolizing one last look back at his family and troops. Taylor was buried near his childhood home in Kentucky.

According to Taylor's youngest daughter, Mary Elizabeth, Whitey lived to old age.

> *You ask about Old Whitey; he was a great pet to us all, and was never ridden after my father's return from Mexico, and when he went to Washington the horse was sent to his plantation. During his term as President there was so much interest and curiosity expressed to see the old charger that he had him brought to Washington, and after my father's death, he was sent back to the plantation, then the home of my brother Richard, where Whitey lived to a good old age.*

53

Stagecoach Travel

The use of four-wheeled, horse-drawn, covered coaches dates back to as early as the 1200s. The first stagecoach route in England was established in 1610. By the mid-1700s, when a few roads were wide enough to permit more than travel on horseback, stagecoaches began to carry passengers between American colonies. By 1832, there were 106 stagecoach lines in Boston alone. Stagecoaches are most often associated with the Old West, but they were used all over the United States.

Each stagecoach passenger was permitted to bring twenty-five pounds of luggage which was stored at the rear of the coach in a covered compartment called the boot. The coach windows had leather roll-down curtains. Stagecoaches were equipped with a brake the driver could engage, particularly on downhill sections of a route. The undercarriage of the coach was often painted yellow with a bright red or green body. The name of the stagecoach line was emblazoned on the sides.

The early coaches, often packed with as many as eighteen passengers—nine inside and nine on top, traveled over primitive, unpaved roads. Inside the coach were three benches, each providing three seats, roughly fifteen inches per person. The middle bench was the most undesirable. It had no back—at best a narrow leather strap was pulled across after everyone was seated.

Passengers seated in the middle found it difficult to decide what to do with their legs. Middle passengers faced those riding in the front seat, who faced backwards. Twelve legs had to be arranged within the limited space. This arranging of legs was referred to as dovetailing—something female passengers in particular found awkward.

The coach was fitted with three seats, and these were occupied by nine passengers. As the occupants of the front and middle seats faced each other, it was necessary for these six people to

—Raphael Pumpelly, a Butterfield Overland passenger

On longer routes, the stagecoaches ran night and day with brief stops at stations to change out
horses or drivers. Passengers could stay overnight at one of the stations, but there was a good chance
of becoming stranded for a week or more before another stage arrived with an available seat. If the
dovetailing of legs was an awkward and embarrassing situation, falling asleep in the coach and
nodding over onto a fellow passenger was even more so. Staying awake as long as possible was the
only solution.

*The fatigue of uninterrupted traveling by day and night in a crowded coach, and in the most
uncomfortable positions, was beginning to tell seriously upon all the passengers, and was
producing in me a condition bordering on insanity.*

—Raphael Pumpelly

Early stagecoaches were known for their rough, uncomfortable rides. One passenger, Abigail
Scott Duniway, gives a vivid description of what must have been a painful journey.

*The stage goes laboring up the mountain, straining, careening, crashing and bumping, almost
whipping bones and muscles to jelly.*

Another passenger described his journey in a similar manner.

*I am here, and without any broken bones, but how my bones happen to be whole after the fearful
ride up and down the Sierra Nevada mountains, I haven't the remotest idea.*

—Nevada Legislature, Carson City, Nevada Territory, September, 1861

*Creeping through the valley, crawling o'er the hill, Splashing through the branches, rumbling o'er
the mill; Putting nervous gentlemen in a towering rage. What is so provoking as riding in a
stage?*

*Spinsters fair and forty, maids in youthful charms, Suddenly are cast into their neighbors' arms;
Children shoot like squirrels darting through a cage; isn't it delightful, riding in a stage?*

*Feet are interlacing, heads severely bumped, Friend and foe together get their noses thumped;
Dresses act as carpets-listen to the sage; "Life is but a journey taken in a stage."*

—Six Horses by Captain William Banning & George Hugh Banning, 1928

In 1828, J. Stephen Abbot and Lewis Downing of New Hampshire devised a new suspension
system that used long, horizontal leather straps called thorough braces that supported the bottom of
the coach on each side. These leather braces allowed the body of the coach to rock back and forth,
producing a swaying motion that was preferable to the former jarring and jolting.

Mark Twain described the Concord Stagecoach as "a cradle on wheels." The Concord became the
new standard for stagecoach design, however the swaying caused motion sickness in some as
passenger William Reed describes.

*The heat could be unbearable; the bodies of the passengers covered with sand, which permeated
every inch of clothing. The rough roads gave to the coaches a motion not only from side to side,*

Of course, stagecoaches weren't climate controlled. In the winter months, they were cold. A hot soapstone, blanket, or buffalo hide could be brought along to keep one's feet warm.

When spring arrived, passengers might have to exit the coach and walk if the wheels became stuck in mud or deep sand. In some cases, they even had to push.

During the sweltering summer months, the passengers, clothed in the long-sleeved attire of the day, already crammed uncomfortably close to each other in the stifling, tight quarters of the coach, had no relief from the heat and dust. Ladies were invited to bring a veil to keep out the dust. Men used a bandanna for the same purpose.

The passengers on top of the coach might not be as hot, but they had to endure the dust clouds kicked up by the horses racing to stay on schedule. Long overcoats known as dusters protected clothing, but only made the passengers even hotter.

In the close quarters of the coach, strangers quickly became annoyed or disgusted by the habits of their fellow passengers.

Most of the men chewed tobacco, and those who occupied centre seats had to exert considerable skill to spit clear of the other passengers. Americans are generally adept in this art, but we had one or two unskilful professors, although it must be admitted that they had hardly a fair opportunity of showing off their proficiency, from the jolting of the coach. Occasionally they would unconcernedly expectorate among the baggage on the floor. The smell caused by this abominable practice was intolerable and sickening at first, until one became somewhat accustomed to it.

—*Edmund Hope Verney, 1865*

In order to maintain civility among their passengers, stagecoach companies developed rules of etiquette. An issue of the Omaha Herald newspaper from 1877 offers a sampling of those guidelines.

- When the driver asks you to get off and walk, do it without grumbling.

- If a team runs away, sit still and take your chances; if you jump, nine times out of ten you will be hurt.

- In very cold weather, abstain entirely from liquor while on the road; a man will freeze twice as quick while under its influence.

- Don't smoke a strong pipe inside especially early in the morning. Spit on the leeward side of the coach.

- Don't swear, nor lop over on your neighbor when sleeping.

- Don't ask how far it is to the next station.

- Never attempt to fire a gun or pistol while on the road, it may frighten the team; and the careless handling and cocking of the weapon makes people nervous.

- Don't discuss politics or religion, nor point out places on the road where horrible murders have been committed.

- Don't grease your hair before starting or dust will stick there.

The Horses

Stagecoaches were usually pulled by a team of four, sometimes six horses. The lead horses were up front. The horses at the back were called wheel horses or wheelers. For teams of six, the middle pair were called the swing horses or pointers. The size of the horses generally increased from font to back.

The wheel horses were responsible for most of the pulling. Teams of all-white horses were highly desirable for their visibility at night.

The horses' work was hard, pulling a loaded coach over rough terrain as fast as was safely possible. The average speed was five to eight miles an hour. Teams were swapped out every ten or fifteen miles at swing or relay stations where the animals rested. The stations normally had toilet facilities for both men and women, however the stops might last only ten minutes—just long enough to unharness and then hitch a new team.

The Drivers

Drivers typically drove the same forty or fifty mile section of a route—out and back. Stagecoaches ran on a schedule, and the drivers did their best to stick to it. When he called out, "All Aboard!" passengers scrambled to find their seats for fear of being left behind.

The drivers were sometimes called Jehu, a name attributed to them from the Biblical character who drove furiously.

> *"the driving is like the driving of Jehu the son of Nimshi, for he drives furiously!"*
>
> *2 Kings 9:20 NKJV*

The lives of the passengers depended upon the driver's skill. Stagecoach drivers were given a respect comparable to airline pilots today. George Monroe was considered one of the most skilled stagecoach drivers. He was born a slave in Georgia in 1844. His father, a barber in the California mining camps, purchased his son's freedom.

Three stagecoach roads were built in the mid-1870s to carry tourists to Yosemite. The area became Yosemite National Park in 1890. Monroe was one of the forty drivers employed by the Yosemite Stage and Turnpike Company. The company had forty stagecoaches and 700 horses. In the busy, summer season, eleven coaches a day ran from the train station to Yosemite. In order to feed all those horses, large freight wagons full of hay and grain were pulled by ten-mule teams.

For twenty years, George Monroe drove a treacherous route along the Wawona Road from Mariposa, California to the Yosemite Valley. Portions of his route contained sharp drop-offs at the side of the road and tight switch-backs, however Monroe never had an accident or injury to any of his passengers.

Three U.S. presidents rode Monroe's coach—Grant, Garfield, and Rutherford B. Hayes. On his trip in 1879, Grant rode beside Monroe rather than inside the coach. Monroe gave the reins briefly to the former president—the only time he allowed anyone else to drive his coach.

Ironically, Monroe died at the age of forty-two when a runaway horse caused a coach, in which he was a passenger, to tip over.

Although nearly all stagecoach drivers were male, there were a few exceptions. Mary Fields was born a slave in Tennessee, owned by the Dunn family. After the Civil War, Mary followed a member of the Dunn family to central Montana where she worked at a convent.

In 1895, the muscular, six-foot-tall woman became a mailcoach driver. Stagecoach Mary, as she was known, and her mule Moses never missed a day's work.

In addition to the skill of the stagecoach driver, the passengers' safety depended to a great extent on the intelligence and sensibility of the horses. One passenger related an account of a surprising discovery he made on one of his journeys.

I rode on the outside with the driver a part of the way during the night, and I am certain that I never saw anybody who could drive so well in his sleep. Up hill and down hill, wiring in and wiring out along "dug-ways" on the mountain sides, where vast piles of rocks impended on one hand and death and destruction a thousand feet deep yawned within six inches of the wheels on the other, it made no difference to him; he still nodded with closed eyes, and bobbed up and down on his seat. Once or twice, in particularly bad looking places, I ventured to rouse him, and finally he very coolly informed me that his horses knew every foot of the way and that was his sleeping ground—that whenever he reached a certain hill he always began to grow sleepy.

—*Nevada Legislature, Carson City, Nevada Territory, September, 1861*

Accidents did happen, though. Artemus Ward, riding alongside the driver in 1881, spotted a wrecked coach off the side of a narrow mountain road.

> *Our roadway is narrow. The ravines beside us are a quarter of a mile deep. At the bottom of one of them I see the fragments of a coach. No wonder that they are fragments only; for, in rolling over down the precipitous side of the mountain, that coach must have fallen five hundred feet. I ask the driver if there were any passengers in it at the time of the accident. He replies that there were; that two of them were killed and three severely injured.*

Stagecoaches brought more than passengers and mail. Prosperity usually followed wherever they went. In addition to the relay stations where teams of horses were exchanged, home stations were located fifty miles apart.

At a home station, drivers were switched. The driver waited at the home station for a coach traveling in the opposite direction. Passengers disembarked here to eat and rest. Area farmers had a market for their horses and products, and enterprising community members provided food and entertainment for the passengers at these stops. The stations were known for their bad food, often consisting of jerky, salt pork, bread, coffee, and beans.

When early railroad routes were developed, running primarily east and west, stagecoaches focused on local routes, particularly those that ran north and south. But the continued expansion of railroads and the development of the automobile eventually meant the end for stagecoach lines. Today, stagecoaches are relegated to museums, history buffs, parades, and western movies.

Note the thorough braces running under the body of the coach. These created the rocking motion.

54

Wells Fargo & Co.

Many stagecoach companies operated in America in the 1800s, however Wells Fargo is the name most would recognize. Henry Wells was born in Vermont in 1805, the son of a Presbyterian preacher. As a teen, Wells worked as a tanner and shoemaker. In 1824, he visited a speech therapist in New York for help with a severe stuttering problem. Wells was able to use what he learned from the therapist to help others with speech problems, but he never overcame his own stuttering. That didn't stop him from becoming a successful businessman.

William G. Fargo, born in 1818 in New York, was the eldest of twelve children. He began delivering mail at the age of thirteen. In 1841, Henry Wells worked as an express messenger for several bankers and businessmen who trusted him to deliver their money, mail, and various packages between Albany and Buffalo, New York. The route required travel on multiple trains and stagecoaches over three days and four nights.

Wells hired William Fargo, and the two expanded their delivery business into the Midwest. In 1850, Wells, Fargo, and John Butterfield merged to create the American Express Company, the same one known today for its credit cards.

The discovery of gold in California and the migration of settlers westward resulted in an increased demand for timely mail and freight deliveries. Wells and Fargo proposed expanding their services to the Pacific Coast. When American Express rejected the idea, the two men formed their own business, Wells, Fargo & Co.

Miners and businessmen in Oregon and California needed a secure way to transport their treasure. The Wells Fargo stagecoaches carried gold and silver coins, money, and important documents in a green, wooden box under the driver's seat. This treasure box was wrapped with iron

bands and padlocked while traveling. The depot men at the origin and the destination were the only ones with keys to unlock it.

In the final months of the Pony Express, Wells Fargo operated its western end, carrying mail from California to Salt Lake City. Business was booming for the company. In 1866, they bought out several other stagecoach lines. Wells Fargo coaches ran in Colorado, Nebraska, Utah, California, Montana, and Idaho, covering over 3,000 miles of routes

The company was known for its high standard of care for its horses. Each day, drivers were required to inspect their animals for signs of injury as well as to check for and replace worn equipment. Horses received water and sponge baths in hot weather and blankets in cold.

The horses enjoyed the standard hay and oats but also molasses, carrots, and alfalfa. A 1913 edition of the Wells Fargo Messenger declared, "Our horses, wagons, and harness are the pride of Wells Fargo service—our best advertisement."

In 1867, the company placed an order for thirty new coaches with Abbot-Downing & Company, a carriage builder in Concord, New Hampshire. Each stagecoach from the Abbot Company was marked with a number to ensure it was delivered to the right customer. By April 15, 1868, the thirty red and gold coaches were finished and loaded onto fifteen rail cars in Concord. Four additional cars carried spare parts and new sets of horse harness.

Residents of the town gathered to watch the impressive display begin its journey to the West. When the train reached Council Bluffs, Iowa, there was no rail bridge over the Missouri River, so the stagecoaches were ferried across to Omaha, Nebraska.

In Omaha, livestock cars were connected to the train pulling the coaches. The cars carried 150 horses to be added to the Wells Fargo stable. A Union Pacific locomotive hauled everything from there, reaching Cheyenne, Wyoming on April 27, 1868.

Since the transcontinental railroad wouldn't be finished until the following year, Cheyenne was the end of the line. In Cheyenne, the horses were harnessed with their new tack and hitched to the shiny new coaches to continue the work of delivering mail, passengers, and other products to Wells Fargo customers.

The stagecoach business dominated the west for only a few more years. When the transcontinental railroad was completed in 1869, railroads took over many of the stagecoach routes. By September 1869, Wells Fargo had transferred most of their deliveries to rail. They continued to use horse-drawn carriages for shorter distances.

Only three of the thirty Abbot-Downing stagecoaches remain. Initially not recognized as a Wells Fargo coach, stagecoach 251 was displayed for many years at Sutter's Fort Historical Park in Sacramento, California.

As workers began to restore the old coach, the number "251" was found stamped on its frame. Stripping each layer of paint revealed a story from the coach's past. It had been used for a while by a San Francisco livery stable. Before that, it was owned by the Coast Line Stage Company, traveling up and down the California coast. Removing another layer of paint revealed, "Wells, Fargo & Company" in gold letters. After the restoration was complete, coach 251 was displayed at the Wells Fargo Museum in San Diego, California.

| Bridget and Her Treats | Nellie Saves the Day | Shamrock the Great Delivery Horse | Take a Ride Around Town With Al a Wells Fargo Pony |

In 2003, Wells Fargo began offering an annual plush pony to honor the horses that had served Wells Fargo. Bridget, one of the honorees, pulled a Wells Fargo wagon in 1894, delivering mail and packages all around Phoenix, Arizona. The chestnut mare had a flaxen mane and tail and a white star. Her route started at the Alhambra Hotel. Bridget could recognize the Wells Fargo card placed in a building's window and knew to stop there. Hancock's General Store was one of her favorite stops as the clerk always brought her a treat.

Mollie, a beautiful, white mare was part of a Wells Fargo stagecoach team working in Roseburg, Oregon. In 1880, President Rutherford B. Hayes was a passenger in Mollie's coach. The President narrowly missed an encounter with the bandit, Black Bart, who three days earlier had robbed the stagecoach.

55

Black Bart

S tagecoach travel could be dangerous. In addition to racing over narrow, mountain roads, there was the possibility of attack by Native Americans. Butterfield's Overland Mail Company displayed a poster, warning their passengers.

YOU WILL BE TRAVELING THROUGH INDIAN COUNTRY AND THE SAFETY OF YOUR PERSON CANNOT BE VOUCHSAFED BY ANYONE BUT GOD.

One of the greatest dangers was stagecoach robberies. Coaches transporting gold were a popular target for thieves. They were mainly after the treasure box stored under the driver's seat. Gold dust, gold bars, gold coins, legal papers, and other valuables were carried in Wells Fargo's green strong boxes. Fully loaded, the boxes might weigh 100 to 150 pounds.

On some occasions, the mail was also stolen and passengers were robbed. More rarely, the driver or passengers were killed. When mail was stolen, the U.S. government became involved. Wells Fargo hired their own detectives to track down the thieves. Often a guard, known as a shotgun messenger, was hired to sit on top of the coach beside the driver. The 10 or 12-gauge double-barreled shotgun he carried, loaded with buckshot, was intended to discourage robbers. Today, this position next to the driver is referred to as riding shotgun, but that terminology wasn't used until the early 1900s.

A Wisconsin Journal of 1891, describes the effectiveness of the stagecoach guard.

Of all the devices and inventions for the protection of treasure and circumvention of the road agent, the only one that has stood the test of time and experience is a big, ugly-tempered man with a sawed-off shotgun on the box.

One of the most successful stagecoach robbers was known as Black Bart. The name conjures up an image of a notorious scoundrel, however no one would have characterized Charles Boles as an outlaw. Born in Norfolk, England in 1829, the third of ten children, his family immigrated to New York when Charles was two.

In 1849, Charles traveled with two of his brothers to Sacramento, California to prospect for gold. His brothers died there a few years later. Charles returned East and was married in 1854. He fought in a Union regiment during the Civil War, was wounded at the Battle of Vicksburg, and was with Sherman on his March to the Sea in 1864.

After the war, Boles returned to prospecting—this time in Idaho and Montana. In 1871, Boles' wife received a letter, informing her of his intention to exact revenge on the Wells Fargo Company. He'd had an unpleasant encounter with some of their agents—possibly a mining deal gone wrong.

Black Bart's first known robbery was committed on July 26, 1875, when he robbed a stagecoach in Calaveras County, California. Boles wore a flour sack over his head with cut outs for his eyes.

He ordered the driver, John Shine, to "throw down the box."

Then Boles shouted, "If he dares shoot, give him a solid volley, boys."

The driver looked around and saw rifle barrels aimed at him from the nearby bushes. Shine handed over the strong box. One of the women passengers threw out her purse as well.

Boles bowed to the woman and returned her purse. "Madam, I do not wish your money. In that respect I honor only the good office of Wells Fargo."

Boles motioned the driver on. When Shine looked back, he saw the robber attacking the strong box with a hatchet. After Boles had vanished, Shine returned to the area and discovered the additional "robbers" with rifles were only sticks Boles had rigged up in the bushes.

Twice, Boles left hand-written poems in the treasure box after cracking it open and removing the contents.

> *Here I lay me down to sleep*
> *To wait the coming morrow,*
> *Perhaps success, perhaps defeat,*
> *And everlasting sorrow.*
> *Let come what will, I'll try it on,*
> *My condition can't be worse;*
> *And if there's money in that box*
> *'Tis munny in my purse.*

> *—Signed Black Bart the PO8 July 25, 1878, After the robbery of the stagecoach that ran between Quincy and Oroville, California*

Black Bart continued to hold up the stages periodically. Usually the drivers tossed down the boxes when ordered to do so at gunpoint.

On July 13, 1882, George Hackett, driving near Strawberry, California, refused Black Bart's polite request to "Please throw down your strongbox."

Instead, Hackett fired a shot at the thief, wounding Boles on the forehead.

Black Bart's last robbery occurred near the site of his first one. The stage was driven by Reason McConnell. Jimmy Rolleri, a nineteen-year-old passenger got off at one point to hunt along a creek.

As the stage approached the top of a hill, Black Bart stepped out from behind a rock and pointed his shotgun at McConnell. When ordered to throw the strong box down, the driver informed Boles that it was bolted to the floor. McConnell was then ordered to unhitch the team and lead them over the hill.

Boles went to work breaking the strongbox loose, which took a considerable amount of time. By then, Rolleri had caught up with McConnell. The driver grabbed Rolleri's rifle and fired at Boles twice, missing both times. Rolleri took the rifle back and hit Boles with the next shot. Black Bart escaped, but he'd been wounded in the hand. He stashed some of the money and his belongings along the way.

Investigators found a few of the items Boles left behind including his derby hat, eyeglasses, food, flour sacks, a razor, and a handkerchief. This time, Henry Morse, sheriff of Alameda County, California and Wells Fargo detective, James Hume, were determined to track down Black Bart. The handkerchief was a vital piece of evidence. It contained a laundry mark—FX07.

There were ninety-one laundries in San Francisco at the time, but the men finally located the one that used that mark. The laundry operator directed them to Boles who lived in a nearby boarding house, where he presented himself as a mining engineer.

Not surprisingly, the dates of the "engineer's" business trips coincided with the Wells Fargo robberies. Boles confessed to robberies committed before 1879, believing the statute of limitations had run out on them. He was only tried for the final robbery.

Between 1875 and 1883, Boles staged at least twenty-eight robberies, only attacking Wells Fargo coaches. He stole a total of $18,000.

It's said that Boles was afraid of horses, and therefore committed all his robberies on foot. He was intelligent, polite, well-dressed, and became known as a "gentleman robber." Although he always carried a gun, there is no record of Boles ever firing a shot in the robberies.

Boles was convicted and sentenced to six years in San Quentin Prison. He was released for good behavior after serving four years. On his release, he claimed to reporters, "I'm through with crime."

Boles was last seen on February 28, 1888. It's unclear what became of him after that.

56

Young, Skinny Orphans Wanted

Although their riders are portrayed as the heroes, there would have been no Pony Express without the horses. Horse Express doesn't have quite the same ring to it, but most of the four-legged participants were horses rather than ponies. They were on the smaller end, about 14.2 hands tall, weighing approximately 900 pounds. Few details were recorded about most of the riders, and even less is known about the amazing horses they rode.

Gold was discovered in California in 1848. So many settlers flocked to the West that by 1850, California had become a state. The Californians wanted to receive news and mail from the East in a timely manner, especially when rumors began to circulate of a civil war.

Delivery by ship involved either sailing around the tip of South America and up the West Coast or to Panama, where the mail would be transported by mule overland, then back to a ship on the other side and up to California. The ship routes sometimes took as long as six months. Stagecoach delivery was faster, but still averaged a month.

William Russell, Alexander Majors, and William Waddell came up with the idea for the Pony Express to speed the delivery of mail to California. Russell had hoped to receive government funds for the project, but when they were turned down, the men decided to proceed on their own. A 1,966 mile trail was agreed upon for the route, running from St. Joseph, Missouri to Sacramento, California. The goal was to deliver the mail in just ten days.

Four hundred horses were purchased initially, with another hundred or more added as time went on. The owners didn't skimp in this area. An average saddle horse at the time sold for $50, but the Pony Express was willing to pay $150 to $200 for a quality animal. The riders' safety depended on the speed and endurance of their mounts. Some breeds were better suited for certain types of terrain— Morgans and Thoroughbreds for the flatter sections of the trail and Mustangs for the rugged areas.

Advertisements for riders indicated the type of young men they sought.

Approximately eighty riders were hired. The pay was good, however it was a dangerous job. Pony Express riders faced extreme weather and difficult terrain—from dry, barren desert to snowy mountain passes.

The trail crossed land that would become eight states. Missouri and California were the only official states on the route. The rest of the trail area belonged to Native Americans, particularly the Paiute tribe, and they were not happy about the invasion of their land. Riders and station masters faced the threat of attacks by bandits as well as by Native Americans.

During the time the Pony Express operated, one rider was killed by Native Americans. Another died in an accident, and two froze to death. One rider disappeared along his route and was never seen again. His mail pouch was found two years later.

In order to allow the horses to run as fast as possible, weight needed to be kept to a minimum. Lightweight saddles were designed that used less leather and wood. The "skinny, wiry" rider typically weighed about 125 pounds. Another forty pounds was allowed for the saddle, mail bag, and the mail itself. The most weight the horses were expected to carry was 165 pounds.

Alexander Majors presented each rider with a special-edition Bible and required them to sign the following oath.

I, (rider's name), do hereby swear, before the Great and Living God, that during my engagement, and while I am an employee of Russell, Majors, and Waddell, I will, under no circumstances, use profane language, that I will drink no intoxicating liquors, that I will not quarrel or fight with any other employee of the firm, and that in every respect I will conduct myself honestly, be faithful to my duties, and so direct all my acts as to win the confidence of my employers, so help me God.

The riders were issued bright red shirts and blue pants, although most preferred to wear their own clothes. Each also carried a Colt revolver and a horn to signal their approach to the next station.

Relay stations along the route were approximately ten miles apart. Some of the more than 180 stations were previously existing structures, such as military forts, while others were built specifically for the Pony Express.

The first Pony Express riders set out on April 3, 1860. There were always riders traveling in both directions simultaneously—from East to West as well as West to East. The identity of the first rider heading west from St. Joseph, Missouri is disputed. However, many agree it was Johnny Fry, riding a horse named Sylph. The first rider heading east from Sacramento, California was James Randall. The Pony Express goal of delivery in ten days was achieved in that first run.

Each rider typically rode 75 to 100 miles at a speed of approximately ten miles per hour. He switched mounts at each relay station. Fresh horses allowed them to keep up the high speed. Switching horses was expected to take no more than two minutes.

No rider rode the entire route. When he reached a special post, called the home station, he would be replaced by another rider on a fresh horse, essentially forming a giant relay race. The riders slept and ate at their home stations, resting until a rider arrived from the opposite direction. Then, the rested rider would take over and return to the station he started from.

Of course, the most important thing about the Pony Express was the mail. Special attention was given to carrying it. Regular saddle bags were too heavy and awkward. The Pony Express mail pouch was called a mochila *(mochee-yuh, Spanish for pouch)*. The leather mochila was rectangular, shaped much like a modern saddle blanket, except it was placed over, rather than under, the saddle.

Two openings in the mochila were positioned so the horn and cantle of the saddle projected through it. The mochila was held in place by the weight of the rider sitting on it. As long as the rider was mounted, there was no danger of losing the mail bag.

Each corner of the mochila had a cantina or box-shaped, leather compartment. Three of these contained mail that would be delivered to the final stop. The fourth pocket held mail for the next station along the route. Each of the four cantinas were locked with a small padlock. The only people with a key to the three pouches were the station keepers at each end of the route. The workers at the home stations had the key to the fourth pocket.

In May of 1860, Paiute Indians attacked Pony Express stations from Carson City, Nevada, to Salt Lake City, Utah. This was known as the Pyramid Lake War. Mail delivery in that area was suspended for a month. For the 1860 presidential election, extra horses and riders were added, so results could be sent to California as quickly as possible. The West received news of Lincoln's election in just seven days and seventeen hours.

The young Pony Express riders did their work with little fanfare or recognition. No one seemed to realize, at the time, how important the Pony Express was. Little information was recorded about the riders or their horses. And, some accounts, such as Buffalo Bill Cody's were later considered untrue.

Once I spent 24 hours in the saddle carrying the mail 120 miles to Fairfield (Nebraska) with snow two or three feet deep and the mercury around zero. I could tell where the trail lay only by watching the tall weeds on either side and often had to get off and lead my horse. There was no rider to go on at Fort Kearny, so I went on to Fairfield 20 miles away.

—*William Campbell*

—William Campbell

—William Frederick Fisher

Charlie Miller claimed he was eleven years old when he joined the Pony Express. He was known as "Bronco Charlie." At the other end of the age spectrum was forty-five-year-old Howard Egan.

Howard's two sons, Ransom and Richard, were also Express riders. It's reported that Lightning, a mare ridden by eighteen-year-old Richard "Ras" Egan, earned her name by traveling west from Salt Lake City, covering the twenty-two-mile trip to the next relay station in only sixty-five minutes!

Robert Haslam (Pony Bob) was one of the best-known riders. He once rode 120 miles, while wounded, in eight hours and twenty minutes, the fastest ride ever for the Pony Express. On that ride, he carried the text of Abraham Lincoln's Inaugural Address.

Jack Keetley is credited with the longest ride, 340 miles in thirty-one hours without stopping to rest or eat. He was taken from the saddle sound asleep.

Fourteen-year-old Billy Tate who rode a route in the Utah/Nevada area was killed by Paiute Indians in 1860. When Billy's horse showed up at the next station with the mail—but without Billy, a search party was sent out.

Sylph, Lightning, and Ragged Jim are a few of the Pony Express horses whose names are known, but there were hundreds of others who sped over the trail, delivering the mail. By April 1861, the Pony Express was nearly out of money. Wells Fargo assumed operation of the western end of the trail.

Western Union completed the transcontinental telegraph line that October. The instantaneous delivery of telegraph messages brought the Pony Express to a sudden halt. During its nineteen months of operation, 35,000 pieces of mail were delivered. Horse and rider teams had traveled more than half a million miles. Never financially successful, the Pony Express lost $200,000 over the course of its operation.

Although short-lived, the Pony Express served an important role in connecting the East and West at a time when the country was splitting apart over the issues of slavery and states' rights.

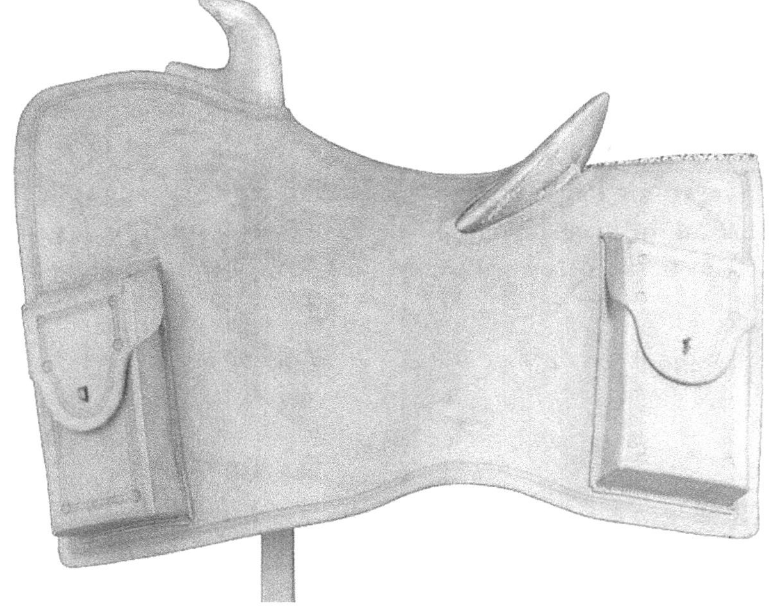

57

Old Bob

In 1819, at the age of ten, one of young Abraham Lincoln's chores was hauling corn to the gristmill where it was ground into flour. The mill was powered by a horse walking in a circle, which turned gears to rotate the large millstones. One day, Lincoln grew more and more impatient with the slow process as he waited for the customers ahead of him to finish. When it was his turn, he hooked his old mare up to the shaft, then hit her with a whip, calling to her to hurry up. As he yelled the words, "Git up" again, the mare kicked out, striking Lincoln in the forehead.

Young Lincoln was knocked down, bleeding and unconscious. A man ran to get Abraham's father, and Thomas Lincoln took his injured son home in a wagon. The boy remained unconscious all night. His father feared Abraham would die, but the boy recovered the following day.

As an adult, Lincoln owned several horses—Tom, Belle, and Old Buck, but his favorite was a chestnut named Robin, also known as "Old Bob." He rode Old Bob during his years as a circuit lawyer.

After winning the presidential election, Lincoln sold Bob to a neighbor, John Flynn. The horse remained in Springfield, Illinois. Fido, the Lincoln's dog, didn't make the trip to Washington either.

Although his sons, Willie and Tad, protested, Lincoln didn't think Fido would do well on the train trip and in Washington. Lincoln gave the dog to two neighbor boys, John and Frank Roll, with a set of stipulations. They were never to scold Fido for entering the house with muddy paws. The dog

wasn't to be tied up alone in the backyard. He was to be allowed into their home whenever he scratched at the front door. The Lincolns gave the Roll family their horsehair sofa to help Fido feel at home.

In Washington, D.C., a new horse was provided for Lincoln's use. Members of the presidential security detail called the horse "Old Abe."

> *He (Lincoln) did not have a saddle horse of his own at all, and when he wished to go out on horseback, as he sometimes did, he would send word to our quarters that when we came, to bring with us a saddle horse for him, and we would rig up one of our Company horses for his use.*
>
> *We had in the Company a long-legged, high-headed horse that was pretty well gaited and fairly well suited for the President's equestrian figure; and because of that horse's tall, angular make-up, the boys called him 'Abe' after the President.*
>
> *Our greatest difficulty was in getting stirrup-straps adjusted for the president. We would let them out to the end hole, and then he would have to kink up his legs to get his feet in the stirrups. When he mounted that horse, with his tall hat extending high in the air, he was indeed an interesting figure. We enjoyed seeing him on his 'high horse,' as we used to say.*
>
> —*Sergeant Smith Stimmel, member of Lincoln's security guard*

In addition to the living quarters at the White House, the Lincolns often stayed in a cottage at the Soldiers' Home which served as a presidential retreat. The complex was built for homeless and disabled soldiers, but also contained several two-story cottages. Although referred to as a "cottage," the two-story home contained thirty-four rooms.

Located three miles from the White House, it offered a little peace and privacy for the family. The Lincolns spent much of their summers at the cottage. The president rode Old Abe back and forth between the Soldiers' Home and the White House, sometimes accompanied by Tad on his pony.

Lincoln described an early assassination attempt experienced on one of those trips.

> *I was jogging along at a slow gait, immersed in deep thought, when suddenly I was aroused—I may say the arousement lifted me out of my saddle as well as out of my wits—by the report of a rifle. Old Abe, with one reckless bound, unceremoniously separated me from my eight-dollar plug-hat, with which I parted company without any assent, expressed or implied, upon my part. At a break-neck speed we soon arrived in a haven of safety.*

The relief felt by many at the surrender of Robert E. Lee and the end of the Civil War was short-lived. On April 14, 1865, Lincoln was assassinated by John Wilkes Booth at Ford's Theatre in Washington, D.C.

On Friday, April 21, the president's funeral train left Washington. After traveling through several Northern states to allow citizens to pay their last respects, the train arrived in Springfield, Illinois on May 3. A team of six black horses with plumes attached to the top of their bridles pulled the hearse.

Behind the hearse came Old Bob, sixteen at the time, with swaying back and round belly. Lincoln's horse was draped in a black mourning blanket trimmed with silver fringe and tassels. He was led by Henry Brown, an African Methodist Episcopal minister. Brown, a former slave, had performed odd jobs for the Lincoln family in the past.

Next, came a carriage carrying Robert Todd Lincoln. Other than Old Bob, Robert was the only immediate family member to travel to the cemetery. After Lincoln's burial, several showmen attempted to purchase Old Bob for exhibition, but John Flynn refused to sell him.

A life-size, bronze statue of Abraham Lincoln and Old Bob was created by Ivan Schwartz. The artist studied a photo of Old Bob to make it as realistic as possible. A Standardbred horse was used as a model for the sculpture which stands at the Soldiers' Home in Washington, D.C.

58

Old Douglas

Jefferson Davis, US Secretary of War under President Franklin Pierce, was a strong proponent of the use of camels to cross the deserts of the American Southwest. Another supporter of this unusual idea, Major Henry Wayne, believed the introduction of camels into the United States would someday be as historic as the importing of horses by the early explorers.

In 1855, the US Congress granted $30,000 for the Camel Corps also known as the Texas Camel Experiment. Davis outfitted a ship, the USS Supply, and Henry Wayne sailed to North Africa to locate camels for the military. Wayne and Lieutenant David Porter purchased thirty-three animals—nineteen females and fourteen males. These included two Bactrian, thirty Dromedary, and one Bactrian/Dromedary cross. They also bought pack saddles for the animals. During the three-month return voyage, one of the males died, but two calves were born. Thirty-four animals landed in Indianola, Texas on March 14, 1856.

Many Texans had never seen camels before and crowded the docks to watch as the strange animals were unloaded. Henry Wayne described the animals' joy at leaving the ship.

On being landed and feeling solid earth beneath them, they became excited to an almost uncontrollable degree, rearing, kicking, crying out, breaking halter, tearing up pickets, and by other fantastic tricks demonstrating their enjoyment of the liberty of the soil.

On a second trip that same year, approximately forty more camels were purchased. Camp Verde, an army facility in Texas became the official camel station with a herd of nearly eighty animals. A large, stone barn was built for them. Early experiments found the camels capable of hauling twice the supplies in less time than mule teams pulling wagons.

They didn't require as much water and were happy to eat plants that horses and mules wouldn't go near. Their

padded feet didn't require shoes and weren't sensitive to the rocky terrain. Camels also lived longer, up to fifty years in captivity.

In the summer of 1857, twenty-five camels successfully completed a 1,200 mile march from Texas to California. Edward Beale, leader of the expedition, reported on the experience.

> *My admiration for the camels increases daily with my experience with them. The harder they are put to the test, the more fully they seem to justify all that can be said of them. They pack water for others four days under a hot sun and never get a drop; they pack heavy burdens of corn and oats for months, and never get a grain; and on bitter grease wood and other worthless shrubs they not only subsist, but keep fat.*

Despite their advantages, the use of camels never took hold in the U.S. Horses and mules tended to panic at the sight or smell of them. Many of the military leaders disliked the camels' temperamental personalities or weren't comfortable working with an animal virtually unknown to them. The beginning of the Civil War drew the attention of the military in a different direction.

In 1861, Confederates captured Camp Verde. Although Jefferson Davis had been instrumental in bringing camels to the U.S., now as president of the Confederacy, he apparently had no time to devise a plan to use the captured animals. A few of the camels were put to work hauling cotton. Others were simply turned loose.

One of the Camp Verde Dromedaries, Douglas, was presented as a gift to Confederate Colonel W. H. Moore. Old Douglas was the only camel used east of the Mississippi River. He was the mascot for the 43rd Mississippi Regiment, which became known as the camel regiment. Despite initially frightening their horses, Douglas became a favorite of the soldiers. He served in battles at Iuka and Corinth as a pack animal, carrying the supplies of the regiment's band.

In June of 1863, Old Douglas was tied inside the Confederate line during the long siege at Vicksburg. When the hungry camel broke loose and wandered out in search of food, he was shot and killed by Union soldiers.

Five thousand Confederate soldiers are buried at the Cedar Hill Cemetery in Vicksburg. Among the tombstones is one honoring Douglas, the "Faithful Patient camel of the 43rd MS Infantry."

The Camel Corps was officially discontinued by Secretary of War Edwin M. Stanton in 1864. Any remaining camels were sold at auction. Most were purchased by circus owners, prospectors, and a few ranchers.

For years, there were occasional sightings of camels in the Southwest desert. In 1885, five-year-old Douglas MacArthur lived at Fort Selden, New Mexico, where his father was the commander. As an adult, General MacArthur recalled a peculiar sight from his childhood at the fort.

> *One day, a curious and frightening animal with a blobbish head, long and curving neck, and shambling legs, moseyed around the garrison.*

The animal young MacArthur had seen was one of the old army camels.

59

The Cavalry

Infantry are soldiers on foot. Calvary are mounted soldiers. Dragoons or mounted infantry are foot soldiers who moved on horseback but dismounted to fight.

In addition to charging the enemy in battle, cavalry soldiers scouted out areas, pursued retreating troops, and raided enemy territory to destroy supplies and communication lines. Initially, Union General Winfield Scott was reluctant to accept cavalry regiments. Certain that the war would be short, Scott didn't believe cavalry would be needed.

But the North was defeated in the first major conflict of the Civil War (The First Battle of Bull Run on July 21, 1861). A Confederate Cavalry regiment, led by J.E.B. Stuart, pursued retreating Union troops to the Potomac River. After Bull Run, Union leaders recognized the importance of the cavalry, and establishing an organized mounted force became a higher priority.

The Battle of Brandy Station, fought on June 9, 1863, involved the largest cavalry forces of the war (17,000 horsemen).

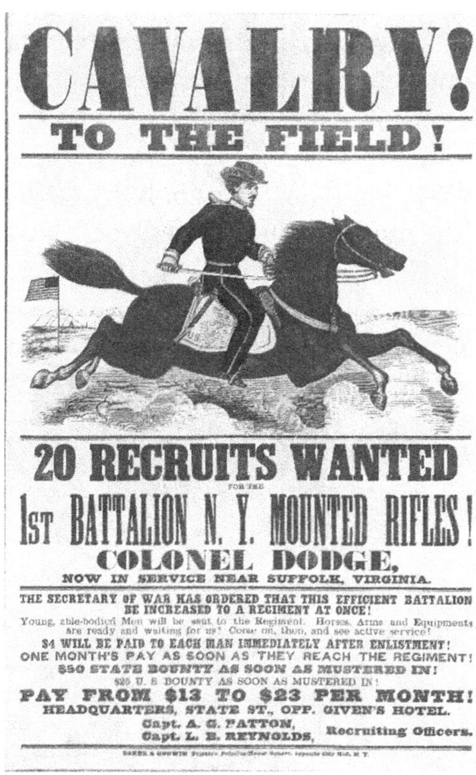

Brandy Station made the Federal cavalry. Up to that time confessedly inferior to the Southern horsemen, they gained on this day that confidence in themselves and in their commanders which enable them to contest so fiercely the subsequent battle-fields.

—*Major Henry B. McClellan*

Naming Cavalry Horses

As many as 10% of the known, named horses from the war included "Old" in their name—perhaps a term of endearment by the soldiers who rode them. Old Bob, Old Billy, Old Dan, Old Joe, and Old Spunk are a few examples. Color were also commonly used, such as Blackie, Blackjack, Black Hawk, Gray Alice, and Gray Eagle.

A mare named "Old Gray" used both naming conventions. The tall mare was an artillery horse with the Cumberland, Ohio Army. Old Gray survived the war and lived a long life, dying at thirty-five in 1893. After the war, thunder and lightning always made Old Gray nervous, apparently a reminder of her battlefield years.

Horses were sometimes named after a place or battlefield. At least three horses were named Chickamauga after that battle. Others included: China, Cincinnati, Decatur, Egypt, and Kentucky.

Using the names of military, political, or historical figures was also common. Six horses were named after the Confederate president, Jefferson Davis. Other examples include Daniel Webster, Don Juan, King Philip, Pocohantas, and Robin Hood.

In terms of common names, some version of Bill or Billy was most frequently used for male horses, while variations of Nelly were popular for mares. Simon was a frequent name for mules. One of the more unusual names was Tom Telegraph, a white stallion ridden by Confederate Turner Ashby.

60

Life in the Cavalry

While encamped, a bugle call alerted the men when it was time to feed and care for their horses. The words associated with this stable call include:

> *Go to the stable, as quick as you're able,*
> *And groom off your horses, and give them some corn;*
> *For if you don't do it the captain will know it,*
> *And then you will rue it, as sure as you're born.*

This call summoned all the drivers in the company to assemble at the grain pile with their pair of canvas nose-bags, where the stable sergeant, so called (his rank was that of a private, though he sometimes put on the airs of a brigadier-general), furnished each with the usual ration of grain, either oats or corn. With this forage, and a curry-comb and brush, they at once proceeded to the picket rope, where, under the inspection of the six sergeants, supervised also by the officer of the day and orderly, the horses were thoroughly groomed. At a given signal, the grooming ceased, and the nose-bags were strapped on. Sometimes the feed was given while the grooming was in progress.

—Billings, John D.. Hardtack & Coffee: The Unwritten Story of Army Life (p. 83)

Some soldiers carried a forage-bag with them as they traveled. It was about a foot wide and three feet long and could hold enough feed for a day or two in case the supply wagons were delayed. These were handmade from grain sacks.

The cavalryman and his horse got very close to each other, not only physically, but also heart to heart. They ate together, slept together, marched, fought and often died together. While the rider slept, the horse cropped the grass around him and got as close up to his rider's body as he could get. The loyal steed pushed the trooper's head gently aside with his nose to get at the grass beneath it.

—Captain George Baylor of the 12th Virginia Cavalry

In an account written several years after the war, cavalryman, Willard Glazier, provides a description of what life as a cavalry soldier was like. Initially, he and his fellow soldiers had no uniforms. Most didn't have horses either.

August 23, 1861: To-day I am happy to make the following entry in my diary, namely: the regiment was furnished with sabres, Colt's revolvers and all the necessary appendages, consisting of belts and ammunition-boxes.

It wasn't until early September that a shipment of horses arrived—not enough for every soldier, but Glazier was one who received a horse that day.

It was my good fortune to be the recipient of a beautiful black mare, only five years old, full of life and fiery metal, fourteen hands high, and weighing ten hundred pounds. She was a gem for the cavalry service, or any thing else, and a friendship was to grow up between us worthy of historic mention.

The loud noise of a bugle was something the horses, as well as the men, had to become accustomed to.

All our movements are now ordered by the bugle. By its blast we are called to our breakfast, dinner and supper. Roll-call is sounded twice a day, and the companies fall into line… By the bugle we are summoned to inspections, to camp-guard, to the feeding and watering of our horses and to drill.

When all the soldiers received their horses, many hours at the camp were spent on mounted drills.

At first we had some exciting times with our young and untrained horses. One of our men received a kick from his horse which proved fatal to his life. Several of our wildest and seemingly incorrigible ones we

Glazier relates one instance where the horses provided an interesting escape for soldiers trapped at a river.

A small force of our infantry and cavalry were surrounded by the enemy on the south bank of the Shenandoah River, which was so high as to be unfordable. As a last resort the cavalrymen plunged into the stream, swimming their horses, and towing across the infantrymen, who clung to the animals' tails!

After exhausting days on horseback, some soldiers fell asleep in the saddle.

Others slept in their saddles, either leaning forward on the pommel of the saddle, or on the roll of coat and blanket, or sitting quite erect, with an occasional bow forward or to the right or left, like the swaying of a flag on a signal station, or like the careenings of a drunken man.

The horse of such a sleeping man will seldom leave his place in the column, though this will sometimes occur, and the man awakes at last to find himself alone with his horse which is grazing along some unknown field or woods.

Glazier lost his black mare in March of 1863 to overwork, exhaustion, and a disease called scratches.

By this cause [scratches] and through hard work my little black mare, which I drew by lot at Camp Sussex in the autumn of 1861, has at last succumbed, and, with a grief akin to that which is felt at the loss of a dear human friend, I have performed the last rite of honor to the dead. The Indian may love his faithful dog, but his attachments cannot surpass the cavalryman's for his

Glazier was assigned a new horse, another black one, but his new gelding was not as well-behaved as the mare had been.

Willard Glazier was captured in October of 1863 and spent a year in a Confederate prisoner of war camp.

Walter G. Jones, a private in the 8th New York Cavalry, was saved twice when bullets shot at him hit the Bible he carried in his shirt pocket. The first incident occurred at Cedar Creek, Virginia, October 19, 1864, and the second at the Battle of Appomatox in April, 1865.

Coffee wasn't a popular beverage in America until the Boston Tea Party in 1773. After that, it became patriotic to drink coffee rather than tea. Coffee was welcomed by Civil War soldiers for the energy boost it gave them.

Confederate soldiers didn't often have access to coffee. Instead, they made due with concoctions derived from acorns, beans, chicory, dandelion roots, rye, or other substitutes. Union soldiers received a ration of coffee beans, which they had to grind, often by smashing the beans against a rock with the butt of a rifle. Lt. Col. Walter King, a cavalry officer, developed a grinding mill that could be incorporated into the stock of a Sharps rifle. The plan was for one man in each cavalry unit to have one of these guns, and he would grind coffee for the rest of the men. The gun coffee grinder was never widely adopted, although apparently up to 100 were made.

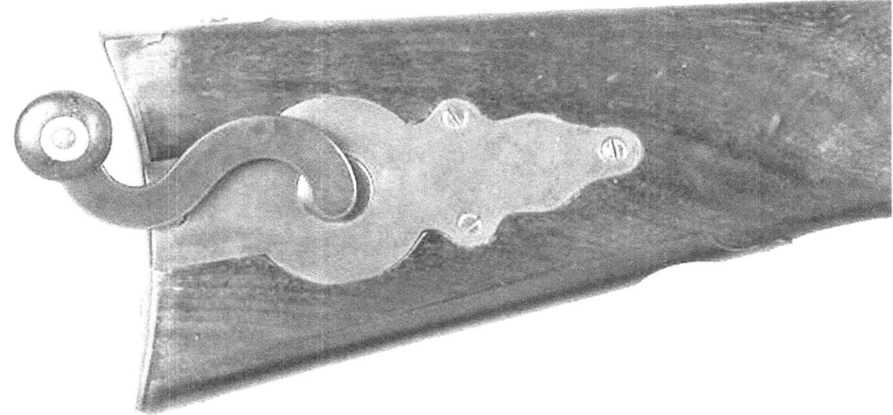

After the First Battle of Bull Run, the United States Christian Commission (USCC) was formed to provide supplies, medical services, and Christian literature to Union soldiers during the war. Initially, women weren't allowed in the Commission, but when that changed, author Louisa May Alcott became one of the volunteers.

When Union armies were encamped, the Christian Commission provided coffee brewed on a large scale through the use of coffee wagons. The wagons, invented by Jacob Dunton, were modified artillery caissons with the ammunition chest used to store coffee beans and grinders.

Each horse-drawn coffee wagon contained three thirty-five gallon, wood-fired chambers that could brew up to 105 gallons of coffee and hot chocolate per hour.

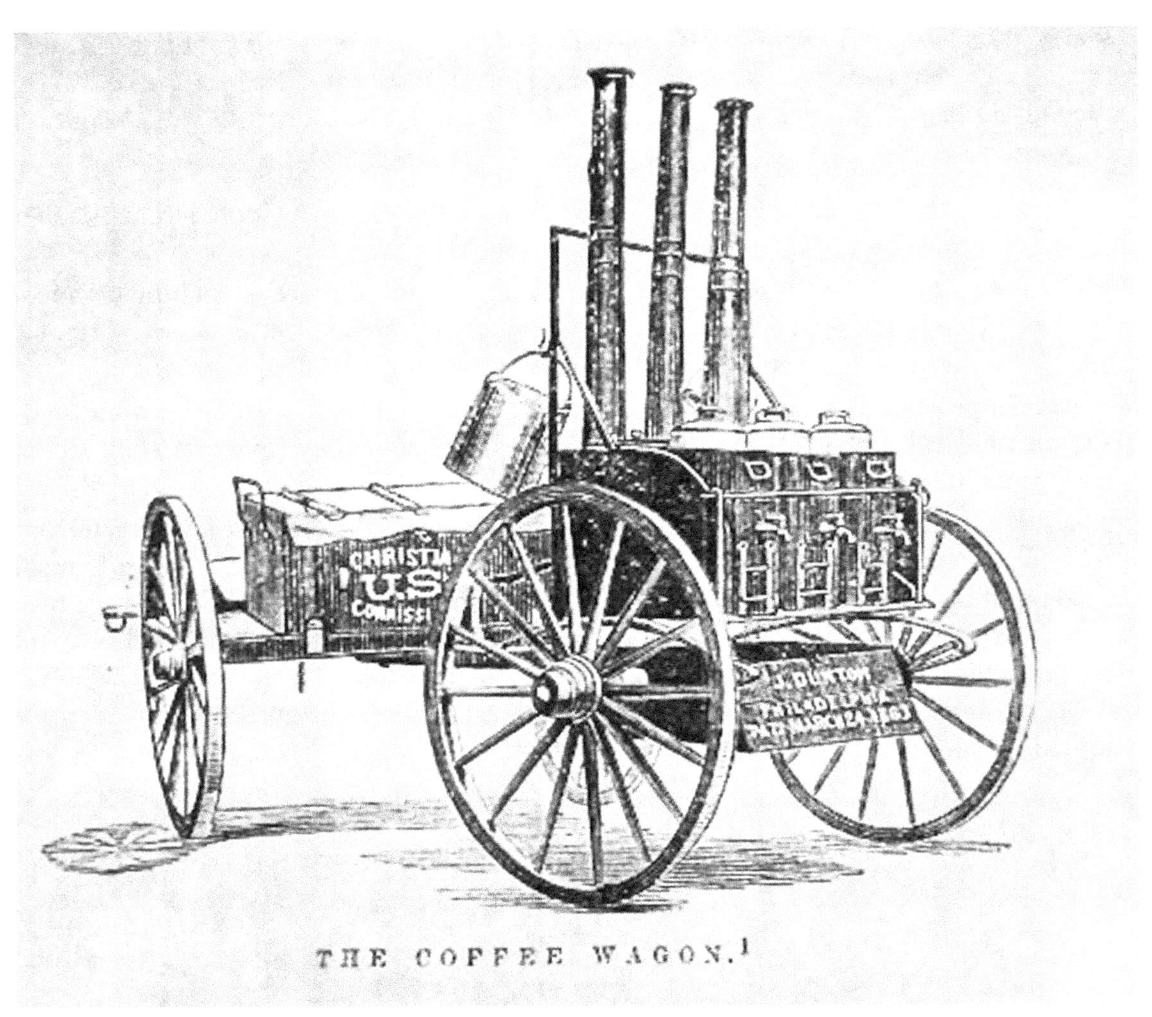

THE COFFEE WAGON.[1]

61

Millions of Brave War Horses

Horse lovers would be sad to learn that three million horses were used in the Civil War, and over half of them didn't survive. But those horses served alongside men. 620,000 soldiers also died in combat or from disease. More Americans died in the Civil War than any other.

War at the best, is terrible, and this war of ours, in its magnitude and in its duration, is one of the most terrible.

—*Abraham Lincoln, 1864*

At the start of the Civil War, the northern states had roughly twice as many horses as the South (3.4 to 1.7 million). There were another 800,000 horses in the border states of Missouri and Kentucky. However, many of the northern horses were used primarily for farming and pulling carriages or wagons. Many Northerners preferred carriages and horse-drawn streetcars for transportation rather than riding horseback.

A lack of good roads in the South meant it was more common for people to ride rather than drive horses. As a result, the average southern man had better horsemanship skills than those in the North.

Early on, the Union Cavalry commanders didn't test new recruits to tell what level, if any, of horsemanship skills the men possessed. At the start of the war, over half the U.S. Cavalry officers (104 out of 176) chose to fight for the Confederacy. In 1861, the Southern Cavalry was superior in nearly every way—the quality of horses, riding ability, and leadership skills of the officers.

A Civil War cavalry regiment consisted of ten to twelve troops (or companies) each containing one hundred men, their horses, and various officers. Each regiment was commanded by a Colonel. Farriers, veterinarians, and equipment and transportation specialists were some of the non-fighting roles each regiment required. Two to six regiments could be combined to form a brigade. Brigades might unite into a division and combined divisions were known as a corps.

Southern cavalrymen had to provide their own mounts. If a Confederate soldier's horse was sick, injured, or killed, the soldier was permitted to return home to find a replacement at his own expense. If he wasn't back with his unit within sixty days with a new horse, he was forced to leave the cavalry to serve as an infantryman.

This is one area where the Union Cavalry had at least a financial advantage. Horses were usually purchased by the Union Army, although a few companies provided their own.

It was the job of the Quartermaster Department to keep the Union Army supplied, including the horses needed for both artillery and cavalry. For a time, this responsibility was assumed by a newly created Cavalry Bureau, but it was later resumed by the Quartermaster. The Union Army had six facilities devoted to the purchase, training, and distribution of military horses. These were called remount depots.

Government contracts were awarded to dealers to obtain suitable animals. Guidelines for Union Army horses included:

- at least 15 hands tall

- minimum weight of 950 pounds

- between 4 and 10 years old

- well-broke to saddle and bridle

- free from defects such as shallow breathing, deformed hooves, spavin, or ringbone

- dark colors preferred

- geldings preferred

Horses for military use were supposed to be inspected before purchase, however corruption was rampant in the system. Some dealers bought old, diseased, blind, or wild horses at extremely low prices then charged the government the full price for each animal. The dealer pocketed the difference—after perhaps paying a corrupt inspector his share. These substandard horses found their way into the cavalry, bringing a whole host of problems with them.

Thoroughbreds were the most common type of cavalry horse.

Morgans, known for their strength, endurance, and courage were also popular. Sheridan's horse, Rienzi, and Stonewall Jackson's, Little Sorrel, were both Morgans. A few Arabians and Indian horses were used also. The "Indian horses" probably came from the Mustang herds in the West.

Initially, the horses were sorted by color, so each regiment would have a similar look, however with the high turnover of horses, that color coding couldn't always be maintained.

The price of a cavalry horse varied over the duration of the war. In 1861, the highest price the government would pay was $119. Toward the end of the war, when horses were scarce, some sold for as much as $3,000. Lincoln once said, "I can make more generals, but horses cost money."

Veterinary services were added into the remount depots in order to rehabilitate horses. Whenever possible, ill, injured, or exhausted horses were sent there for medical care and rest until the animals were healthy enough to return to battle.

The largest remount depot was Giesboro Point in Maryland, near Washington, D.C. The Army purchased the 624-acre property from George Washington Young, the area's largest slave owner. With thirty-two stables, Giesboro could hold 30,000 horses, although the largest number at any given time was 21,000. It's estimated 200,000 horses went in and out of this depot over the course of the war. Each fifteen-acre corral held 1,000 horses.

The facility had a staff of 1500, including 100 farriers. Giesboro included a veterinary hospital with 2,500 stalls. Cavalry soldiers waiting for a new mount stayed at Camp Stoneman adjacent to the Giesboro Depot.

The high military demand for horses and mules meant a shortage of work horses for those who relied on them to make a living, such as farmers. This became more of a problem, especially in the South, as the conflict wore on. Both armies confiscated any horses they could find. Families hid their horses in swamps, caves, mines, and sometimes even in the cellar when they knew troops were in the area.

Care & Feeding

War horses were subjected to long, strenuous marches. The recommended daily feed for each horse was fourteen pounds of hay and twelve pounds of grain. In addition to food, the horses needed shoes. In the North, supplies were carried by rail or ship as close to the army locations as possible, then supply wagons pulled by teams of horses or mules hauled the provisions the rest of the way.

The horses rarely received full rations, particularly toward the end of the war. To improve care for the animals, Congress created the rank of veterinary sergeant in 1863, but few qualified men were

available to fill the role. Malnutrition made the animals susceptible to disease. More horses died from disease, exhaustion, and starvation during the war than were killed in battle.

> *Every opportunity at a halt during a march should be taken advantage of to cut grass, wheat, or oats and extraordinary care should be taken of the horses upon which everything depends.*
>
> —*William T. Sherman*

McClellan's Contribution to the Cavalry

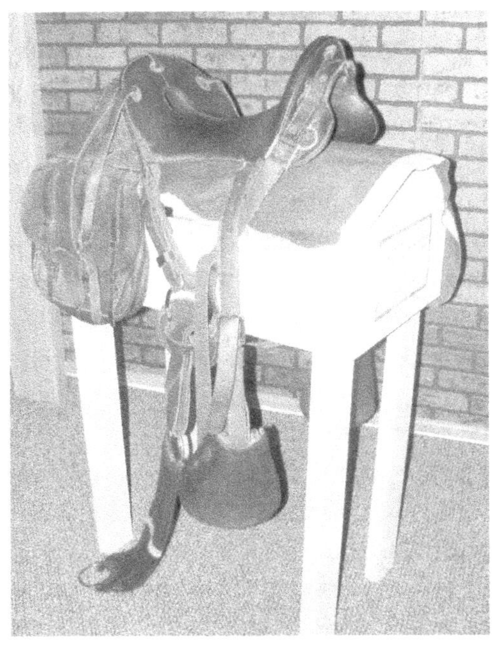

In November of 1861, Union General Winfield Scott retired. Scott had been reluctant to use cavalry as he assumed the war would be short. Lincoln appointed George B. McClellan to replace Scott. The president quickly grew dissatisfied with McClellan's lack of action, and he was removed from command several months later.

Although a failure as a general, McClellan left a lasting contribution to the cavalry. In 1859, he had designed a saddle that was adopted for use by the Army. The saddle was light, so it didn't add unnecessary weight, but was strong and sturdy enough to provide support for the rider. The seat had an open design and was covered with rawhide or leather. It also had wooden stirrups, and a wool girth strap. Optional accessories included a nose bag for horse feed, curry comb, picket pin and rope for picketing the horse, saddlebag, and a holder for a rifle or carbine. McClellan saddles were used throughout the war.

Other Equine Roles

Saddle horses were used by messengers to convey information between military leaders. At the start of the war, the postal system in the North halted mail service to recipients in the Confederate states. But mail continued to be delivered by horse-drawn wagons to Union soldiers throughout the war. Letters sent from soldiers didn't require stamps. The Confederacy established its own postal system in 1861.

Reception was most reliable when soldiers were encamped at the same location for an extended time. This was one of the easiest jobs for a Civil War horse. Between battles, the soldiers longed for letters from their family and friends back home.

Newton Scott, from Iowa, wrote to his childhood friend, Hannah Cone, throughout the war. An excerpt from one of those letters, written shortly after Christmas, 1864 reads,

222

The war letters created a bond between Newton and Hannah, and they married in 1866.

Mules weren't typically used in cavalry, but teams of four to six mules were popular for pulling supply wagons. The Union Army used about one million mules in the war. The best source of mules at the time was Kentucky.

The wagons pulled by the mules were filled with vital provisions—food, clothing, medicine, and ammunition. Supply trains were the lifeline of the army. Feed for the thousands of horses comprised a large percentage of the space in the supply wagons.

Railroads moved troops and provisions, but trains were limited in terms of their reach. The supply wagons were the link from the railroads to the troops. Thirty supply wagons were required for every 1,000 men.

My train now comprises 103 army waggons and eleven ambulances, and 781 horses and mules; the grand total of carriages of all sorts is 225, which when on the march, allowing fifteen yards to each, will cover just about two miles of road.

—Colonel Charles Wainwright

It has often been said that the South could not have been worsted in the Rebellion had it not been for the steady re-enforcement brought to the Union side by the mule. To just what extent his services hastened the desired end, it would be impossible to compute; but it is admitted by both parties to the war that they were invaluable.

—Billings, John D.. Hardtack & Coffee: The Unwritten Story of Army Life (p. 142)

Billings describes the suitability of mules for draft animals rather than in battle.

The horse was good for any kind of service, as a beast of burden, up to the limits of his endurance. Not so his half-brother the mule. The latter was more particular as to the kind of service he performed.

—Billings, John D.. Hardtack & Coffee: The Unwritten Story of Army Life (p. 143)

Artillery horses had one of the worst jobs of the war, hauling heavy field guns into place. The average life of an artillery horse was just seven months. The horses or mules that hauled supplies or artillery were frequent targets of the opposing army, since cutting off weapons, ammunition, and supplies was an effective strategy for weakening or stopping the enemy.

Approximately 30,000 horses were used in the war by medical personnel. Two types of ambulances were used on the

224

battle fields—a two-wheeled cart pulled be a single horse and a four-wheeled one pulled by a team of four horses.

A sutler was a peddler or merchant who followed the army and sold goods to soldiers—items such as clothing, tobacco, coffee, flour, and sugar. Sutler pies could be purchased for twenty-five cents a piece. According to one soldier the pies were "moist and indigestible below, tough and indestructible above, with untold horrors within."

Photography was invented in the early 1800s. Over the following decades, improvements continued to be made to cameras and image processing. The Civil War was one of the first to be captured in photos. The best-known photographer of the war was Mathew Brady, an Irish immigrant.

Horses pulled the photographer's darkroom on wheels, carrying cameras, the glass plates that served as negatives, the processing chemicals, and a light-proof tent. The wagon looked so unusual, most who encountered it for the first time asked, "What is it?" These horse-drawn mobile darkrooms became known as "What's-it wagons."

Matthew Brady spent $100,000 of his own money over the course of the war and died penniless in 1896. In 1940, his Civil War images became part of the National Archives. Brady photographed Abraham Lincoln as well as other presidents and Union officers. Brady's photographs were used on the five-dollar bill and the Lincoln penny.

After the War

Confederate soldiers and many of the Union troops were allowed to keep their horses to use for farming or other work. Fifty thousand surplus horses from the Union Army were sold at public auctions held at the Giesboro Remount Depot.

Tens of thousands of them have fallen and died and gone to the eternal pastures of the horse heaven that we trust is in reserve for all good, loyal horses and mules that have discharged their burdens and duty in this world.

—*The Richmond Examiner*

In response to the Examiner article, General Robert E. Lee stated, "Eternal pastures—a horse heaven? I wonder. I would like to believe there are such. Poor creatures! They suffered and died in our service."

A statue honoring the horses and mules that served during the Civil War stands outside the Virginia Historical Society in Richmond. Copies of the statue are found in Middleburg, Virginia and Fort Riley, Kansas.

The monument is inscribed with these words:

In memory of the one and one
half million horses and mules
of the Union and Confederate
armies who were killed, were
wounded, or died from disease in the Civil War.

62

Military Mishaps

Although the horses were trained with rattling pans, firecrackers, and gunshots in order to prepare them for war, some never became accustomed to the noise and chaos of battle. Most horses run when they are frightened. Although it often works for self preservation in the wild, running in fear is dangerous on the battle field. A horse bolting toward the rear, at best might make his owner appear to be a coward. At worst, he could cause other soldiers to follow in a panic. A horse bolting in the other direction—toward the enemy line—would put his rider in danger of being killed.

Sam Watkins of Company H described a runaway mule.

> *One fellow, a courier, who had had his horse killed, got on a mule he had captured, and in the last charge, before the final and fatal halt was made, just charged right ahead by his lone self, and the soldiers said "Just look at that brave man, charging right in the jaws of death." He began to seesaw the mule and grit his teeth, and finally yelled out, "It arn't me, boys, it's this blarsted old mule. Whoa! Whoa!"*
>
> —Sam Watkins, Battle of Shiloh, Co. Aytch, 1882

John Billings relates the experience of a cook with another contrary mule.

> *On the road to Harper's Ferry, after the Antietam campaign in 1862, the colored cook of the headquarters of the Sixtieth New York Regiment picked up a large and respectable looking mule, to whom, with a cook's usual foresight and ambition, he attached all the paraphernalia of the*

cook-house together with his own personal belongings, and settled himself down proudly on his back among them.

All went on serenely for a time, the mule apparently accepting the situation with composure, until the Potomac was reached at Harper's Ferry. On arriving in the middle of the pontoon bridge upon which the army was crossing, from some unexplained reason, perhaps because, on looking into the water, he saw himself as others saw him—the mule lifted up his voice in one of those soul-harrowing brays, for which he is famous—or infamous—and, lifting his hind legs aloft, in the next moment tossed his entire burden of cook and cook-house into the river, where, weighted down with mess-kettles and other utensils of his craft, the cook must have drowned had not members of the regiment come to his rescue.

Not at all daunted by this experience, the cookey harnessed the mule again as before, led him across the remaining portion of the bridge, where he remounted and settled himself among his household goods once more, where all was well till the Shenandoah was reached. Here, with another premonitory blast of his nasal trumpet, the mule once more dumped his load into the rapid rolling river, when the cook lost all confidence in mules as beasts of burden, and abandoned him.

—Billings, John D.. *Hardtack & Coffee: The Unwritten Story of Army Life* (pp. 145-146)

At Gettysburg, Union General George Meade rode a borrowed horse, Bill, for an inspection of his troops. A shot was fired at the general.

The great ball went high and harmlessly struck the ground beyond. But the whizzing missile had frightened the charger of General Meade into an uncontrollable frenzy. He reared, he plunged. He could not be quieted. Nothing was possible to be done with such a beast except to let him run; and run he would, and run he did. The staff straggled after him; and so General Meade, against his own will, as I then believed and afterwards ascertained to be the fact, was apparently ingloriously and involuntarily carried from the front at the formal opening of the furious engagement of July 2, 1863.

—Major Henry Tremain, 1905

Even though he was considered one of the best horseman of the Civil War, Ulysses S. Grant was thrown from a horse on September 4, 1863 in New Orleans. The general was returning from a meeting, riding a horse that wasn't his own. When a locomotive blew its whistle, the horse shied and fell, injuring Grant's leg and rendering him unconscious. A witness of the incident, General Lorenzo Thomas, wrote that Grant's horse "threw him over with great violence."

The General, who is a splendid rider, maintained his seat in the saddle, and the horse fell upon him. Grant was carried to a nearby inn, where he regained consciousness, but it was many weeks before he had full use of his leg again.

On February 19, 1864, Confederate General William Edwin Baldwin was killed when a stirrup broke, causing him to fall off his horse near the Dog River in Alabama.

Fortunately, nothing bad happened, but this case could have turned into a disaster. Colonel Charles Marshall was an aide to General Robert E. Lee and fought alongside him for the Confederacy. When Marshall's horse was killed in battle, he received a new mount (name unknown).

The following day, the colonel started off with his new horse toward the battlefield. As they crossed an area that contained numerous tree stumps, guns and cannons began to roar. The air was soon filled with smoke.

Before Colonel Marshall knew what was happening, the horse leaped on top of one of the stumps. With all four feet on the stump, the animal pranced in a circle. As the intensity of the battle increased, Marshall's fear grew. All the while, his horse continued the strange dance, completely ignoring the colonel's commands to move on.

When a lull in the fighting occurred, Marshall convinced the horse to step down from the stump, and the two continued on their way. According to Colonel Marshall, "It was not until afterward that I found the horse had belonged to a circus and had been trained to do this act amid the firing of cannon."

—The Saturday Evening Post, Vol. 173

Colonel Marshall never rode the horse in battle again.

The life of Walter G. Jones, a private in the 8th New York Cavalry, was saved twice when bullets aimed at him hit the Bible he carried in his shirt pocket. The first incident occurred at Cedar Creek, Virginia, October 19, 1864, and the second at the Battle of Appomatox in April, 1865.

In 1861, Wilmer McLean's farm near Manassas, Virginia was the site of the First Battle of Bull Run. In fact, a cannonball dropped through the kitchen fireplace of his home. Wanting to avoid the war, the retired McLean and his wife moved to Appomattox, Virginia.

But, McLean hadn't gotten away from the war after all. General Robert E. Lee surrendered to Ulysses S. Grant in McLean's house in Appomattox. McLean later said, "The war began in my front yard and ended in my front parlor."

Despite McLean's protests, members of the Union Army took furniture and other possessions from his Appomattox home as souvenirs of the surrender. Major General Philip Sheridan took the table on which Grant had written the terms of the surrender. Sheridan paid the equivalent of $327 for it and had George Armstrong Custer carry it away on his horse.

Union Horses

Although millions of horses served in the Civil War, many losing their lives, they were never rewarded for that service, and most are unknown today. Particularly anonymous are the thousands of artillery horses and the teams who pulled the supply wagons that kept the armies running. Of the relatively few horses that are remembered, most were cavalry mounts or the saddle horses of officers. Even for those, few details were recorded.

When he was born, Ulysses Grant went unnamed for several weeks until the name Ulysses was selected by drawing names from a hat. Ulysses grew up around horses. Early on, Grant's father recognized his son's unique ability with them. It's said that at age five, Ulysses could ride standing on the back of a trotting horse. He purchased his first horse at the age of nine and was training horses for others before reaching his teens.

Ulysses entered West Point Military Academy at seventeen. A mix up on his paperwork listed his name as Ulysses S. Grant rather than his birth name, Hiram Ulysses Grant. He adopted this new variation from then on.

At West Point, Grant and a horse named York set a high-jump record that stood at the school for twenty-five years. Despite being an excellent horseman, after graduation, Grant was assigned to the infantry rather than the cavalry. President Lincoln went through several generals before he gave command of the Union Army to Ulysses S. Grant.

When Grant is mentioned, the horse that comes to mind is Cincinnati. However, Grant's first Civil War horse was Jack, a cream-colored stallion purchased from an Illinois farmer. Jack served with Grant until 1863, then the eleven-year-old horse was donated to the Sanitary Fair in Chicago where he was auctioned for $4,000 (equal to $200,000 today).

Grant rode Fox, a spirited roan, in the battles of Fort Donelson and Shiloh. General Grant adopted a starving, raw-boned Thoroughbred found abandoned on the Shiloh battlefield. The horse was called Kangaroo because of his awkward appearance. When given feed, care, and time to rest, Kangaroo proved to be a fine mount that Grant rode at Vicksburg.

During the Siege of Vicksburg, a raiding party captured a large, black pony from the plantation of Joe Davis (brother of the Confederate president). The animal was known to kick and bite, but he had a very smooth gait. Grant purchased the pony, naming him Jeff Davis or Little Jeff. He rode Little Jeff often to check on his troops. Grant claimed the pony had incredible endurance.

> *This animal exceeds any horse-flesh I ever saw for endurance. I have taken this horse out at daylight and kept in the saddle till dark, and he came in as fresh when I returned as when I saddled him in the morning. Gold could not buy him.*
>
> *—Ulysses S. Grant*

When asked if he would trade Little Jeff for the Confederate president, Grant replied, "I would exchange it for the rebel chief, but for nothing else under heaven."

Grant kept Little Jeff after the war, giving him a home until the pony died.

In 1863, when a man named S.S. Grant became ill, he wanted General U.S. Grant to have the horse he considered the finest in the world.

> *The name excited my father's curiosity and he called at the hotel to meet the gentleman who told him that he had, he thought, the finest horse in the world, and knowing General Grant's great liking for horses he had concluded, inasmuch as he would never be able to ride again, that he would like to give his horse to him; that he desired that the horse should have a good home and tender care and that the only condition that he would make in parting with him would be that the person receiving him would see that he was never ill-treated and should never fall into the hands of a person that would ill-treat him. This promise was given and General Grant accepted the horse and called him 'Cincinnati.'*
>
> *—Frederick Grant, Ulysses' son*

The 17-hand chestnut was a son of Lexington, the fastest four-mile Thoroughbred in the United States. Grant named the horse Cincinnati, after the Ohio city.

In 1864, people in Illinois found a beautiful horse they sent to Grant. The horse was named Egypt since he came from an area of the state known by that name.

Egypt was a great horse, but was overshadowed by Cincinnati, the animal that became Grant's favorite mount. The General considered Lincoln to be a skilled horsemen, so the president was one of the few people permitted to ride Cincinnati.

> *Lincoln spent the latter days of his life with me. He came to City Point in the last month of the war and was with me all the time. He was a fine horseman and rode my horse Cincinnati every day.*
>
> *—Ulysses S. Grant*

Cincinnati was the horse Grant rode to Appomattox Court House where Robert E. Lee surrendered. It's possible that while there, Grant's Cincinnati met Robert E. Lee's horse, Traveller.

Grant was once offered $10,000 for Cincinnati, but he refused the offer. When elected president, Cincinnati traveled with Grant to Washington where he lived in the White House stable. When he became too old, Cincinnati was moved to the Maryland farm of Grant's friend, Admiral Daniel Ammen. The great horse spent his last days there, dying in 1878.

Rutherford B. Hayes

Old Whitey was owned by Rutherford B. Hayes who later became the nineteenth president. (Not to be confused with Zachary Taylor's Old Whitey) Whitey was reported to have survived anywhere from nineteen to thirty Civil War battles. After the war, he enjoyed a well-deserved retirement. When Hayes ran for president in 1876, the Cleveland Leader newspaper accused Hayes of stirring up hostility toward the South by keeping the old war horse.

But Old Whitey didn't seem to have a preference for the North or South. Apparently, the people weren't offended by Old Whitey either, since Hayes won the election. After Old Whitey's death in 1879, at the age of twenty-nine, the Fremont Journal (Ohio), provided the following details about the Civil War horse.

Too spirited to pull supply wagons, Old Whitey found his place as the personal mount of Hayes' friend and aide, Major Russell Hastings. In battle after battle, the big white horse proved himself fearless under fire. His speed, stamina, and ability to clear any fence or creek were legendary among the soldiers of the 23rd Ohio.

Only his color prevented Old Whitey from becoming the perfect war horse. Time and again, the big, white steed became the target of enemy sharp shooters. Somehow horse and rider always managed to escape unharmed. But their luck ran out at the Battle of Opequan, when a Rebel bullet found its mark, shattering Major Hastings' right leg. Unscathed, Old Whitey carried his badly wounded rider to the rear.

From that day forward, Old Whitey resided at Hayes' headquarters, receiving special treatment from the entire regiment. At war's end, surrendering Rebels asked about the "big white horse." When Hayes proudly produced him, Old Whitey immediately became the "hero of the moment." Admiring Confederates gathered about the gallant steed, swearing they had fired at him "ten thousand times!"

The brave war horse was buried at Hayes' farm, Spiegel Grove, with a grave marker reading, "Old Whitey A Hero of Nineteen Battles 1861-1865."

General George B. McClellan

General McClellan's favorite horse was a 17-hand, dark bay named Daniel Webster. His staff called the horse Devil Dan, because he was so fast it was difficult to keep up with him. McClellan rode Daniel Webster in the battle of Antietam.

No soldier ever had a better horse than I had in Daniel Webster.

—George B. McClellan

When McClellan retired, he took Dan with him to the family farm in Orange, New Jersey. Dan died there at the age of twenty-three. McClellan also had a black horse, Burns, named for an army friend who'd given him the animal.

Burns was a good horse—as long as he was ridden early in the day. When it came close to evening, Burns became obsessed with thoughts of his dinner and would bolt in whatever direction he thought the meal would be served.

General George Meade

It's believed Old Baldy came from out West. The chestnut with a white face was used in the First Battle of Bull Run by General Hunter. Wounded twice in that battle, Hunter turned the horse back in to the Quartermaster Department.

Later in 1861, the horse recovered, and General Meade acquired him. Meade called him Old Baldy. Although Meade isn't as well known as Ulysses Grant, General George Meade was vital to the success of the Union Army. Meade led the force that defeated Robert E. Lee at the Battle of Gettysburg—considered the turning point of the Civil War. Meade's leadership was instrumental in many other battles as well.

Old Baldy was left for dead after being wounded in the neck at Antietam. He recovered, but was shot in the chest at Gettysburg. Then, he was shot in the ribs at Petersburg. After being wounded again in the 1864 Battle of Weldon Railroad, Meade retired Old Baldy to his farm in Pennsylvania.

Various accounts exist as to the number of times Old Baldy was wounded. Some indicate as many as fourteen times, but the horse's story has a happy ending; he survived every shot.

The horse outlived the general by ten years. Meade died in 1872; Old Baldy in 1882. After his death, Old Baldy's head was stuffed and mounted. It's now on display at the Civil War Museum in Philadelphia, Pennsylvania.

General Philip H. Sheridan

While stationed at Rienzi, Mississippi in 1862, General Philip Sheridan was given a three-year-old Morgan. The horse was a descendant of Black Hawk, a son of the foundation sire Figure or Justin Morgan.

He was named Rienzi after the town. Rienzi was tall for a Morgan at 16 hands. He was jet-black with three white fetlocks and a small star. Sheridan and Rienzi participated in a large number of

battles: Perryville, Stones River, Chickamauga, the Wilderness, Yellow Tavern, and Cold Harbor. Rienzi received superficial wounds several times. General Sheridan said of Rienzi.

I could at any time control him by a firm hand and a few words, and he was as cool and quiet under fire as one of my soldiers. I doubt if his superior as a horse for field service was ever ridden by any one.

It was the Battle at Cedar Creek in Virginia that made Rienzi a celebrity. Confederate General Jubal Early led a surprise attack against the Union Army on the morning of October 19th, 1864. General Sheridan was in Winchester, Virginia. When he received word of the battle, Sheridan had Rienzi saddled.

The general raced toward Cedar Creek on Rienzi, along with a 300-man cavalry escort. On the way, they met Union troops retreating from the battle. Sheridan rallied them, and the soldiers turned around to resume the fight.

When Sheridan arrived at Cedar Creek, the sight of their general on his splendid horse renewed the courage of the Union soldiers. By nightfall, it was the Confederates who were in retreat.

Thomas Buchanan Read wrote a poem about the Union victory, "Sheridan's Ride." A portion follows:

Hurrah! hurrah for Sheridan!
Hurrah! hurrah for horse and man!
And when their statues are placed on high
Under the dome of the Union sky,
The American soldier's Temple of Fame,
There, with the glorious general's name,
Be it said, in letters both bold and bright:
Here is the steed that saved the day
By carrying Sheridan into the fight,
From Winchester—twenty miles away!

In honor of his role in the victory, Rienzi's name was changed to Winchester, the town from which Sheridan began his ride. Sheridan and Winchester also participated in the Battle of Appomattox Courthouse, when Confederate General Robert E. Lee surrendered.

After the war, Winchester went to Sheridan's home in Chicago. When the horse died in October, 1878, Sheridan had him preserved. He was on display at a museum in New York until 1922, fitted with Sheridan's saddle, bridle, and blanket. Later, Winchester was moved to the Smithsonian National Museum.

General William T. Sherman

Early in the war, Sherman was given command of the Union Army in the West. Later, he and a company of 60,000 men made the March to the Sea. Marching from Atlanta to Savannah, Georgia, the men cut Confederate supply lines and left a swath of destruction behind them intended to render the Confederacy unable to continue the war. During the march, Sherman's men captured 5,000 horses and 4,000 mules.

Sherman's troops took possession of Savannah on December 21, 1864. Sherman sent a message to President Lincoln. "I beg to present to you, as a Christmas gift, the city of Savannah."

Through the war, Sherman used several horses. Sam, a bay, half-Thoroughbred 16.2 hands tall, was injured several times, but survived the war and was retired to an Illinois farm where he died of old age in 1884. Sam was Sherman's second favorite horse.

Another of Sherman's horses was Lexington, however it was not the famous racehorse with the same name. Lexington, the racehorse, was eleven years old and possibly blind when the Civil War began. The racehorse was hidden to save him from being forced into the war. Sherman rode a feisty mare, Dolly, until she was captured by Confederate soldiers in Tennessee. But his favorite horse was Duke.

> *I take pleasure in saying that my favorite horse during the war was the one I rode at Atlanta, and whose name was Duke. He was a bright bay, had a white star on his forehead, and one white foot (left hind foot). I have a good portrait of him by Trotter of Philadelphia now hanging in my office.*
>
> *—William T. Sherman*

Sherman's riding style was described as follows:

> *General Sherman was a nervous and somewhat careless rider. He wore his stirrup-leathers very long, seeming to be almost all the time standing in the irons. This appearance was intensified by his habit of rising in the stirrups on reaching a turn in the road or some advantageous point of observation. While always careful of his animals, Sherman did not appear to have that fondness for them that is so common among good horsemen.*
>
> *He was constantly on the go, and his eye seemed to be everywhere except where his horse was treading. Sherman's rein was a rather loose one, for he trusted apparently, the natural sagacity of his steed, rather than to his own guidance. Seen at the head of a column of troops, or giving orders for their disposition on the field, Sherman presented a remarkable figure. Riding along the road, he was constantly gazing about him, noting the lay of the land passed over, as if internally planning how a battle could be fought there.*
>
> *—The United Service, A Monthly Review of Military and Naval Affairs, 1892*

Charlie

Charlie was ridden by William H. Spencer to carry the message from General Slocum to General William T. Sherman announcing the surrender of Atlanta, Georgia to the Union Army. Spencer rode Charlie the rest of the way to Savannah with Sherman's men. After the war, Spencer traded another of his horses to the army quartermaster for Charlie and brought him to his home in New York.

Mary Ann Bickerdyke

Inspired by her pastor, abolitionist Edward Beecher, Mary Ann Bickerdyke wanted to do her part to help the North during the Civil War. Bickerdyke's nursing experience was valuable to the army. She provided medical care for Civil War soldiers in the field hospitals and improved sanitation in the army camps.

I have a commission from the Lord God Almighty to do all I can for every miserable creature who comes in my way; he is always sure of two friends, God and me.

—Mary Ann Bickerdyke

At the battle of Iuka, Mississippi, on September 19, 1862, a stray horse was captured. The malnourished animal was covered in sores. Mrs. Bickerdyke had the same compassion for the horse as for the wounded soldiers, and she did all she could to restore his health.

When the horse she named Old Whitey had recovered, he became Bickerdyke's mount. Although she used a regular army saddle, she rode sidesaddle, not considering it appropriate for a lady to ride astride like a man. Mrs. Bickerdyke rode Old Whitey in the Grand Review in Washington, D.C. after the war.

The Lightning Mule Brigade

While the North typically didn't use mules under saddle, there was one significant exception. In March of 1863, Union Colonel Abel D. Streight was chosen to lead 1,700 soldiers in a raid across northern Alabama into northwest Georgia. The brigade would ride mules.

Named the Lightning Mule Brigade, this unusual force experienced problems right from the start. Many of the mules proved to be sickly, old, or totally untrained.

On April 19th, 400 of the brigade's mules stampeded into the countryside. Streight's campaign was delayed while waiting for a shipment of replacement animals. On the 26th, a heavy rainstorm made the roads impassable.

The brigade was being monitored by Confederate cavalry led by General Nathan Bedford Forrest. The braying of the mules continually alerted the Confederates as to Streight's location.

Convinced that he was surrounded and greatly outnumbered by the Confederates, Streight surrendered to Forrest on May 3, 1863 at Cedar Bluff, Alabama.

After surrendering, Colonel Streight learned he hadn't been outnumbered after all. Forrest only had 500 men. He'd tricked Streight by having his troops march in a circle around them. Colonel Streight and most of his men were imprisoned in Richmond, Virginia. In 1864, the colonel and 107 of his men escaped.

Confederate Horses

The most famous horse of the Confederacy, and perhaps of the entire Civil War is General Lee's Traveller. Traveller wasn't Lee's first or only horse. Ajax was ridden by General Lee early in the war. However, Lee considered the horse too large, and Ajax was returned to the family's farm. Richmond, a bay stallion, died in 1862 after the Battle of Malvern Hill. Brown Roan, another of Lee's horses went blind and was left with a farmer.

Lucy Long was Lee's second-favorite horse. He rode the mare in the Battle of Chancellorsville, but lost track of her after the evacuation of Richmond. In 1866, she was found and joined Traveller at Lee's farm. Lucy outlived General Lee, dying at the age of thirty-three.

Traveller was known by three different names in his lifetime. Sired by Grey Eagle, a 16-hand racehorse, the colt was first named Jeff Davis by James Johnston, the Virginia farmer, who raised him. As a two and three-year-old, Jeff Davis was a prize-winning colt at the 1859 and 1860 Greenbrier County Fair.

In 1861, the gelding was purchased by Captain Joseph M. Broun who named him Greenbrier for the county in Virginia in which the colt was born. The tall gray's smooth gaits, strength, and willing temperament made him a favorite with the soldiers in Broun's Virginia regiment.

Confederate General Robert E. Lee purchased the horse from Broun in February, 1862 for $200. He changed his name to Traveller because of the horse's fast walk. Lee preferred to spell the name with two Ls. Traveller is considered to have been present at more battles than any other horse in the Civil War.

Lee described Traveller in a letter to a relative who wanted to paint a portrait of the horse.

> *If I was an artist like you, I would draw a true picture of Traveller; representing his fine proportions, muscular figure, deep chest, short back, strong haunches, flat legs, small head, broad forehead, delicate ears, quick eye, small feet, and black mane and tail. Such a picture would inspire a poet, whose genius could then depict his worth, and describe his endurance of toil, hunger, thirst, heat and cold; and the dangers and suffering through which he has passed.*

> *He could dilate upon his sagacity and affection, and his invariable response to every wish of his rider. He might even imagine his thoughts through the long night-marches and days of battle through which he has passed. But I am no artist Markie, and can therefore only say he is a Confederate gray.*

Lee was injured by Traveller in August 1862. As he stood holding the reins, the horse spooked and knocked him down, injuring both of the General's wrists, possibly breaking his right hand. It was at least a month before Lee could ride again.

Later, Traveller redeemed himself by saving the general's life. On May 11, 1864, in a battle at Spotsylvania, Union forces began to fire on the Confederates. Traveller reared wildly, but Lee remained on the horse and tried to calm him. When Traveller reared again, a musket ball passed just under Lee's stirrups.

General Lee rode Traveller when he surrendered at Appomattox Court House. After the war, the gray horse accompanied Lee to Washington College in Lexington, Virginia where Lee served as president. The horse was permitted to graze on the college grounds. Traveller occupied one stall in the college stable with Lucy Long in an adjoining one. Traveller was nearly as famous as General Lee. The horse lost many tail hairs to souvenir-hunting students.

> *The boys are plucking out his tail, and he is presenting the appearance of a plucked chicken.*

> —*Robert E. Lee*

When Lee died in October, 1870, Traveller, draped in black crepe, followed the casket in the funeral procession. In June of 1871, Traveller developed tetanus after stepping on a nail, and the horse had to be put down.

Turner Ashby

In 1862, Virginian, Turner Ashby was the commander of General Stonewall Jackson's cavalry. By the end of that year, Ashby was promoted to brigadier general. He rode a white stallion, Tom Telegraph, who was admired by soldiers on both sides of the war.

GENL. TURNER ASHBY

Tom Telegraph was killed on April 17, 1862 during the Shenandoah Valley Campaign. Henry K. Douglas, an officer present at the battle, remarked, "The most splendid horseman I ever knew lost the most beautiful war-horse I ever saw."

Two months later, Turner Ashby was killed in battle.

Nathan Bedford Forrest

General Nathan Bedford Forrest claimed to have killed thirty Union soldiers and had twenty-nine horses shot out from under him during the Civil War. Forrest's nickname during the war was "The Wizard of the Saddle." In 1867, Forrest became the first grand wizard of the Ku Klux Klan. Later in life, he claimed to no longer be involved with the group.

One of Forrest's favorite horses was a racehorse named Roderick. When Roderick was killed at Thompson's Station, Forrest acquired King Philip. The striking, iron-gray horse with a dark mane and tail was wounded in battle, but survived the war. King Philip was said to charge and snap his teeth at anyone wearing Union blue. On one occasion after the war, General Forrest rode in a wagon pulled by King Phillip. When they approached several police officers in blue, the horse immediately charged at them.

—General Thomas Jordan and J. P. Pryor, 1866

King Philip died of colic later in 1865 at Forrest's plantation and was buried wrapped in a Confederate Army blanket.

Thomas Jonathan "Stonewall" Jackson

When young, Thomas Jackson was close to his sister, Laura. However as an adult, Laura Jackson Arnold became a staunch Unionist. It was difficult for her when her brother, Thomas, joined the Confederate Army. When she heard of Stonewall's death, Laura said she "would rather know that he was dead than to have him a leader in the rebel army."

In 1861, Confederates captured a train load of supplies and horses at Harper's Ferry. Thomas Jackson selected two of the horses, both sorrel geldings. He kept the larger horse for himself and intended to give the smaller one, whom he named Fancy, to his wife.

When Jackson discovered his new horse, Big Sorrel, was afraid of gunfire and unreliable in battle, he began to ride the smaller gelding. Although others called him Little Sorrel, Jackson continued to call the 15 hand Morgan, Fancy.

Such endurance I have never seen in horse flesh. We had no horse at Hd. Qrs. that could match him. I never saw him show a sign of fatigue.

—Henry Kyd Douglas describing Little Sorrel

242

At least one of Jackson's soldiers didn't think much of the general's horsemanship skills.

He wore a cap pulled down nearly to his nose and was riding a rawboned horse that did not look much like a charger, unless it would be on hay or clover. He certainly made a poor figure on horseback, with his stirrup leather six inches too short, putting his knees nearly level with his horse's back, and his heels turned out with his toes sticking behind his horse's foreshoulder. A sorry description of our most famous general, but a correct one.

—Georgia volunteer William Andrews

Jackson was known to be "fanatical" about his Christian faith and was a strict observer of the Sunday Sabbath. "My religious belief teaches me to feel as safe in battle as in bed."

Jackson earned his nickname at the First Battle of Bull Run in July, 1861. Urging the Confederate soldiers to regroup, someone called out, "There is Jackson standing like a stone wall."

After Bull Run, he was promoted to general and became known as Stonewall Jackson. Jackson and Little Sorrel fought together in many battles: First and Second Manassas, Front Royal, Winchester, Cross Keys, Port Republic, Harpers Ferry, Fredericksburg, and the Seven Days Campaign.

Their last battle was at Chancellorsville in Virginia in 1863. There, Jackson led a successful attack against Union forces. When he returned to the Confederate line, riding Little Sorrel, he was mistaken for a Union cavalryman and was shot by his own soldiers.

Jackson was hit in the left arm by two bullets and in the right hand by a third. Little Sorrel was unharmed. Jackson's wounds weren't life-threatening, but his left arm had to be amputated. He developed pneumonia and died on May 10th.

As Jackson lay dying, General Robert E. Lee sent a message to attending Chaplain Lacy, "Give General Jackson my affectionate regards, and say to him: he has lost his left arm but I my right."

After Jackson's death, Little Sorrel was retired to the Jackson farm in North Carolina. Later, he became the mascot of the Virginia Military Institute. After the war, Little Sorrel was exhibited at fairs and exhibitions. In 1885, Little Sorrel was retired to the Confederate Soldier's Home. The following year, he died at the age of thirty-six.

A stuffed version of Little Sorrel is on display at the Virginia Military Institute Museum in Lexington, Virginia.

John Hunt Morgan

Confederate general, John Hunt Morgan, led a band of more than 2,000 raiders across Ohio and Indiana in July 1863. This campaign became known as Morgan's Raid and served to distract Union forces as they tried to catch the marauders.

Morgan's favorite horse was a glossy-black, 15-hand mare, Black Bess. Given to Morgan by an admirer from Kentucky, she was described as a paragon of beauty.

Black Bess was captured by Union forces at the Cumberland River. After that, Morgan was given a horse named Glencoe. Morgan's troops reached farther north than any other Confederate troops would during the war. On July 26, near Salineville, in northeastern Ohio, Morgan and his men were forced to surrender.

Morgan was imprisoned in the Ohio Penitentiary in Columbus, Ohio, but he and six Confederate officers tunneled out of the prison in November 1863. Morgan was killed by Union troops the following year.

At the unveiling of the John Hunt Morgan statue in Kentucky in 1911, attendees of the ceremony were surprised to find Morgan mounted on a stallion rather than his favorite horse, the mare, Black Bess. The sculptor, Pompeo Coppini, didn't consider a mare a worthy mount for a general. He used his sculpting skills to transform Bess into a stallion. In 2018, the statue was moved to Lexington Cemetery.

65

Clarintha Draper

Soldiers weren't the only ones who relied on horses during the Civil War. Clarintha Draper also required the help of a faithful horse. Mrs. Draper was born Clarintha Choate on January 6, 1838 near Nashville, Tennessee. At three, she moved with her family to Fannin County, Texas. In 1860, at sixteen, she married George Washington Draper. The Drapers moved to Arkansas and raised cattle on a small farm.

When the Civil War began, her husband joined the Confederate army. While George Draper was away fighting, Clarintha remained on the farm, tending the cattle and caring for her young son, Dawson, and daughter, Lucinda.

One day, Union soldiers stormed in to raid the Draper's farm. Clarintha hid in the brush with her children. Fortunately, they were not discovered. As Clarintha watched, the raiders set the family's cabin ablaze. The destruction of their home left them with the clothes on their backs and a little food she'd hidden away. The Drapers' horse was at a neighbor's at the time of the raid and was not stolen.

Clarintha made the difficult decision to leave Arkansas and return to her relatives in Texas, a distance of over two hundred miles. She believed it was the only way she and the children would be safe.

> *I just saddled up my horse, put my little boy on behind me, held my little girl on the saddle in front of me, and struck out for Texas. The boy was four, the little girl, two. I didn't have much food to carry along for them. I could only hope that I would come across farms or settlements often enough along the way, and trust in the kindness of human nature that they would feed us, for I had no money.*

It was a difficult journey in more ways than one. A trip of two hundred miles in a car would be challenging enough with two children that young, let alone on horseback with little to eat. But things quickly became worse. When they approached Walden, Arkansas, they came upon a skirmish between Confederate and Union troops. With cannon balls whizzing around them, Mrs. Draper retreated to relative safety under a cliff on the bank of a creek. An occasional cannonball still fell close to them.

> *They were shooting all around us, the cannon balls were falling thick as hail—my little boy burned his hand when he picked one up, it was so hot. He saw it fall in the sand and thought it was so pretty he wanted to pick it up.*

After the battle ended, Clarintha resumed her journey. When the trio reached the Arkansas River on their horse, soldiers on guard duty were on the lookout for spies. They refused to allow her to cross on the ferry. With no bridge in sight, Mrs. Draper plunged into the river on horseback.

When they reached the other side, Confederate soldiers built a fire so they could warm
themselves and dry their clothes.

As an adult, Dawson Draper remembered some of their journey. He described a time when his
mother was forced to give up her horse to a group of Union soldiers.

When they set off again, the worn-out horse wasn't strong enough to carry an adult, so Mrs.
Draper led the animal and walked. Dawson rode in the saddle, holding his younger sister in front of
him.

Mrs. Draper stopped at the first house they came to and asked whether they could stay there to
rest. The family already had a house full of visitors and, at first, refused her. But when the men
became aware of her desperate situation, they moved out of the house to make room for the young
mother and her children. The Drapers ended up staying with the family for six weeks. In return for
their hospitality, Clarintha wove cloth for her hosts.

246

At some point, Clarintha was able to trade the run-down horse for a better one. Unfortunately, the names of all three horses who carried them on their journey have been lost to history.

Finally, the travelers reached the Red River. It wasn't as deep or treacherous as the Arkansas River had been, and the horse swam them across into Texas. They met friends who helped them on to Fannin County. When Mrs. Draper reached her family, she found that her mother's property and cotton had been confiscated by Union soldiers, and her mother was nearly starving. It had been so long since she'd heard from her husband; Clarintha feared he had been killed in the war.

George Draper was alive, but he had been captured by Union soldiers and held as a prisoner of war. Once released, he walked to Arkansas and discovered their burned cabin. He learned from neighbors that Clarintha had returned to Texas. George borrowed a mule and a saddle and made the same long trip in search of his family. He joined Clarintha there a year after her arrival.

George and Clarintha Draper settled in Cold Creek, Texas. In addition to raising ten children, Clarintha helped herd cattle on the open ranges, riding alongside the men. She continued to ride horses into her nineties.

> *Just give me a good horse and put me on it, and I'll show you how I can ride. I've rounded up many a cow; we had to do it.*

66

White House Stable Fire

Abraham and Mary Todd Lincoln had four sons. Only the first, Robert, lived to old age. Robert passed away in 1926 at eighty-two. The Lincoln's second son, Edward (Eddie), born in 1846, died a month before his fourth birthday. The Lincoln's third and fourth sons, Willie, born in 1850, and Thomas (Tad), born in 1853, were ten and nearly eight, when Lincoln took office.

Tad was born with a cleft palate which caused him to speak with a lisp. The two boys were only loosely disciplined by their parents. Mrs. Lincoln hired a tutor for her sons. Willie enjoyed learning. Tad, although intelligent and imaginative, was more rambunctious and didn't like to study like his brother.

John Hay, Lincoln's secretary, said that Tad had, "a very bad opinion of books and no opinion of discipline."

Tad Lincoln

Willie and Tad enjoyed playing soldier, wearing military uniforms specially made for them. They had a fort on the roof of the White House with logs painted to look like cannons. Each of the boys had a pony that lived in the White House Stable.

A variety of animals found their way into the Lincoln White House—cats, rabbits, and even goats. The boys once harnessed two goats, Nanko and Nannie, to a dining room chair and drove them through the middle of a party Mrs. Lincoln was hosting in the East Room.

In 1863, President Lincoln established Thanksgiving as an annual holiday. Tad took a liking to a live turkey that had been sent to the White House as a gift. When he asked his father not to kill Jack, as he had named the bird, Lincoln wrote a pardon for him. Pardoning a turkey became a tradition at the White House each Thanksgiving.

Secretary John Hay would later write of Tad.

He was a fearless rider, while yet so small that his legs stuck out horizontally from the saddle. He had that power of taming and attaching animals to himself, which seems the especial gift of kindly and unlettered natures. "Let him run," the easy-going President would say. "He has time enough left to learn his letters and get pokey."

Early in 1862, both boys became ill, perhaps with typhoid fever. Tad recovered, but Willie continued to grow weaker. On February 20, 1862, he passed away at the age of eleven. Willie's death devastated the family. After Willie's passing, President Lincoln and Tad grew closer.

My poor boy. He was too good for this earth. God has called him home. I know that he is much better off in heaven, but then we loved him so. It is hard, hard to have him die!

—Abraham Lincoln

A fire at the White House Stable on February 10, 1864 was to bring even more sadness to Lincoln and his son.

Sergeant Smith Stimmel, on duty that night, wrote.

It was a brick stable, and evidently had been burning for some time before it was discovered. The carriages, in a different section of the barn, were recovered, but all six horses died. Two were Mr. and Mrs. Lincoln's carriage horses. Two bay horses belonged to one of Lincoln's secretaries, John George Nicolay. Tad Lincoln lost his ponies—his own bay and a gray that his brother Willie used to ride. Lincoln consoled his son by saying, "the horses had gone where all good horses go."

The security detail suspected that someone had intentionally started the fire.

Although the fire had apparently been deliberately set, it wasn't part of an assassination plot. Most believe it was the work of the coachman, Patterson McGee. Earlier that day, Mrs. Lincoln had fired McGee. He was arrested and charged with arson but was released for lack of evidence.

Congress quickly approved $12,000 for a new stable, but no amount of money could replace Tad's ponies.

Chasing the Assassin

On April 9, 1865, Confederate General Robert E. Lee surrendered, and the long, deadly Civil War came to an end. Abraham Lincoln was inaugurated to a second term. Spirits were lifting in the North, but optimism about the country's future didn't last long.

Just days after the war officially ended, President Lincoln was assassinated by John Wilkes Booth.

A horse provided the means for Booth's escape, and horses assisted in his capture. Several livery stable employees offered testimony that identified Booth's accomplices by means of the horses they shared. John Surrat, George Atzerodt, and David Herold were known to be friends of Booth, having often been seen together at the stables. A half-blind horse connected Booth to both Lewis Powell and Doctor Samuel Mudd.

Although he despised the North, John Wilkes Booth never joined the Confederate Army. In 1864, several Confederates and Southern sympathizers agreed to assist Booth in a plan to kidnap President Lincoln, however the kidnapping proved too difficult to carry out. With the surrender of Robert E. Lee, Booth became desperate. When he learned Lincoln was to attend the play, "Our American Cousin", at Ford's Theatre on April 14th, Booth's plan became more sinister.

John Wilkes Booth was an actor as were his father and brothers, Edwin, and Junius Jr. He was a regular at the theater in Washington, D.C. where many of the employees knew and liked him. He rented a shed behind the building, in which Ford's employee, Ned Spangler, built stalls where Booth kept his horses.

On April 14, 1865, a Good Friday, Booth was staying at the National Hotel a few blocks from Ford's. At noon, he went to James Pumphrey's livery stable to arrange for a horse. Booth's favorite, a sorrel, wasn't available. He selected a different one—a bay mare with a white star. Pumphrey warned him that she was high-spirited. If Booth tried to tie her, the mare would pull back until she broke her halter or bridle.

Booth, an excellent horseman, agreed to rent the horse anyway. He didn't take her immediately, but returned to his hotel room. That afternoon, Booth visited Lewis Powell and George Atzerodt to confirm their assignments—to kill Secretary of State, William Seward and Andrew Johnson, the vice president. David Herold would guide Powell to Seward's home. Powell would ride the tall, one-eyed horse Booth provided for him. The attacks were to occur simultaneously at 10:15 p.m.

Atzerodt and Herold rented horses from John Fletcher at Nailor's stable. Atzerodt used a dark-bay mare; Herold, a roan, racking horse named Charley. At four o'clock, Booth picked up the bay mare from Pumphrey's livery, rode her to his shed behind Ford's, and turned her loose in the stall.

Around 9:30 p.m., he led the saddled and bridled mare to the back of the theater. The alley was known as Baptist Alley because the theater had originally been the First Baptist Church of D.C.

Remembering Pumphrey's warning that the mare wouldn't stand tied, Booth asked Ned Spangler to hold her. The last thing Booth needed that night was for the horse to break loose and leave him stranded. But the play was in progress, and Spangler was needed inside to help change sets. He handed the reins to a young man, Joseph Burroughs. According to a later statement by Spangler, Joseph often fed and exercised Booth's horses when the actor was out of town.

Burroughs was known as Peanut John, because part of his job was to sell peanuts to theater-goers. While Booth was inside, Burroughs walked the restless mare back and forth in the alley.

At 10:15, John Wilkes Booth entered the presidential box and shot President Lincoln with a small, single-shot deringer. After he fired the gun, the assassin wrestled briefly with the president's guest, Major Henry Rathbone. Booth wounded the major with his knife, then climbed over the banister and dropped onto the stage.

Most accounts indicate Booth landed awkwardly and broke the fibula in his left leg just above the ankle. However, a few researchers contend the assassin broke his leg later that night after a fall from his horse. Pandemonium broke out inside the theater. In the confusion, Booth escaped out a back door into Baptist Alley and shouted for his horse.

> *I heard the report of the pistol. I was still out by the bench, but had got off when Booth came out. He told me to give him his horse. He struck me with the butt of a knife, and knocked me down. He did this as he was mounting his horse, with one foot in the stirrup: he also kicked me, and rode off immediately.*
>
> *—Joseph Burroughs, Peanut John*

Booth galloped away while the attention of the shocked people in the theater was focused on the president. Lincoln was carried across the street to the Petersen Boarding House.

Because of the time he'd spent with the spirited horse, Burroughs was able to provide a detailed description of her to investigators. She was a light-bay mare with an uneasy temperament. Her mane fell on the left side. She had a long, wavy tail, a thin, arched neck, small ears, and a sloping rump.

For Booth to mount the horse required inserting his left leg into the stirrup with his full weight on it. In Burroughs' statement, he never mentioned Booth appearing to be in pain.

From the window of her home behind Ford's, Mary Jane Anderson also witnessed Booth's escape.

> *I saw Booth come out of the door with something in his hand, glittering. He came out of the theater so quick that it seemed as if he but touched the horse and it was gone like a flash of lightning.*

Additionally, several witnesses at the theater stated Booth swung over the rail of the Presidential Box and dropped no more than six feet to the stage.

Those testimonies give credence to the theory that Booth's leg wasn't broken at the theater.

Booth and his horse were stopped at the Navy Yard Bridge at 10:45. Due to war security measures, it was illegal to cross the bridge after 9:00 p.m. The guard, Sergeant Silas Cobb, questioned Booth, then allowed him to cross. Not long after, Cobb allowed David Herold, riding the roan horse, to pass over the bridge as well.

The Navy Yard Bridge crossed by Booth and Herold

Earlier that day, John Fletcher, an employee at the Nailor Stable, had rented the roan, racking horse gelding, Charley, to Herold for five dollars. The horse was due back at 9:00 pm, but hadn't been returned. Fletcher was the third rider to visit Cobb that night. He was chasing Herold, trying to get the horse back. Charley was one of the stable's best horses, and Fletcher knew he'd be in trouble if the animal was lost. Cobb informed Fletcher that he could cross the bridge, but if he did, he wouldn't be allowed back until the following morning. Fletcher gave up his chase and decided to report the stolen horse to the police.

According to Herold's later testimony, when he caught up with him, Booth said he'd been thrown from his horse and sprained his ankle. The two continued riding south across Maryland, heading toward Virginia where Booth assumed he would be hailed as a Confederate hero. Booth wrote in his diary that he, "rode sixty miles that night, with the bones of my leg tearing the flesh at every jump."

In reality, the pair rode half that distance.

Back in Washington D.C., a large, bay, one-eyed gelding, dripping sweat, was found east of the Capitol. He wore a saddle and bridle but was riderless. Some investigators, unaware of Burrough's detailed description of Booth's horse, thought the mysterious horse had been ridden by the assassin. They searched the area where the animal was found, giving Booth additional time to escape to the south.

The one-eyed horse belonged to Booth, but that night, it was ridden by Lewis Powell. Several months earlier, while visiting Dr. Samuel Mudd, the doctor had taken Booth to a neighbor's farm to purchase the large bay.

After attacking Secretary of State Seward, Powell mounted the bay and galloped toward the Navy Yard Bridge, intending to join Booth

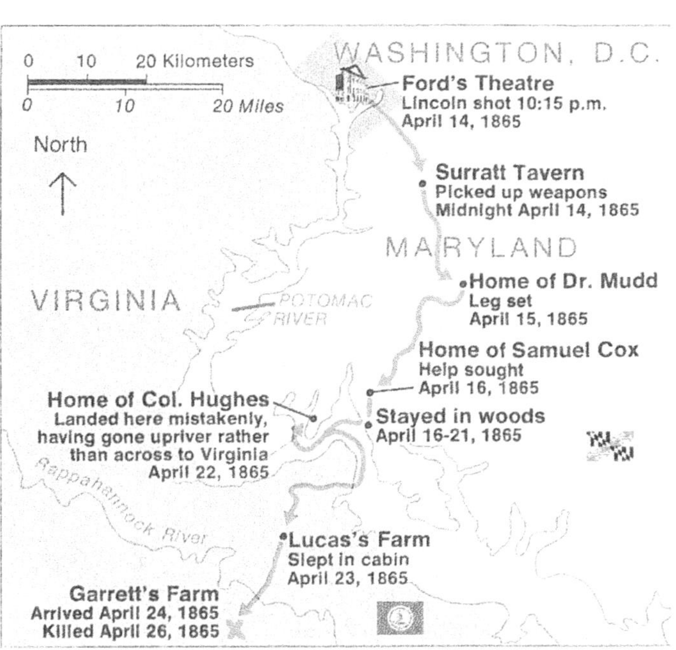

in his escape. But at some point, Powell was thrown from the horse. John Fletcher later identified the horse's saddle and bridle as belonging to George Atzerodt.

The third accomplice, Atzerodt, couldn't go through with his assignment to kill Vice President Johnson. Instead, he returned his horse to Nailor's stable and spent the evening drinking in a tavern.

Booth and Herold's first stop was the Surratt Tavern. Around midnight, the tavern keeper gave them rifles Mary Surratt had delivered earlier in the day. The two men continued on, arriving at the farm of Dr. Samuel Mudd at four o'clock Saturday morning.

Dr. Mudd invited them in, and Booth stretched out on the parlor sofa. When later questioned, Mudd claimed not to have known either of the men.

In addition to his leg, Booth complained of pain in his back. He told the doctor he'd fallen from his horse. After Mudd cut Booth's boot off, he set his broken leg and applied a splint. While Booth rested in an upstairs bedroom, Mudd's servants cared for the two horses. A servant, Thomas Davis, noticed that one of the horses had a swollen shoulder and part of his back was raw and bloody.

Dr. Mudd's later insistence that he hadn't recognized Booth that night aroused suspicion, since the two were known to have met on several occasions in the past.

At 7:22 a.m. on Saturday, April 15th, President Lincoln died.

That morning, Booth and Herold were eager to continue further south. They tried to get a carriage from Dr. Mudd. A carriage would allow Booth to travel more comfortably, but none could be found. The two fugitives seem to have switched horses at this time. Charley's smooth gait would cause Booth less pain than the excitable, bay mare.

By Saturday afternoon, hundreds of soldiers and civilians scoured the countryside for the assassin. The 16th New York Cavalry, led by Lieutenant Edward P. Doherty, joined the search. On April 20th, Secretary of War Edwin Stanton offered a reward of $50,000 for the capture of Booth and $25,000 each for the accomplices John Surratt Jr. and David Herold. Stanton's proclamation also stated that anyone harboring the suspects would be considered accomplices and could face punishment by death.

From April 16th (Easter Sunday) to the 21st, Booth and Herold hid in an area of thick pine trees near the Potomac River, waiting for a boat and the opportunity to cross over into Virginia. A Confederate sympathizer, Thomas Jones, brought them food and newspapers. Booth was eager to read about people's reaction to what he considered a heroic deed. He was dismayed by reports that called him a coward and a traitor. Booth continued to write in his diary while in the pine thicket.

As the cavalry began to close in on the criminals, Booth and Herold feared their horses might call out to the soldier's animals

and reveal their location. Samuel Cox, another Confederate who had assisted the escapees, testified that Herold led both horses to Zekiah Swamp and shot them, leaving their bodies to sink there. An alternate account by a Maryland farmhand claimed the two horses were sold.

On Wednesday, April 19th, Lincoln's funeral was held at the White House. Mrs. Lincoln was so grief stricken, she didn't attend. Tad Lincoln was there with his older brother, Robert. On the 21st, a train left Washington, carrying the coffins of Lincoln and his son, Willie, who had passed away in 1862 at the age of eleven. Thirty million people viewed the train over the next two weeks as it traveled to Lincoln's hometown of Springfield, Illinois.

On April 23rd, the tenth day, Thomas Jones decided circumstances were favorable for Booth and Herold to cross the Potomac River into Virginia. The two men helped Booth onto Jones' horse, a gray mare named Kit. Jones led the way to the shore where he'd arranged to have a boat waiting. Jones helped Booth into the small boat, and Herold began rowing. On the first attempt, the two became disoriented and landed back in Maryland. On the second try, they reached Virginia.

Booth and Herold arrived at Richard Garrett's farm on the 24th. Booth convinced the family he was a wounded Confederate soldier and Herold was his cousin. The Garretts permitted the men to stay in their house that night. But after listening to more of their story, Garrett's sons, John and William, both Confederate soldiers, suspected the men were lying.

The Garretts allowed them to stay a second night, but not in the house. Booth and Herold were sent to the tobacco barn. Worried the men might steal their horses in the middle of the night, Garrett's sons locked the barn doors from the outside. The brothers spent the night in a nearby corn crib to keep an eye on their suspicious guests.

The 16th New York Cavalry caught up with Booth around 2 a.m. the next morning. The unit contained twenty-six cavalrymen, Lieutenant Doherty, and two detectives—Everton Conger and Luther Byron Baker.

Conger knocked at the farmhouse door, and Richard Garrett opened it. The man had been awakened from a sound sleep and stood, frightened, on the porch with minimal clothing. When questioned, Garrett claimed Booth was in the woods. Conger didn't believe him and threatened to hang the man right then. Garrett's sons emerged from the corn crib to save their father. John told Conger the men were in the tobacco barn.

Early on the morning of April 26th, the soldiers formed a circle around the barn. Herold was quick to surrender. Booth denounced him as a coward but allowed Herold to leave the barn. Federal investigator, Everton Conger, set fire to a handful of hay and stuck it through a crack in the barn to burn Booth out.

As the fire spread, Cavalry Sergeant Thomas (Boston) Corbett kept an eye on Booth through the narrow gaps between the vertical boards in the barn wall. When it appeared to Corbett that Booth was coming toward him, Corbett fired.

Baker and Conger rushed into the barn to pull the wounded Booth out. Lincoln's assassin was carried to the front porch of the farmhouse where he died a few hours later.

Boston Corbett insisted he intended only to wound Booth, but his shot struck the man in the neck. The officers weren't pleased. They'd hoped to capture Booth alive for questioning.

Corbett was offered one of Booth's pistols as a memento, but he declined, saying he, desired no reminder of the sad duty he had performed and wanted to have it banished from his mind as soon as possible. Corbett was offered $100 for the pistol he'd shot Booth with, but he refused, saying it belonged to the government. If the government wanted to reward him, Corbett preferred to have the cavalry horse he'd ridden the past few days. The reward money was divided among the men present at Booth's capture, with the officers receiving the largest share. Corbett received $1,653.85.

Booth's diary was among the belongings taken by the officers that day, but it wasn't made public until two years later. Ironically, both Corbett and Booth felt their actions were directed by God.

God simply made me the instrument of his punishment.

—*John Wilkes Booth*

Providence directed my hand.

—*Boston Corbett*

Lieutenant Baker was one of the detectives who participated in the capture of John Wilkes Booth. Baker had ridden his horse, Old Buckskin, to the Garrett farm. The former Union Cavalry officer related that tears came to his eyes upon hearing Booth's last words. "Tell mother I died for my country. I did what I thought was best."

I thought of a mother's sacred love, of a mother's despairing sorrow, and I knew that Booth was thinking of it, too, with eternity's wide gate before him; invisible hands rolling back the massive portals; a just God to be met and answered.

—*Luther Baker*

Old Buckskin had been Baker's mount through many battles as part of the 1st D.C. Cavalry. In 1864, Old Buckskin was wounded in the shoulder, but the brave horse kept on. At the end of the war, Baker purchased him from the U.S. government.

With a portion of the reward money received for the capture of Booth, Baker bought land in Lansing, Michigan, bringing Old Buckskin with him to the new farm. The two participated in parades together. Baker traveled and gave lectures describing the assassination of Lincoln and the hunt for his killer. Baker loved his horse and claimed he wouldn't part with him for any price. Old Buckskin lived to be thirty. After his death, the horse was stuffed and displayed at the Michigan Agricultural College.

68

Buffalo Soldiers

When the Civil War began in 1861, African-American men were not accepted as soldiers in the Union Army. Frederick Douglass, former slave and a leader of the abolitionist movement, was one who urged President Lincoln to allow the men to fight. Lincoln's main objective was to preserve the Union—not to eliminate slavery. But he realized allowing blacks to join the Union Army could help accomplish both goals. The Emancipation Proclamation permitted blacks to serve in the Union Army. In May of 1863, the War Department created African-American regiments known as United States Colored Troops or USCT.

The acceptance of African-American soldiers during the Civil War laid the groundwork for the first black regiments in the regular U.S. Army. Both infantry and cavalry regiments were formed. Soldiers enlisted for five years and were paid thirteen dollars a month plus room, board, and clothing.

The black regiments became known as Buffalo Soldiers. There are several theories as to the origins of the name.

- The black soldiers' hair reminded Comanche or Apache warriors of the hair of a buffalo.

- The name was given out of respect for their fierce fighting ability.

- The Plains Indians gave them the name because of the bison coats they wore.

In the early years, many of the horses used by the Buffalo Soldiers of the 9th and 10th Cavalry were ones left over from the Civil War. The motto of the 9th Cavalry was, "We can, we will." And the 10th's, "Ready and Forward."

The Buffalo Soldier units served on the western frontier, attempting to maintain peace between westward-bound settlers and Native Americans. They patrolled a wide territory, including the area of the present states of Montana, North and South Dakota, Kansas, Oklahoma, Colorado, Texas,

Arizona, New Mexico, and California. The black regiments participated in battles periodically with Native Americans until 1898. They explored and mapped new territory and served as stagecoach guards, riding on top of the coaches to protect them from robbers. Buffalo Soldiers also fought in the Spanish-American War.

The U.S. Army administered national parks from 1891 to 1913. In 1899, Buffalo Soldiers from the 9th Cavalry Regiment became some of the first national park rangers in California. Approximately 500 Buffalo Soldiers served in Yosemite and Sequoia National Parks where their duties included capturing hunters poaching the parks' wildlife, stopping timber thieves, and extinguishing forest fires. They also constructed roads, trails, and other park facilities.

Isaiah Mays

Isaiah Mays was born in Virginia in 1858. Mays served as an infantry Buffalo Soldier. On May 11, 1889 he was one of a

group of eleven soldiers guarding two wagons with a strongbox that carried $28,000 in gold and silver coins. The coins weighed 250 pounds with a value today of nearly half a million dollars. The money was to pay soldiers' salaries at several Arizona forts. Army Paymaster Major Wham's caravan included two wagons pulled by a dozen mules.

Near Pima, Arizona, the wagons stopped when they came to a large boulder in the middle of the road. When several soldiers laid down their rifles to move the rock, gunshots sounded from a nearby hill. The ensuing gun battle became known as the Wham Paymaster Robbery. The thieves wounded eight of the soldiers and got away with the payroll.

Corporal Isaiah Mays was shot in both legs, but made it to a nearby ranch to get help. The bandits hadn't covered their faces and were recognized. One, thought to be the head of the gang, was the mayor of Pima.

The thieves were not charged with any of the shootings, but were charged with robbery. They were not convicted, and the money was never recovered. The area consisted largely of polygamist Mormons, and many of the locals considered the robbers to be "Latter-Day Robin Hoods."

Mays was awarded the Medal of Honor for bravery. Another Buffalo Soldier, Benjamin Brown, also received the medal for his heroic actions that day.

Colonel Charles Young

Colonel Young, born in 1864, was the first black to graduate from a white high school in Ripley, Ohio at the age of sixteen. He taught school in Ripley for two years before being accepted into West Point Military Academy. He was the third black to graduate from the Academy. After graduation, he was assigned to the 9th Cavalry, serving in Nebraska and Utah in the early 1890s.

Young led a troop to Sequoia National Park in 1903 to extend a road to the park's Giant Forest. He later served in Haiti, Liberia, the Philippines, and Mexico.

When the U.S. entered the First World War, Young was fifty-four and already retired. He applied for a command, but was refused because of his age and health. He had suffered a bout with malaria several years earlier, and a medical examination revealed kidney problems.

Determined to prove that he was capable of serving in the war, Charles came up with a plan to ride horseback to Washington, D.C. He believed completing the long journey would demonstrate his ability to serve as a commander.

On June 6, 1918, Colonel Young mounted his bay mare, Dolly, in Wilberforce, Ohio and began the ride to Washington D.C. The sixteen-day journey of 497 miles took him across parts of Ohio, West Virginia, Maryland, and Virginia.

At the end of his ride, Young met with Secretary of War, Newton Baker, but Baker still refused to grant him a command. When Young persisted, he was finally recalled to active duty but assigned a non-combat role. By the time his reinstatement became effective, the war was near its end.

Mark Matthews

Mark Matthews was born in Alabama on August 7, 1894, but grew up in Mansfield, Ohio. He gained his early riding experience by delivering newspapers on his pony. While working with horses at a racetrack in Kentucky, Matthews met members of the 10th Cavalry Buffalo Soldier unit. At fifteen, he joined the regiment. The minimum age was seventeen, but Matthews forged documents to alter his age. During World War I, he served with the 10th Regiment on the Mexican border.

In 1931, Matthews was transferred to Fort Myer in Virginia (near Arlington National Cemetery, across from Washington D.C.). Matthews organized horse shows to sell war bonds during World War II. He also cared for First Lady Eleanor Roosevelt's horses. At the age of fifty, he served in World War II. In 2005, Matthews was recognized as the oldest living Buffalo Soldier. He died in September of that year at the age of 111.

Beautiful Jim Key—Book 2 Preview

Beautiful Jim Key is only one of the amazing horses you'll meet in Volume II of *Horsestory*. Enjoy this preview taken from chapter twenty of the second volume.

In the late 1800s and early 1900s, there were several horses whose abilities seemed to indicate they possessed near-human levels of intelligence. These horses were exhibited in various areas and performed feats that went beyond the usual trick-trained horses. For example, many of the horses could paw a number of times to show answers to math problems.

Why there was this surge in "educated" horses during this time period is unclear, but they became the subjects of psychological and behavioral studies. The consensus was that horses do not possess intelligence on the level of humans, but they are far more intelligent than people had given them credit for. The first of this group was Beautiful Jim Key.

Jim Key wasn't always beautiful. In fact, when the bay colt was born in the spring of 1889, his owner, William Key, said the foal was "the most spingled, shank-legged animal I ever did see!" He'd planned to give the colt a fine name from the Bible, but William was so disappointed in him he named the foal, Jim, after a drunken man who lived nearby.

Born a slave in Winchester, Tennessee in 1833, William was given the last name of his owner, Captain John Key. Upon John Key's death, five-year-old William was bought by the captain's nephew, also named John Key.

The animals on the Key farm seemed to sense young William was a friend. They greeted the boy affectionately each time he entered the barnyard. Because of his skill with animals, as William grew older, he was sent to neighboring farms to train horses or mules. Usually within a week's time, he had the animal tamed and ready to ride or drive.

It was uncommon in the South to teach slaves to read, but William learned alongside John Key's children. When the Civil War began, William joined the Confederate army with the Key sons in order to protect them.

After the war, William Key was a free man, and his ability with animals served him well. Considered a veterinarian, despite a lack of formal training, William was called Doc Key. One of Doc's dreams was to raise a successful racehorse. Lauretta, Jim Key's mother, was a full-blooded Arabian, formerly owned by a Persian sheikh. The beautiful gray mare was stolen from the sheikh and sold to P. T. Barnum's circus while it toured Europe. Lauretta came to America, and for years, was exhibited as the Queen of Arabian Horses.

It's uncertain whether the part about the sheikh is true, but years later, William Key found Lauretta abused and neglected at a ramshackle circus in Mississippi. He purchased the mare, and over the next year, using the Keystone liniment he'd developed, Lauretta's health was restored.

Many horsemen traveled to races at the track on Doc Key's farm. When Doc spotted the horse, Tennessee Volunteer at one of those races, he knew right away that was the horse who should sire Lauretta's foal. Volunteer, a Standardbred, was a descendant of the famed racer Hambletonian.

Lauretta was the smartest horse Doc Key had ever known, and Tennessee Volunteer was the fastest. How could those two produce anything but a champion foal?

But the night Lauretta's foal arrived, Doc's hopes were dashed. As he surveyed the scraggly colt, Doc wasn't sure the weak, wobbly thing would be able to walk, let alone race. As if the little colt hadn't gotten off to a bad enough start, Lauretta died when Jim Key was young.

His beloved mare's death was devastating. As he grieved, Doc kept to himself—except for the presence of Jim Key. The colt seemed to sense Doc's sadness and wouldn't leave the man's side. A few days later, Doc was standing in the yard when he felt something nudge his arm. When he turned around, there was Jim Key, holding a stick in his mouth. The colt pushed it toward Doc as if he wanted him to throw it. Doc did. The colt raced after it and brought it back. It was as if Jim had seen Doc play fetch with the family dog, and he wanted to play the game, too. Perhaps he thought playing fetch might make his master smile again. For the first time, Doc realized there was something special about Jim.

That night, the colt refused to be led to his stall. Instead, he followed Doc into the house. Apparently, Jim now considered himself a member of the family. Doc made a deep pile of straw and covered it with blankets for Jim's bed. The colt was house-trained and always went out behind the house for his bathroom needs. Doc began to teach the colt to identify and retrieve household items. Jim Key even taught himself a trick. He learned to open the gate, so he could wander down the road.

By the time he was a yearling, in 1890, Jim Key's legs had straightened. He truly was a beautiful horse now—a big one—too big to remain in the house. Jim was not happy about returning to the barn. He threw such a fit that Doc set up a cot outside his stall and slept near him. What Doc had intended as a temporary arrangement, to help Jim Key adjust to living in the stable, ended up lasting the rest of Doc's life. He even moved his desk to the barn to create an office.

The next revelation of Jim's intelligence came when Doc stored a supply of apples in his desk drawer. For the next few days, each time he returned to the barn, Doc found the drawer closed and its contents missing. He questioned his wife and the stable help, but none of them knew what had become of the apples.

Doc refilled the drawer, exited the barn, and watched through a window. Sure enough, Jim Key strolled inside, grabbed the drawer handle, and pulled it open. The horse ate every apple, closed the drawer, and moseyed back outside.

One day, Doc's wife, Lucinda, was in the barn eating Jim's favorite fruit. She asked him if he wanted an apple, and the horse nodded his head. Stunned, she ran to tell Doc. From that point on, Doc began working with Jim more earnestly. In addition to answering questions by nodding "yes," he learned to move his head side to side for "no."

When Jim Key was a year and a half old, Doc brought him along as he traveled the countryside selling his Keystone Liniment. The colt's ability to fetch and several other tricks drew crowds.

Doc trained the horse to act as if he were sick—kicking at his stomach, staggering, then dropping to the ground to roll and kick violently, as if he were in pain. When Doc gave Jim Key a dose of the liniment, the horse's symptoms immediately vanished. The colt's antics helped Doc sell more liniment.

Next, Doc taught Jim to recognize the letter "A" on a tin square. He coated the square containing the correct letter with sugar, so Jim was rewarded by licking the right one. It took six months for Jim to learn to pick out that specific letter and bring it to Doc. Over the next years, Jim learned to recognize all the letters and the numbers from one to thirty. He could spell out words and solve simple mathematical problems with answers up to thirty.

Doc enjoyed reading passages from the Bible to Jim, especially those that mentioned horses. He trained the horse to pick up a card containing the Scriptural reference that matched the passage being read.

> *Jim likes the prophets. The prophets had visions of horses. John says he looked up and beheld a white horse in heaven, and what Jim wants to know is, if there are white horses in heaven, why can't a good bay horse go there also?*
>
> *—Dr. William Key*

In 1896, Doc and Jim Key toured county fairs across the state of Tennessee, performing a variety of the horse's tricks. Doc was a Republican, but at these events, Jim Key always claimed to be a Democrat.

The following year, Jim Key was one of the most popular exhibits at the Tennessee Centennial and International Exposition. President William McKinley attended one of their performances. Jim bowed to women in the audience. He selected letter blocks one at a time to spell his own name. The horse retrieved letters from simulated post office mailboxes and filed them in the correct drawers. He could pick out coins that added up to values called out by members of the audience. Jim could even write his name on a chalkboard. Actually, the horse held an eraser in his mouth and erased his name from the chalk-covered board.

Doc came up with a variation of Jim's old trick of feigning lameness they'd used during their days on the road, selling liniment. When someone in the crowd offered to buy the horse, Jim Key would suddenly act as though he were deathly ill. But he would miraculously recover when Doc refused to sell him.

When a presidential cabinet member's name was called out, Jim selected the card containing that man's name. Doc asked him where the president was seated, and Jim Key turned and bowed to McKinley. The Republican president was determined to change the horse's political persuasion. When McKinley asked him whether he was a Republican, Jim Key moved his head from side to side, insisting he was not. The president was quoted in a newspaper,

> *This is certainly the most astonishing and entertaining exhibition I have ever witnessed. It is indeed a grand object lesson of what kindness and patience will accomplish.*

When that article caught the eye of Albert Rogers, a young promoter, he decided he had to own Jim Key. Rogers met Doc Key at the Centennial Exhibition and offered $100,000 for the horse. Doc turned him down. As a former slave, Doc knew what it felt like to be bought and sold. He wouldn't do that to Jim Key. But the two men worked out a deal. A substantial initial payment went to Doc, and

Rogers would receive a percentage of the proceeds from each exhibit he arranged. Jim Key would travel in his own private rail car with only the best hay.

Albert Rogers proved to be an effective promoter. Doc and Jim soon rose to national prominence. Both Rogers and Doc Key wanted to promote the ethical treatment of animals as well. As part of their events, Doc explained the gentle methods he used to train the horse.

The book, *Black Beauty*, written by Anna Sewell twenty years earlier in England, was awakening people to the plight of abused horses. Jim Key's act caught the attention of George Angell of the American Humane Education Society. He endorsed the act, making Jim Key an honorary agent of the organization. Angell gave Doc a copy of *Black Beauty*, which Doc promised to read aloud to Jim Key.

In 1901, at an exhibition in Atlantic City, New Jersey, a small black-and-white dog appeared one day in Jim's stall. The dog barked menacingly, preventing the stable help, and even Doc, from approaching the horse. The dog then leaped onto Jim Key's back.

Doc named the dog Monk, short for monkey. When no one claimed him, Monk began to travel with Jim Key. He never appeared on stage, but was a constant companion in the horse's stall. From his perch atop Jim's back, Monk served as the horse's bodyguard, threatening to bite strangers who came too close.

What was the secret of Jim Key's abilities? Did the horse really have a level of intelligence that allowed him to think and reason—or were his feats merely sophisticated tricks?

In October 1901, a group of professors from Harvard College attended two of Jim's performances. They concluded the act was not a hoax. Neither Doc Key nor anyone in the audience was consciously giving the horse cues. Jim Key's unique upbringing and close relationship to Doc, as well as the gentle training he had received, seemed to play a role in the horse's ability to sense what Doc wanted him to do.

Doc and Jim Key were one of the most popular acts at the 1904 St. Louis World's Fair. The Silver Horseshoe Pavilion was specially constructed for their exhibit.

Five million visitors attended Doc and Jim's performances. Two million children joined the Jim Key Band of Mercy and signed a pledge that stated, "I promise to be kind to animals."

After their 1906 season, Jim Key began to suffer from arthritis. Doc and his horse returned to their home in Shelbyville, Tennessee to rest. Over the next few years, Doc and Jim performed for small groups who visited their farm, but due to the declining health of both, the pair never traveled again.

In 1909, Doc died at seventy-six. Jim Key was lost without the man he'd rarely been apart from. Mrs. Key's brother, Stanley Davis, who had traveled for years with the show, took over Jim's care. Three years later, at twenty-three, Beautiful Jim Key passed away.

References and Credits

Chapter 1 - Arrival in America

marshtacky.info

corollawildhorses.com

floridacrackerhorseassociation.com

chincoteague.com

kigermustangs.org
upload.wikimedia.org/wikipedia/commons/3/32/de_soto_tampa_bay_1539.jpg

upload.wikimedia.org/wikipedia/commons/c/cb/bodmer_--_blackfoot_indian%2c_1840-1843.jpg

Chapter 2 - The Weather God

mesoweb.com/maler/conquistador.html

loc.gov/resource/cph.3c01695

Chapter 3 - Thoroughbred Family Tree

en.wikipedia.org/wiki/Byerley_Turk

en.wikipedia.org/wiki/Darley_Arabian

en.wikipedia.org/wiki/Godolphin_Arabian

newscientist.com/article/dn7941-95-of-thoroughbreds-linked-to-one-superstud

horsefund.org/horse-racing-breeding-for-trouble-part-2.php
commons.wikimedia.org/wiki/file:byerly_turk.jpg

upload.wikimedia.org/wikipedia/commons/1/12/darley_arabian.jpg

upload.wikimedia.org/wikipedia/commons/b/b1/daniel_quigley_-_the_godolphin_arabian_-_google_art_project.jpg

Chapter 4 - Old Billy

historic-uk.com/CultureUK/Old-Billy-The-Barge-Horse

en.wikipedia.org/wiki/Old_Billy

Chapter 5 - Eclipsing the Competition

upload.wikimedia.org/wikipedia/commons/1/1d/Eclipse%28horse%29.jpg

Chapter 6 - Delivering the Good News

Francis Asbury Circuit Rider, Benge, Janet and Geoff. YWAM Publishing 2013

Peter Cartwright Pioneer Circuit Rider, Veglahn, Nancy. Charles Scribner's Sons 1968

christianhistoryinstitute.org/uploaded/564154452a9e41.32228711.pdf

archive.org/details/autobiographyofp01cart/page/n10

upload.wikimedia.org/wikipedia/commons/thumb/a/a2/the_circuit_preacher_-_drawn_by_a.r._waud._lccn98506148.tif/lossy-page1-3292px-the_circuit_preacher_-_drawn_by_a.r._waud._lccn98506148.tif.jpg

upload.wikimedia.org/wikipedia/commons/0/0c/circuit_rider_illustration_eggleston.png

upload.wikimedia.org/wikipedia/commons/c/cd/circuit_rider_statue_oregon_state_capitol.jpg

upload.wikimedia.org/wikipedia/commons/c/c6/oregon_historical_quarterly_vol._25_circuit_rider.jpg

Chapter 7 - Arriving With Bells On

history.com/topics/westward-expansion/conestoga-wagon

colonialsense.com/Society-Lifestyle/Signs_of_the_Times/Conestoga_Wagon.php

radnorhistory.org/archive/articles/ytmt/?p=404
loc.gov/resource/cph.3a25345/

commons.wikimedia.org/wiki/file:smithsonian_national_museum_of_american_history_-_conestoga_wagon_(8307591214).jpg

Conestoga Horse - U.S. Department of Agriculture

Chapter 8 - A Midnight Ride

paulreverehouse.org

upload.wikimedia.org/wikipedia/commons/e/e2/Paul_Revere%27s_ride.jpg

Chapter 9 - Independence

mountvernon.org

en.wikipedia.org/wiki/Blueskin_(horse)

commons.wikimedia.org/wiki/File:Portrait-of-george-washington-taking-the-salute-at-trenton-john-faed.jpg

Chapter 10 - First in the Heart of His Mules?

mountvernon.org/george-washington/farming/the-animals-on-george-washingtons-farm/father-of-the-american-mule
upload.wikimedia.org/wikipedia/commons/e/e3/American_farming_and_stock_raising%2C_with_useful_facts_for_the_household%2C_devoted_to_farming_in_all_its_departments_%281892%29_%284782248575%29.jpg

Chapter 11 - Morgan's Figure

uvm.edu/cals/morganhorsefarm/history

morganhorse.com/upload/photos/905TMH_Jan2015_Justin-Morgan.pdf

morganhorse.com/upload/photos/905TMH_Oct2016_HISTORICAL_EthanAllen.pdf

loc.gov/item/91795905

loc.gov/item/2004667209

loc.gov/item/2003662852

Chapter 12 - All Men Are Created Equal

monticello.org

en.wikipedia.org/wiki/Thomas_Jefferson

commons.wikimedia.org/wiki/File:American_stallion_register_-_including_all_stallions_prominent_in_the_breeding_of_the_American_roadster,_trotter_and_pacer,_from_the_earliest_

records_to_1902._And_this_includes_nearly_all_imported_
(17973577598).jpg

Chapter 13 - Lewis & Clark

lewis-clark.org/

monticello.org/thomas-jefferson/louisiana-lewis-clark/origins-
of-the-expedition
commons.wikimedia.org/wiki/Sacagawea#/media/File:Lewis_
and_clark-expedition.jpg

commons.wikimedia.org/wiki/File:Alfred_Jacob_Miller_-_
Shoshone_Indian_and_his_Pet_Horse_-_Walters_37194062.jpg

Chapter 14 - Marengo & Napoleon

en.wikipedia.org/wiki/Napoleon

en.wikipedia.org/wiki/Napoleon_Crossing_the_Alps

Chapter 15 - Copenhagen at Waterloo

en.wikipedia.org/wiki/Copenhagen_(horse)

en.wikipedia.org/wiki/Copenhagen_(horse)#/media/File:
Copenhagen_(Wellington%27s_horse).jpg

Chapter 16 - The Dream Horse

warhistoryonline.com/history/5-famous-horses-military-histo-
ry.html

en.wikipedia.org/wiki/Palomo_(horse)

upload.wikimedia.org/wikipedia/commons/3/3f/Equestrian_
portrait_of_Sim%C3%B3n_Bol%C3%ADvar.jpg

Chapter 17-23 - Horse Jobs

victorianlondon.org/publications6/horse-11.htm

The Horse World of London, W.J. Gordon; Chapter XI, The Black
Brigade, p. 138-147, 1893

1900s.org.uk/1900s-coal-deliveries.htm

poulingrain.com/blog/poulinpowered-highlight-draft-trash

Chapter 24 - Andrew Jackson

thehermitage.com

Chapter 25 - Sea Rescue

trove.nla.gov.au/newspaper/article/74227657

Chapter 26 - Romanis

thevintagenews.com/2018/06/22/romani-vardo-wagons
upload.wikimedia.org/wikipedia/commons/1/1b/Gypsy_cara-
van.jpg

upload.wikimedia.org/wikipedia/commons/6/6b/Appleby_
Horse_Fair.jpg

upload.wikimedia.org/wikipedia/commons/9/90/Solid_chest-
nut_coloured_Gypsy_Cob_Horse_1.jpg

Chapter 27 - Bathing Machines

en.wikipedia.org/wiki/Bathing_machine

womenofbrighton.co.uk/martha-gunn.html

victorianweb.org/history/victoria/7.html

Queen Victoria's Bathing Machine, Gloria Whelan. Simon &
Schuster 2014

Chapter 28 - The Woolly Horse

lostmuseum.cuny.edu/archive/barnum-on-the-woolly-horse-
the-life-of-p-t
ia902804.us.archive.org/5/items/lifeofptbarnum00barn/lifeofpt-
barnum00barn.pdf

Chapter 29 - Hambletonian

harnessmuseum.com/content/hambletonian

americanhistory.si.edu/petersprints/objects/small/2003-19660.
jpg

Chapter 30 - Speedy Mares

vault.si.com/vault/1954/08/16/the-belle-of-the-seventies

loc.gov/resource/pga.00729

Chapter 31 - Horse Thieves

*Bullets, Badges, and Bridles - Horse Thieves and the Societies That
Pursued Them*, John K. Burchill. Pelican Publishing Company
2014

en.wikipedia.org/wiki/Horse_theft

netposse.com

magnoliareporter.com/collection_a720c78c-b131-11e1-9bff-
001a4bcf887a.html

Chapter 32 - The Untamable Horse

thompsonrarey.com/jsrarey/index.html

dispatch.com/story/news/history/2022/12/18/john-rarey-of-
groveport-area-was-master-at-subduing-vicious-horses/
69722530007

Chapter 33 - Livery Stables

wnyhistory.org/portfolios/businessindustry/millers_livery/
millers_livery.html

truewestmagazine.com/livery-stables-west

dailyprogress.com/entertainment/lifestyles/livery-stables-were-
staples-in-community/article_9d2b1e77-892f-5832-9d72-
4c23ffd95c32.html

gvshp.org/blog/2014/10/15/horsing-around-the-village
sherrlock.files.wordpress.com/2010/09/langstons-livery-then-
web1.jpg

Chapter 34 - Horse Boats

History of horse whims, teamboats, treadwheels, and treadmills,
Erickson, H. H. 2006. pubmed.ncbi.nlm.nih.gov/17402397

kshs.org/p/ferries-in-kansas-part-i-missouri-river/12571

en.wikipedia.org/wiki/Impulsoria

en.wikipedia.org/wiki/Cycloped

Chapter 35 - Along the Tow Path

nps.gov/choh/learn/kidsyouth/children.htm

en.wikipedia.org/wiki/Chesapeake_and_Ohio_Canal

gutenberg.org/files/14964/14964-h/14964-h.htm

The Amazing Impossible Erie Canal, Harness, Cheryl. Simon &
Schuster 1995

From Canal Boy to President, the Boyhood and Manhood of James A. Garfield, Horatio Alger. American Publishers 1881
gutenberg.org/ebooks/14964

upload.wikimedia.org/wikipedia/commons/9/9a/Horse_drawn_cruising_on_the_Montgomery_Canal_-_geograph.org.uk_-_846074.jpg

loc.gov/resource/cph.3b15770

upload.wikimedia.org/wikipedia/commons/6/63/Children_on_C_and_O_Canal_Boat_in_Cumberland.jpg

Chapter 36 - More Powerful Than a Locomotive

en.wikipedia.org/wiki/Tom_Thumb_(locomotive)

fhwa.dot.gov/rakeman/1830.htm

upload.wikimedia.org/wikipedia/commons/7/75/The_Horse_Wins_The_Race_%28NBY_416209%29.jpg

Chapter 37 - Mass Transportation

midcontinent.org/rollingstock/builders/stephenson1.htm

cable-car-guy.com/html/cchorse.html

en.wikipedia.org/wiki/Horsebus

6sqft.com/worlds-first-streetcar-began-operation-in-lower-manhattan-on-november-14-1832

en.wikipedia.org/wiki/Carville,_San_Francisco

sparkletack.com/2005/10/21/carville-a-lost-neighborhood
en.wikipedia.org/wiki/Horsebus#/media/File:Bundesarchiv_Bild_146-1973-030C-18,_Pferdeomnibus,_Berlin.jpg

commons.wikimedia.org/wiki/File:Horse_Drawn_Streetcar.jpg

en.wikipedia.org/wiki/Carville,_San_Francisco

Chapter 38-41 - Pit Ponies/Coal Mining

Pit Pony Heroes, Squires, Eric. David & Charles 1974

Pit Ponies, Bright, John. Batsford Book 1986

Voices in the Dark, Hollows, Derek. Lulu.com, 2010

ncm.org.uk

victorianweb.org/history/ashley.html

pitponyexperience.com.au

atlasobscura.com/places/sultan-the-pit-pony

Bess, the mule, historylink.org/File/8651

cdn.loc.gov/service/pnp/nclc/01100/01110v.jpg

http://sixtownships.org.uk/derbyshire.html

commons.wikimedia.org/wiki/Pit_pony#/media/File:Pit_Pony_Lowered.jpg

upload.wikimedia.org/wikipedia/commons/9/9e/Cheval_mine_descente.jpg

flickr.com/photos/31134362@N07/3238984868

historylink.org/Content/Media/Photos/Large/bess-the-mule-at-franklin-coal-mine-king-county-march-17-1914.jpg

en.wikipedia.org/wiki/Penallta_Colliery#/media/File:Penallta_pit_pony_-_geograph.org.uk_-_90215.jpg

Chapter 42 - The Whitman Mission

pbs.org/weta/thewest/resources/archives/two/whitman0.htm

Across the Plains in 1844, Pringle, Catherine Sager. CreateSpace, 2016 (original written in 1860)

nps.gov/whmi/index.htm

archive.org/stream/marcuswhitmanpat00eell/marcuswhitman-pat00eell#page/n17/mode/1up

upload.wikimedia.org/wikipedia/commons/a/a2/Oregon_Trail_Whitman_Mission_WA_NPS.jpg

commons.wikimedia.org/wiki/File:Marcus_Whitman_sets_out.png

Chapter 43-46 - The Oregon Trail

If You Traveled West in a Covered Wagon, Levine, Ellen. Scholastic 1986

oregontrailcenter.org

history.com/topics/westward-expansion/oregon-trail

historynet.com/oregon-trail

littlethings.com/life-on-the-oregon-trail

en.wikipedia.org/wiki/Oregon_Trail

gutenberg.org/ebooks/23066 (Randolph Marcy, Prairie Traveler)

loc.gov/item/wpalh002000/ (J. Henry Brown account)

upload.wikimedia.org/wikipedia/commons/4/45/Ezra_Meeker_arrives_in_Los_Angeles_area_by_oxcart_to_witness_first_great_airmeet%2C_1910_%28CHS-105%29.jpg

loc.gov/resource/hec.36000

loc.gov/resource/cph.3c26267

pixabay.com/photos/oregon-trail-covered-wagon-prairie-4217528

commons.wikimedia.org/wiki/File:Covered_wagon_at_the_High_Desert_Museum_Outside.jpg

upload.wikimedia.org/wikipedia/commons/6/6e/Bierstadt_Albert_Oregon_Trail.jpg

upload.wikimedia.org/wikipedia/commons/7/78/Polygamy%3B_or%2C_The_mysteries_and_crimes_of_Mormonism%2C_being_a_full_and_authentic_history_of_this_strange_sect_from_its_origin_to_the_present_time._%281904%29_%2814755319266%29.jpg

upload.wikimedia.org/wikipedia/commons/3/34/Yoke_%28PS-F%29.png

Chapter 47-51 - The Gold Rush

Two Burros of Fairplay, Bancroft, Caroline. Johnson Publishing Company 1968

Prunes and Rupe, Griffin, Lydia. Filter Press 2007

americanhistory.si.edu/onthewater/goldrush/gold_rush.html

en.wikipedia.org/wiki/California_Gold_Rush

history.com/topics/westward-expansion/gold-rush-of-1849

pbs.org/wgbh/americanexperience/features/goldrush-california

loc.gov/resource/cph.3a20657

loc.gov/item/2018646288

upload.wikimedia.org/wikipedia/commons/6/6a/Three_miners%2C_wearing_prospector_outfits%2C_standing_next_to_a_burro_cart_loaded_with_camp_supplies%2C_Goldfield%2C_Nevada%2C_ca.1900-1905_%28CHS-5411%29.jpg

parkcoarchives.org/photos/photos1/photos_burros.html

Chapter 49 - Brighty of the Grand Canyon

http://grandcanyonhistory.org/Publications/TheOlPioneer/
TOP_2012_3.pdf

grandcanyonhistory.org/Publications/TheOlPioneer/TOP_
2012_3.pdf

grandcanyonnews.com/news/2015/oct/27/myths-legends-and-
facts-from-grand-canyons-past

en.wikipedia.org/wiki/Brighty_of_the_Grand_Canyon

atlasobscura.com/articles/who-was-brighty-the-burro-grand-
canyon

americanwildhorsecampaign.org/media/about-burros

Brighty of the Grand Canyon, Henry, Marguerite. Rand McNally
1961

Chapter 50 - Jack Packer

animasmuseum.org/historylaplata2013.pdf

animasmuseum.org/hlp_2016.pdf

Photos courtesy of the Center of Southwest Studies, Fort Lewis
College

fortlewis.edu/finding_aids/SWimages/P01503304.jpg

swcenter.fortlewis.edu/finding_aids/images/P015/P01503322-
Page.htm

swcenter.fortlewis.edu/finding_aids/inventory/LittleOlga.htm

Chapter 51 - Faster Than a Speeding Burro

Photos courtesty of the Western Pack Burro Association: pack-
burroracing.com

packburroracing.com/graphics/bv_burro_race04.jpg

packburroracing.com/graphics/bv20061(13).jpg

Chapter 52 - Old Whitey

americacomesalive.com/zachary-taylors-white-house-pet-a-
horse

presidentialpetmuseum.com/pets/old-whitey-zachary-taylor

whitehousehistory.org/photos/photo-8-6

loc.gov/item/2012649706

Chapter 53 - Stagecoach Travel

*Shotguns and Stagecoaches: The Brave Men Who Rode for Wells
Fargo*, Boessenecker, John. Thomas Dunne Books 2018

yellowstonenationalparklodges.com/connect/yellowstone-hot-
spot/stagecoaches-in-yellowstone

en.wikipedia.org/wiki/Stagecoach

hansenwheel.com

loc.gov/item/92515074

en.wikipedia.org/wiki/Stagecoach#/media/File:Concord_
Coach_no._251.jpg

newsroom.wf.com/multimedia

commons.wikimedia.org/wiki/File:Wells,_Fargo_%26_Co.
%27s_Express_Office,_C_Street,_Virginia_City_LCC-
N2002719065.jpg

loc.gov/resource/cph.3a14154

loc.gov/resource/cph.3a13466

Chapter 54 - Wells Fargo & Co.

en.wikipedia.org/wiki/Wells_Fargo_(1852–1998)

wellsfargo.com/about/corporate/stagecoach

history.wf.com/in-1868-this-was-a-sight-never-before-seen

history.wf.com/stagecoach

* the plush ponies and story books were discontinued, but you
may find some at sites like ebay

Chapter 55 - Black Bart

en.wikipedia.org/wiki/Black_Bart_(outlaw)

Chapter 56 - Young, Skinny Orphans Wanted

Bronco Charlie and the Pony Express, Brill, Marlene. Carolrhoda
Books 2004

They're Off: The Story of the Pony Express, Harness, Cheryl.
Aladdin 1996

Whatever Happened to the Pony Express? Kay, Verla. G.P.
Putnam's Sons 2010

ponyexpress.org

nationalponyexpress.org

postalmuseum.si.edu/research/topical-reference-pages/the-
pony-express.html

americancowboy.com/people/heroes-pony-express-24260

britannica.com/topic/Pony-Express

nationalgeographic.org/news/pony-power

en.wikipedia.org/wiki/Pony_Express#/media/File:Riders_Pony_
Express.jpg

upload.wikimedia.org/wikipedia/commons/7/74/Pony_Ex-
press_Across_the_Plains.png

commons.wikimedia.org/wiki/File:Pony-express-statue.jpg

en.wikipedia.org/wiki/Pony_Express_mochila#/media/File:
Pony_Express_mochila_exhibit.jpg

Chapter 57 - Old Bob

An Affectionate Farewell The Story of Old Abe and Old Bob,
Krisher, Trudy. Bunker Hill Publishing Inc. 2015

militaryimages.atavist.com/highly-honorable-and-strictly-con-
fidential-service-summer-2016

en.wikipedia.org/wiki/Old_Bob

loc.gov/pictures/resource/ppmsca.10880

loc.gov/item/2017659606

Chapter 58 - Old Douglas

texascamelcorps.com

gettysburgcompiler.org/2018/05/30/the-camel-corps-experi-
ment/

expressnews.com/sa300/article/Military-s-Texas-camel-experi-
ment-was-a-short-12178557.php#photo-14062524

commons.wikimedia.org/wiki/File:%22Old_Douglas%22.jpg

commons.wikimedia.org/wiki/File:Camel_Corps,_Carl_Rake-
man_(NBY_435547).jpg

Chapter 59-62 - The Cavalry and War Horses

ehistory.osu.edu/exhibitions/Regimental/cavalry

essentialcivilwarcurriculum.com/the-evolution-of-union-cavalry-1861-1865.html

Horses and Mules in the Civil War, Armistead, Gene C. McFarland & Company, Inc. 2013

Three Years in the Federal Cavalry, Glazier, Willard W. Public Domain (originally published 1870)

Horses in Gray, Hawkins, J.D.R. Pelican 2017

Fly Like the Wind, Savage, Bridgette. Buckbeech Studios 2006

civilwartalk.com

agreenhorse.blogspot.com/2009/12/horses-of-military-war.html

civilwarhome.com/warhorses.html

loc.gov/item/2012648037

upload.wikimedia.org/wikipedia/commons/b/b4/McCellan_Saddle_Fort_Kearny_2006_C.jpg

loc.gov/resource/ppmsca.33210

loc.gov/item/2012649238

loc.gov/item/2013647870

loc.gov/resource/ppmsca.20640

loc.gov/resource/cwpb.01143

loc.gov/resource/ppmsca.20769

Chapter 63 - Union Horses

en.wikipedia.org/wiki/Cincinnati_(horse)#/media/File:Grant's_horses.jpg

commons.wikimedia.org/wiki/File:Old_Whitey_(horse_of_Rutherford_B._Hayes).jpg

loc.gov/resource/cph.3c00810

loc.gov/item/2018672367

loc.gov/item/2017660644

digitalcollections.nypl.org/items/510d47e1-c4e2-a3d9-e040-e00a18064a99

loc.gov/resource/ppmsca.20587

loc.gov/item/2017659661

Chapter 64 - Confederate Horses

loc.gov/pictures/resource/pga.02835

Turner Ashby image from non-copyrighted, old history book

upload.wikimedia.org/wikipedia/commons/a/a9/General_Nathan_Bedford_Forrest.jpg

upload.wikimedia.org/wikipedia/commons/d/d5/Forrest_Park_Memphis_TN_16.jpg

commons.wikimedia.org/wiki/File:Stonewall_Jackson_Bendann.jpg

upload.wikimedia.org/wikipedia/commons/e/eb/MorganWashington.jpg

upload.wikimedia.org/wikipedia/commons/4/4c/John-Hunt-Morgan-and-horse.jpg

Chapter 65 - Clarintha Draper

ancestors.familysearch.org/en/L4YQ-HWJ/clarintha-choate-1836-1943

lrgaf.org/journeys/clarintha.htm

Chapter 66 - White House Stable Fire

mrlincolnswhitehouse.org/the-white-house/the-white-house-grounds-entrance/white-house-grounds-entrance-stables

civilwartalk.com/threads/fire-at-the-white-house-stables-patterson-mcgees-revenge-1864.155982

rogerjnorton.com/Lincoln100.html

commons.wikimedia.org/wiki/File:Little_%22Tad%22_Lincoln_LCCN2004678587.jpg

loc.gov/item/2011660268

Chapter 67 - Chasing the Assassin

Assassination of Abraham Lincoln, Baker, Lieutenant Luther. Historical Society of Greater Lansing 2015

The Great American Myth: The True Story of Lincolns Murder, Bryan, George S. Americana House 1990 (original 1940)

Twenty Days, Kunhardt, Dorothy & Philip. Harper & Row 1965

The Madman and the Assassin, Martelle, Scott. Chicago Review Press 2015

Manhunt The 12-Day Chase For Lincoln's Killer, Swanson, James L. William Morrow 2006

fords.org

boothiebarn.com

historynet.com/abraham-lincoln-assassination

ushistoryimages.com/john-wilkes-booth.shtm

loc.gov/resource/ppmsca.40668

Purchased Alamy Stock Photo alamy.com/stock-photo-the-killing-of-john-wilkes-booth-the-assassin-the-dying-murderer-drawn-58255210.html

Chapter 68 - Buffalo Soldiers

Buffalo Soldiers Heroes of the American West, Baker, Brynn. Capstone Press 2016

nps.gov/yose/learn/historyculture/buffalo-soldiers.htm

en.wikipedia.org/wiki/Buffalo_Soldier

nationalparks.org/connect/blog/retrace-legacy-buffalo-soldiers-national-parks

thelongridersguild.com/charlesyoung.htm

en.wikipedia.org/wiki/File:Buffalo_Soldier_9th_Cav_Denver.jpg

myyosemitepark.com/park/buffalo-soldiers

Beautiful Jim Key - Horsestory Volume II Preview

teva.contentdm.oclc.org/digital/collection/jimkey

Beautiful Jim Key, Rivas, Mim Eichler. Harper Collins 2005

Step Right Up, Bowman, Donna Janell. Lee & Low Books Inc. 2016

History of Horses, General Information

Famous Horses and Their People, Evans, Edna. The Stephen Greene Press 1975

100 Horses in History, Stewart, Gayle. Four-Setters LLC 2018

Military Horses, Sandler, Michael. Bearport Publishing 2007

Heroes: Incredible True Stories of Courageous Animals, Long, David. Faber & Faber 2014 (a couple horses, mostly other animals)

Horsestory

Through their bond with humans,
horses shaped our past in ways no machine ever could.
Their contribution has been all but forgotten—
until **Horsestory!**

The Horsestory series continues with **Volume II,** beginning with the cattle drives in the old West to the 1920s.

Horsestory concludes with **Volume III,** covering the 1920s to modern times.

sonrisestable.com/horsestory

Horses, one of God's most magnificent creations, offer many insights into the nature of our Creator as well as our relationship to Him. This full-color, Christian devotional features a variety of stories, drawn from the author's experiences with her horses and Sassy, a lovable but cantankerous mule. Other famous, and not-so-famous, horses help illustrate Scriptural principles.

Available at sonrisestable.com

viii

SONRISE STABLE

Wholesome and horsey with strong Christian themes, the Sonrise Stable series is unique among modern children's literature.

Read the books alone or use the Companion Guides for additional activities to supplement the series.

sonrisestable.com

www.ingramcontent.com/pod-product-compliance
Lightning Source LLC
Chambersburg PA
CBHW080357030726
47598CB00010B/2783